INSTRUCTION BOOK
MATCHLESS

500 c.c.   TWIN CYLINDER MODELS   600 c.c.

===== 1956 =====

Price

TWO SHILLINGS and SIXPENCE

Factories:
BURRAGE GROVE and MAXEY ROAD
PLUMSTEAD, S.E.18

Telephone: WOOlwich 1223 (7 lines)
Telegrams: "MATCHLESS, WOL-LONDON"
Cables: "MATCHLESS, LONDON"
Codes: A.B.C. 5th and 6th Edition; Bentley's; and Private Codes

Registered Offices:
PLUMSTEAD ROAD, PLUMSTEAD
LONDON, S.E.18   ..   ENGLAND

———————— Issued by: ————————

MATCHLESS MOTOR CYCLES
LONDON S.E.18

Proprietors: ASSOCIATED MOTOR CYCLES LTD.

ERRATA

Page 13

Gear Box Lubrication Table

Extreme Cold Column

For SAE 20 read SAE 30.

Page 42

Front Chain Adjustment

Refer to Illustration 15.

Remove engine plate cover.

Slacken the nut of bolt (5).

Slacken the nut (3).

Screw the bolt (1) into the crosshead (2) to take up slack in the chain.

Pull on the rear chain to move the gear box and tighten the front chain.

Remove the inspection cap from the chaincase and check tension by applying upward pressure, with a finger, to the chain.

The correct amount of whip is $\frac{3}{8}$ inch. Check the adjustment in several positions and adjust for the tightest point.

When the correct adjustment has been obtained, tighten nuts (3) and (5), and replace cover.

If the chain is tight, screw the bolt (1) out of the crosshead (2).

After making adjustments to the front chain always check the adjustment of the rear chain. Slacken or tighten as necessary.

CONTENTS

	Page
Carburetter	33
Controls	8
Data	6
Driving	10
Electrical Equipment	64
Engine	23
Forks and Frame	44
Free Service	80
Guarantee	84
Index	85
Information	74
Lubrication	13
Maintenance	21
Repairs and Service	77
Spare Parts	81
Tools and Special Equipment	82
Transmission	36
Wheels and Brakes	53

ILLUSTRATIONS

	Illustrations	Page
A.V.C. unit	31	69
Battery	32	70
Brake adjustment, front	24	59
Brake adjustment, rear	25	60
Brake pedal adjustment	26	61
Brake shoe adjustment	23	58
Carburetter	12	34
Clutch	14	40
Contact breaker	28	64
Controls	1	9
Crankshaft	11	31
Engine Non-Return Oil Valve	5	17
Engine lubrication	9	27
Fork exploded view	17	48
Fork damper details	16	45
Front chain adjustment	15	42
Gearbox	13	36
Gear lever positions	2	10
Head lamp	33	71
Hub bearing details, front	21	55
,, ,, ,, rear	22	57
Hubs	20	55
Lubrication chart	6	20
Magneto, exploded view	29	65
Oil tank	4	15
Oil pumps	3	14
Rear Brake Anchorage	27	61
Rocker adjustment	7	23
Sparking plug	30	66
Spring frame	18	50
Tank fixing details	8	24
Teledraulic leg, rear	19	51
Tools	36	82
Valve timing gear	10	30
Wire connector, snap type	34	72
Wiring diagram	35	73

MATCHLESS

"SUPER CLUBMAN"
VERTICAL TWINS

Model G9   498 c.c.

Model G11   592 c.c.

THE MODERN MOTOR CYCLE unquestionably provides one of the most healthy, economical and pleasant means of transport. In addition by reason of its superb braking, high power to weight ratio and ease of control it is, if used with due care, one of the safest vehicles on the road.

It is our sincere desire that every owner should obtain from his mount the service, comfort and innumerable miles of low cost travel that we have earnestly endeavoured to build into it.

It must be borne in mind however, that although of simple design and construction, it is nevertheless a highly specialised piece of engineering and must in consequence be intelligently and efficiently maintained in order to provide unfailing reliability.

In this book we provide non-technical instructions for carrying out all the maintenance operations likely to be called for in normal service, together with assisting illustrations.

To owners of long experience we tender apologies for the elementary nature of some of the contents of this handbook, but owners whether novice or expert are advised to read the contents from beginning to end. We are at all times pleased to give owners the full benefit of our wide experience in matters relating to motor cycles of our manufacture and elsewhere will be found details of the particulars required when making enquiries of our Service Department.

Safety on the Road

IN the interest of Safety on the Road a few words of warning will not be out of place.

The outstanding manoeuverability of a motor cycle over all other vehicles on the road makes it necessary to exercise caution at all times.

There are unfortunately a few motor-cyclists whose reckless driving constitutes a menace not only to themselves but also to other road users resulting in the totally false impression in some quarters that motorcycling is a dangerous pastime.

Take a pride in your riding technique and never rely upon the other fellow doing the right thing.

Your example of careful, courteous and unobtrusive riding will materially contribute to road safety and to the reputation of a fine sporting pastime.

DATA

Identity

Engine number	On crankcase in front of left cylinder
Frame number	On seat lug of main frame, right side (below saddle)
Number of cylinders	Two
Bore (nominal) 500 c.c.	66 mm. (2·6 ins.)
Bore (nominal) 600 c.c.	72 mm. (2·84 ins.)
Stroke, all models	72·8 mm. (2·868 ins.)
Engine capacity 500	498 c.c. (30·459 cu. ins.)
Engine capacity 600	592 c.c. (36·13 cu. ins.)

Capacities

Location	British	Metric
Engine 500 c.c.	30·459 cu. in.	498 c.c.
Engine 600 c.c.	36·13 cu. in.	592 c.c.
Gear box	1 pint	568·2 c.c.
Front fork (each side)	6½ fl. ozs.	184·6 c.c.
Rear leg (each leg)	3 fl. ozs.	85 c.c.
Rear wheel fork hinge bearing	1½ fl. ozs.	42·6 c.c.
Fuel tank	3¾ gallons	17·04 litres
Oil tank	4½ pints	2·557 litres

Carburetter

	500 c.c.	600 c.c.
Type ... Monobloc	376/6	376/6
Main jet (no air filter)	240	270
Main jet (air filter fitted)	230	260
Pilot jet	30	30
Throttle valve	4	4
Needle position	Centre notch	4th notch from top
Needle jet	·1065	·1065

Compression Ratios

	500 c.c.	600 c.c.
With standard pistons	7·7 to 1	7·5 to 1
With alternative pistons	7 to 1	7 to 1

Connecting rod

Internal diameter small end	Internal diameter big end (liner situ)	Centres
¾ + ·0005 in. (H) − ·0000 in. (L)	1·7715 in. (H) 1·7710 in. (L)	5·75 in.

Gudgeon Pin ¾ in. −·0001 to −·0003.

Crankshaft external diameters

	Crankpin H—1·62525 L—1·62475	Centre bearing H—1·62625 L—1·62575

Cylinders

Nominal bore	Actual bore
66 mm.	2·598 +·0005 (H) −·0005 (L)
72 mm.	2·835 +·0005 (H) −·0005 (L)

Gear box ratios

First gear	Second gear	Third gear	Fourth gear (top)
2·65 to 1	1·70 to 1	1·308 to 1	1 to 1

Gear ratios

Engine sprocket	First gear	Second gear	Third gear	Fourth gear (top)
19	14·55 to 1	9·33 to 1	7·18 to 1	5·49 to 1
20	13·91 to 1	8·91 to 1	6·86 to 1	5·25 to 1
21	13·25 to 1	8·50 to 1	6·54 to 1	5·0 to 1

The standard size of engine sprocket is the 20 tooth

Shock absorber spring

Free length ... 1¾ in. ± 1/32 in.

Lighting (bulbs)

Location	Type	Voltage	Wattage	Part number
Head lamp (Pre-focus) ...	Double filament	6	30 × 24	312
Pilot	Single contact	6	3	988
Rear lamp	Double filament	6	18 and 3	352
Speedometer	Single contact	6	1·8	53205

Oversize or undersize parts

The following are the only "oversize" variations provided for the Vertical Twin machines.

Big-end and crankshaft centre main bearings :
  Undersize ... ... ·010 below normal (Journals to be reground to suit).

Cylinder re-bore :
  ·020 inch and ·040 inch oversize.

Pistons and rings :
  ·020 inch and ·040 inch oversize.

Pistons

	500 c.c.		600 c.c.
Top of skirt diameter	Bottom of skirt diameter	Top of skirt diameter	Bottom of skirt diameter
2·5976 inches (H)	2·5984 inches (H)	2·8341 inches (H)	2·8349 inches (H)
2·5969 inches (L)	2·5969 inches (L)	2·8334 inches (L)	2·8342 inches (L)

Bore of gudgeon pin boss $\frac{3}{4}$ in. $\begin{array}{c}+ \cdot 0005 \\ - \cdot 0000\end{array}$

Piston rings

Piston ring gap—Normal	·006 inch
Permissible maximum	·030 inch
Piston ring clearance in groove	·002 inch

Sparking plug

Make	Type	Thread	Reach	Point gap
K.L.G.	FE80	14 mm.	$\frac{3}{4}$ in.	·020–·022 in.

Sprockets

Location	Number of teeth	Chain pitch	Chain width	Part number
Engine	19	½ inch	·305 inch	015203
Engine	20	½ inch	·305 inch	015204
Engine	21	½ inch	·305 inch	014294
Clutch	40	½ inch	·305 inch	G-34-2
Gear box	16	⅝ inch	·380 inch	G-31-1
Rear wheel	42	⅝ inch	·380 inch	010293

Valve springs

Outer valve spring		Inner valve spring	
Free length	Part number	Free length	Part number
1⅞ inches	011769	1$\frac{13}{16}$ inches	011770

Renew valve springs when $\frac{3}{16}$ to $\frac{1}{4}$ inch less than normal free length

Valve timing

All timing gears are marked for ease of setting (See illustration 10) with marks coinciding correct timing is assured.

Valve timing pinion

Retained by bolt threaded ½ inch by 20 threads per inch. Right hand thread.

Ignition (Magneto)

Make	Type	Rotation	Point Gap	Setting Fully Advanced
Lucas	K2F	Anti-clock	·012	39°—⅜ inch

Camshaft gears

Retained by nut. Left hand thread.

Weight

Weight of machine with empty tanks ... ... 400 lbs. (approx.)

Wheels (bearing end play)

Bearing end play ... ... ·002 inch (just perceptible rim rock).

CONTROLS

Refer to Illustration 1

(1) **Throttle twist grip.** On right handlebar. Twist inwards to open. When fully closed engine should just idle when hot.

(2) **Air lever.** Small lever on right handlebar. Pull inwards to increase air supply to carburetter. Once set, when engine has warmed up, requires no alteration for different road speeds. Should be fully closed when starting engine from cold.

(3) **Ignition lever.** Small lever on left handlebar. Advances and retards ignition point. Pull inwards to retard. Retard two-fifths of total movement for starting.

(4) **Magneto cut-out switch.** Push switch on magneto contact breaker cover. A press action switch which, when operated, short circuits the magneto, thereby stopping the engine from firing. Place gear foot lever in neutral position before using cut-out switch to stop engine.

(5) **Clutch lever.** Large lever on left handlebar. Grip to release clutch so that drive to rear wheel is disconnected.

(6) **Front brake lever.** Large lever on right handlebar. Grip to operate front wheel brake and, for normal braking, use in conjunction with rear brake application.

(7) **Rear brake lever.** Pedal close to left side foot rest. Depress with left foot to apply rear brake. Apply gently and use increasing pressure as the road speed decreases.

(8) **Gear change lever.** Pedal in horizontal position close to right foot rest. Controls selection of the four speeds, or ratios, between engine and rear wheel revolutions, with a " free," or neutral, position. See illustration 2, page 10.

(9) **Kick-starter lever.** Vertical pedal on right hand side of gear box.

(10) **Lighting switch.** In top of head lamp. Controls lamps by a rotating lever which has three positions :
    (1) " OFF " Lamps not on.
    (2) " L "   Pilot lamps, rear lamp and speedometer lamp on.
    (3) " H "   Main headlamp, rear lamp and speedometer lamp on.

(11) **Ammeter.** In top of head lamp. Indicates flow of electric current, in, or out, of battery. (" Charge " or " Discharge.") 1 division = approx. 2 amps.

(12) **Horn switch.** Press switch on left handlebar.

(13) **Gear box filler cap.** Located on top edge of kick-starter case cover. Allows insertion of lubricant and access to clutch inner wire and internal clutch operating lever.

(14) **Footrest for rider.**

(15) **Petrol tank filler cap.** Located in top of fuel tank. To release, slightly depress, turn fully to the left, and then lift away. There are two locking positions. The middle position, between the fully tightened down and "lift away" positions, is in the nature of a "safety" device to prevent loss that might be occasioned by unauthorised meddling.

(16) **Oil tank filler cap.** Located on top edge of oil tank. To remove, unscrew.

(17) **Dipping switch.** Trigger switch on left handlebar. Used to select normal or "dipped" beam of head lamp when main lighting switch lever is in the " H " position. (The main head lamp bulb has two filaments.)

(18) **Dummy grip.** The fixed grip on the left handlebar.

(19) **Speedometer hand.** The rotating hand in speedometer head. Indicates speed in miles per hour to a maximum of 120 miles per hour. (Certain machines for export have the head calibrated in kilometers per hour to a maximum of 180 k.p.h.)

(20) **Total mileage recorder.** The top set of figures located in the speedometer dial. Indicates the number of miles (or kilometres) travelled to a total of 100,000 and then automatically re-sets to zero.

(21) **Trip mileage recorder.** The bottom set of figures located in the speedometer dial. Indicates the number of miles (or kilometres) travelled since the recorder was set to zero. Can be re-set at any time. Used to measure the length of individual trips. The red figures indicate tenths of a mile. Unless re-set, indicates a total of 1,000 miles and then automatically re-sets to zero.

(22) **Re-set knob.** Protrudes from lower part of speedometer head. Pull and turn to right till "000·0" appears to re-set the trip mileage recorder.

(23) **Gear indicator.** Disc on gear box with periphery marked 1,N,2,3,4. Moves under the control of the gear change lever and the number registering with a line on gear box indicates gear in engagement (or neutral).

(24) **Pillion foot rest.** Fold upwards to a vertical position when not in use.

(25) **Fork top bolt.** One at top of each fork main inner tube. Must be raised to allow insertion of hydraulic fluid.

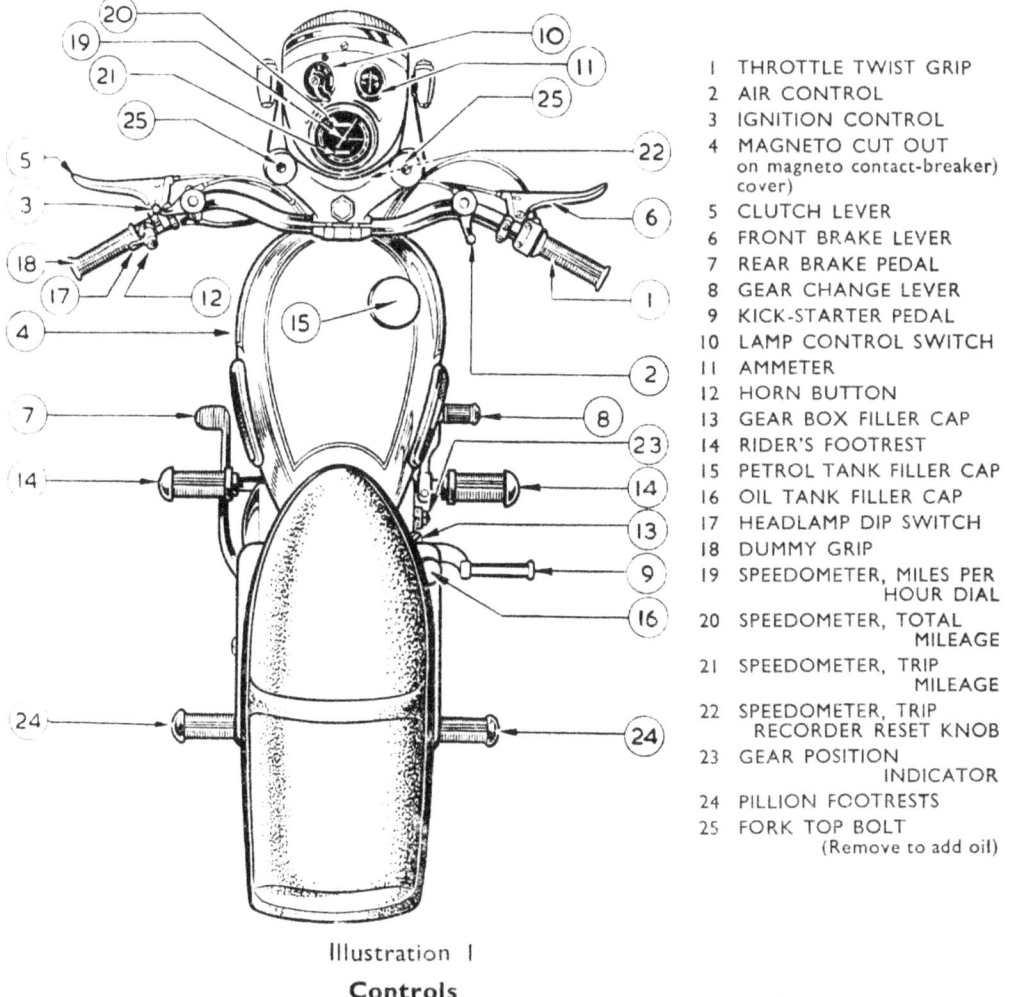

1 THROTTLE TWIST GRIP
2 AIR CONTROL
3 IGNITION CONTROL
4 MAGNETO CUT OUT
  on magneto contact-breaker) cover)
5 CLUTCH LEVER
6 FRONT BRAKE LEVER
7 REAR BRAKE PEDAL
8 GEAR CHANGE LEVER
9 KICK-STARTER PEDAL
10 LAMP CONTROL SWITCH
11 AMMETER
12 HORN BUTTON
13 GEAR BOX FILLER CAP
14 RIDER'S FOOTREST
15 PETROL TANK FILLER CAP
16 OIL TANK FILLER CAP
17 HEADLAMP DIP SWITCH
18 DUMMY GRIP
19 SPEEDOMETER, MILES PER HOUR DIAL
20 SPEEDOMETER, TOTAL MILEAGE
21 SPEEDOMETER, TRIP MILEAGE
22 SPEEDOMETER, TRIP RECORDER RESET KNOB
23 GEAR POSITION INDICATOR
24 PILLION FOOTRESTS
25 FORK TOP BOLT
  (Remove to add oil)

Illustration 1
Controls

Before using the machine, sit on the saddle and become familiar with the position and operation of the various controls. Pay particular attention to the gear positions.

If any adjustment is made to the rear brake pedal make certain the brake does not bind and also see there is not excessive free pedal movement before the brake comes "on."

DRIVING

FUEL

Although various quality fuels are again available, owners are advised to use only the best. The small economy that might be considered to accrue by using the cheaper grades is more than offset by the advantages obtained by using only Number One Grades.

FUEL SUPPLY

Two fuel feed taps are situated underneath the rear end of the petrol tank. (One each side). Both must be shut off when the machine is left standing for more than a few minutes.

The tap plungers work horizontally. To open, pull plunger out, push in fully to close.

Normally, only use the tap on the right hand side of the machine and then the other side will act as a reserve supply. Always re-fuel as soon as possible after being forced to call upon the reserve (approx. $\frac{1}{2}$ gallon) and then, at once, close the " reserve " tap.

It will be noted that, by fitting two petrol feed taps, it is possible to remove the petrol tank from the machine without the necessity of first draining it of fuel.

STARTING THE ENGINE FROM COLD

(a) Check that there is sufficient fuel in the petrol tank.
(b) Check that there is sufficient oil in the oil tank.
(c) Check that the gear pedal is in the neutral position.
(d) Pull outward the plunger of the off side petrol tap.
(e) Check that the air control lever is in the fully closed position.
(f) Fully advance the ignition and then pull inwards the control lever two-fifths of its total movement.
(g) Open the throttle not more than one-sixth of the total movement of the twist grip.
(h) Depress the plunger on the top of the carburetter float chamber until it can be felt the chamber is full of petrol.
(i) Operate the kick-starter by giving it a long swinging kick and the engine should immediately fire.

The kick-starter mechanism must be allowed to engage properly before putting heavy pressure on the kick-starter crank pedal pin. That means there are two definite and separate movements when operating the mechanism by depressing the crank.

The first is a slow and gentle movement which ends when it is felt the quadrant has engaged with the teeth on the ratchet pinion.

The first slow and gentle movement is essential to avoid damage to the teeth of the kick-starter quadrant.

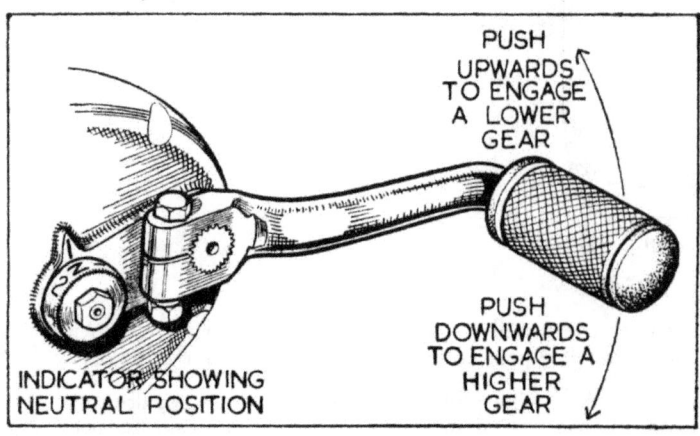

Illustration 2

The gear indicator drum which upon assembly is set to record the various gears and neutral position, as the respective figure or letter N registers with index mark on the gearbox shell.

Upon re-assembly, after dismantling for any purpose, the index disc should be correctly re-set for future reference.

After the engine has started, slowly open the air lever until it runs evenly. Then set the throttle so that the engine is running at a moderate speed (neither racing nor ticking over) and allow to warm up. While doing this, check the oil circulation as detailed in page 15. The machine can then be taken on the road.

NOTE—Do not race up the engine from cold and do not flood the carburetter to such an extent that petrol is dripping, because then, in the event of a backfire, there is a danger of such loose petrol igniting. This cannot possibly happen if the starting instructions are carefully followed, but, in the event of a fire, there is no cause for panic. Merely turn off the petrol tap to isolate the main supply, open wide the throttle and turn over the engine by operating the kick-starter pedal when suction will extinguish the fire.

STOPPING THE ENGINE

To stop the engine, close the throttle, depress the magneto cut-out press switch on the contact breaker cover and keep it depressed until the engine has ceased to revolve.

ON THE ROAD

Having started and warmed up the engine, take the machine off the stand, sit astride it, free the clutch by pulling up the large lever on the left bar and engage lowest gear. Next, slowly release the clutch lever and the machine will commence to move forward. As it does this, the engine speed will tend to drop as it picks up the load so it will be necessary to increase the throttle opening, gradually, to keep the engine speed gently rising.

When well under way, disengage the clutch, slightly close the throttle, engage second gear and release the clutch lever, then open up the throttle to increase the speed of the machine. Repeat these operations in order to engage third and top gears.

To engage a higher gear the pedal is pressed downward with the toe and a lower gear is obtained by raising the pedal with the instep. To engage first gear, from the neutral position, the pedal is therefore raised. After each pedal movement, internal springs return the pedal to its normal horizontal position.

The pedal must be moved to the full extent of its travel when selecting a gear, either up or down. It must not be "stamped down" or jabbed, but firmly and decisively moved till it stops. A half-hearted movement may not give full engagement. Keep the foot off the pedal when driving and between each gear change because, unless the lever can freely return to its normal central position, the next gear cannot be engaged. Finally, fully advance the ignition and leave it in that position unless it is necessary to retard in order to ease the engine and so prevent "pinking" when pulling hard on a gradient.

STOPPING THE MACHINE

To stop the machine, close the throttle, declutch by lifting the large lever on the left handlebar, and gently apply both brakes, increasing the pressure on them as the road speed of the machine decreases. Place the gear change foot pedal in the neutral position and stop the engine.

Before leaving the machine, turn off the fuel supply.

Important

*Never drive away at **high speed** when starting a run with a **cold** engine. **Give** the oil a **chance** to warm up and thin out, **particularly** when the engine is **cold**. Until the oil reaches its **normal running temperature** the circulation is **restricted**. Seizures can be avoided by taking this simple **essential precaution**.*

RUNNING IN

Although it is customary to quote permitted maximum speeds on the various gears during the period of running in, these are really no guide to overdriving, the only essential thing to avoid being the use of large throttle opening.

If the precaution is taken of limiting the use of the throttle to about one third of its opening during the first 1,000 miles, irrespective of the road speed, and whether on the level or climbing, the necessary conditions for running in will have been observed.

Special attention must be given, during the running in period, to such details as valve rocker adjustment, chains, brakes, contact breaker points, and steering head bearings, all of which tend to bed down in the first hundred miles or so. Particular note must be made of the adjustment of steering head bearings, which, if run in a slack condition, will be quickly ruined. After this bedding down process has taken place, adjustments to such details will only be necessary at lengthy intervals.

After about 1,000 miles has been covered larger throttle openings may be gradually indulged in for short bursts only.

Until at least 2,000 miles have been covered the owner of a new machine is strongly advised to curb his natural desire to learn the mount's maximum capabilities. Restraint in this direction will be amply repaid later.

NOTES ON DRIVING

If, at first, the lowest gear will not engage, release the clutch lever and after a second or two, make another attempt. This condition may exist in a new machine, but it tends to disappear after a little use.

Always endeavour to make the movements of hand (on the clutch) and foot (on the gear pedal) as simultaneous as possible, and remember, in all gear changes, a steady pressure of the foot is desirable. This pressure should be maintained until the clutch is fully released. It is not sufficient just to jab the foot pedal and then release the clutch lever. When actually in motion, it will be found sufficient to merely free the clutch a trifle, to ease the drive when changing gear and, with reasonable care, changes of gear then can be made without a sound.

Do not unnecessarily race the engine or let in the clutch sufficiently suddenly to cause the rear wheel to spin. Take a pride in making a smooth silent get-away.

When changing up to a higher gear, as the clutch is freed, the throttle should be slightly closed so that the engine speed is reduced to keep in step with the higher gear ratio. Conversely, when changing down to a lower gear, the throttle should be regulated so that the engine speed is increased to keep in step with the lower gear ratio.

Do not slip the clutch to control the road speed.

The clutch is intended to be used only when starting from a standstill and when changing gear. It must **NOT** be operated to ease the engine, instead of changing gear, or be held out, in order to " free-wheel."

When travelling slowly, such as may occur in traffic or on a hill, and the engine commences to labour, it is then necessary to change to a lower gear. Engine " knocking " or " pinking " and a harshness in the transmission are symptoms of such labour and although relief can sometimes be found by retarding the ignition, it is generally much better to change down. A good driver is able to sense such conditions and will make the change before the engine has reached the stage of distress. The gear box is provided to be used and consequently full use should be made of the intermediate gears to obtain effortless running and smooth hill climbing.

Keep the feet clear of the brake and gear pedals when not actually using them and keep the hand off the clutch lever when not in use.

Drive as much as possible on the throttle, making the minimum use of the brakes.

When using the machine on wet or greasy roads, it is generally better to apply **BOTH** brakes together, because sudden or harsh application of either brake only, under such conditions, may result in a skid.

In all conditions, it is advisable to make a habit of always using both brakes together rather than habitually using the rear brake and reserving the front brake for emergency.

LUBRICATION

LUBRICANTS TO USE

Efficient lubrication is of vital importance and it is false economy to use cheap oils and greases.
We recommend the following lubricants to use in machines of our make.

FOR ENGINE LUBRICATION

HOT above 50° F	COLD 32° F to 50° F	EXTREME COLD below freezing point (32° F)
SAE 50	SAE 30	SAE 20
Mobiloil **D** Castrol **Grand Prix** **Energol SAE 50** **Essolube 50** Shell **X-100** Motor Oil **50**	Mobiloil **A** Castrol **XL** **Energol SAE 30** **Essolube 30** Shell **X-100** Motor Oil **30**	Mobiloil **Arctic** Castrolite **Energol SAE 20** **Essolube 20** Shell **X-100** Motor Oil 20/20W

NOTE—For the British Isles and much of Europe the **Cold** and **Hot** recommendations approximate to **Winter** and **Summer** conditions respectively. The **Extreme Cold** recommendations refer to wintry conditions in parts of Northern Europe, Canada, the Baltic and Scandinavian countries, and high mountainous districts where extreme cold is the average condition.

FOR GEAR BOX LUBRICATION

HOT above 50° F	COLD 32° F to 50° F	EXTREME COLD below freezing point (32° F)
SAE 50	SAE 50	SAE 20
Mobiloil **D** Castrol **Grand Prix** **Energol SAE 50** **Essolube 50** Shell **X-100** Motor Oil **50**	Mobiloil **D** Castrol **Grand Prix** **Energol SAE 50** **Essolube 50** Shell **X-100** Motor Oil **50**	Mobiloil **A** Castrol **XL** **Energol SAE 30** **Essolube 30** Shell **X-100** Motor Oil **30**

NOTE—For the British Isles and much of Europe the **Cold** and **Hot** recommendations approximate to **Winter** and **Summer** conditions respectively. The **Extreme Cold** recommendations refer to wintry conditions in parts of Northern Europe, Canada, the Baltic and Scandinavian countries, and high mountainous districts where extreme cold is the average condition.

FOR HUB LUBRICATION AND ALL FRAME PARTS USING GREASE

Mobilgrease No. 4   **Castrolease Heavy**   **Energrease C3**
Esso Pressure Gun Grease   Shell **Retinax A.** or **C.D.**

FOR TELEDRAULIC FRONT FORKS AND TELEDRAULIC REAR LEGS

Mobiloil **Arctic** (SAE-20)   **Castrolite** (SAE-20)   **Energol SAE 20**
Essolube 20 (SAE-20)   Shell **X-100** Motor Oil **20/20W** (SAE-20)

FOR REAR CHAINS

Mobilgrease No. 2   **Esso** Fluid Grease   **Energrease A.O.**
Castrolease Grease Graphited
Heated Until Just Fluid

See Application Instructions, page 19.

When buying oils and greases it is advisable to specify the **Brand** as well as the grade and, as an additional precaution, to buy only in sealed containers or from branded cabinets.

ENGINE LUBRICATION SYSTEM

This is of the **dry sump** type. Two separate gear type oil pumps are used, one for delivery and the other for returning oil to the tank. Oil feeds by gravity to the delivery pump, by which it is forced, under pressure, to various parts of the engine, from whence it drains back to the crankcase sump to be collected by the return pump and returned to the tank. The return pump has a much larger capacity than the delivery pump to ensure that the crankcase is kept clear of excess oil.

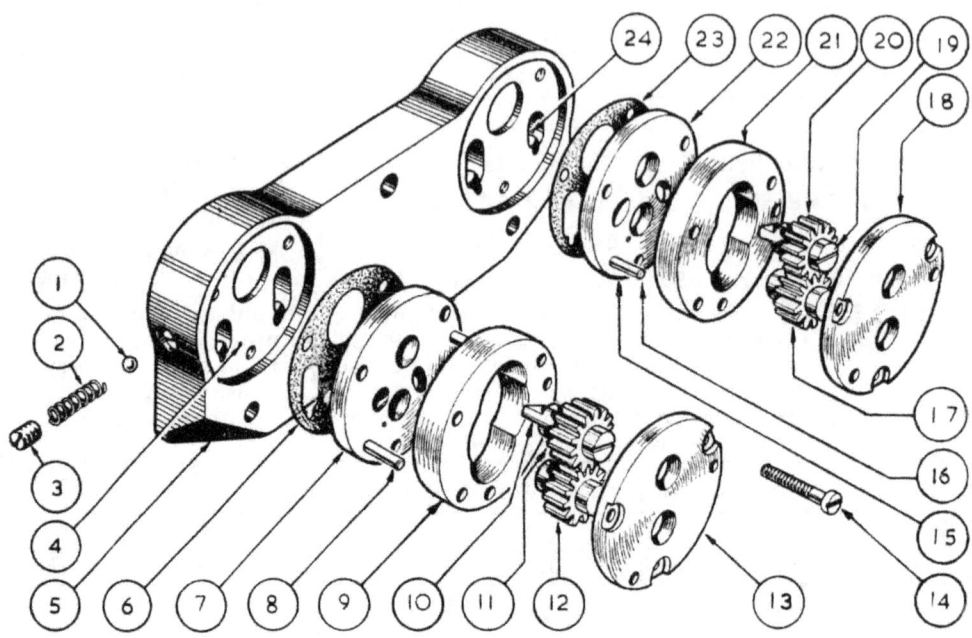

Illustration 3

Delivery Oil Pump (on the right)   **Return Oil Pump** (on the left)

1. BALL, FOR NON-RETURN VALVE.
2. SPRING, FOR NON-RETURN VALVE.
3. PLUG, RETAINING NON-RETURN VALVE SPRING AND BALL.
4. BLEED HOLE.
5. PLATE, CARRYING OIL FEED AND RETURN PUMPS.
6. PAPER WASHER FOR OIL RETURN PUMP.
7. BACK PLATE OF OIL RETURN PUMP.
8. DOWEL PIN, LOCATING PUMP PLATES AND BODY.
9. BODY OF OIL RETURN PUMP.
10. DOG END OF PUMP GEAR TO ENGAGE IN END OF CAMSHAFT.
11. DRIVING GEAR, FOR OIL RETURN PUMP.
12. DRIVEN GEAR, FOR OIL RETURN PUMP.
13. FRONT PLATE OF OIL RETURN PUMP.
14. SCREW (1 OF 6) USED TO RETAIN PLATES AND BODIES OF OIL PUMPS TO THE CARRYING PLATE.
15. BACK PLATE OF OIL FEED PUMP.
16. DOWEL PIN, LOCATING PUMP PLATES AND BODY.
17. DRIVEN GEAR, FOR OIL FEED PUMP.
18. FRONT PLATE OF OIL FEED PUMP.
19. SCREWDRIVER SLOT, TO ENABLE DRIVING GEAR TO BE CORRECTLY POSITIONED DURING ASSEMBLY.
20. DRIVING GEAR, FOR OIL FEED PUMP.
21. BODY OF OIL FEED PUMP.
22. BACK PLATE OF OIL FEED PUMP.
23. PAPER WASHER FOR OIL FEED PUMP.
24. BLEED HOLE.

ENGINE OIL PUMPS

Each pump is independently driven, at half engine speed, from the ends of the two camshafts. They each consist of a pair of close fitting gear wheels in a cast iron body. The gears of the delivery pump are considerably narrower than those of the return pump, giving the latter the necessary extra capacity to ensure efficient scavenging.

CHECKING OIL CIRCULATION

Provision is made to observe the oil in circulation and it is advisable to do this before each run.

If the filler cap on the oil tank is removed the end of the oil return pipe will be noticed below the level of the filler cap orifice and the returning oil can be seen running from it. This check should be made immediately after starting the engine from cold. This is because while the engine is stationary, oil from all parts of the interior of the engine drains back into the crankcase sump, so that, until this surplus is cleared, the return flow is very positive and continuous. Therefore, if the oil circulation is deranged, the fact is apparent at once by the lack of a steady return flow.

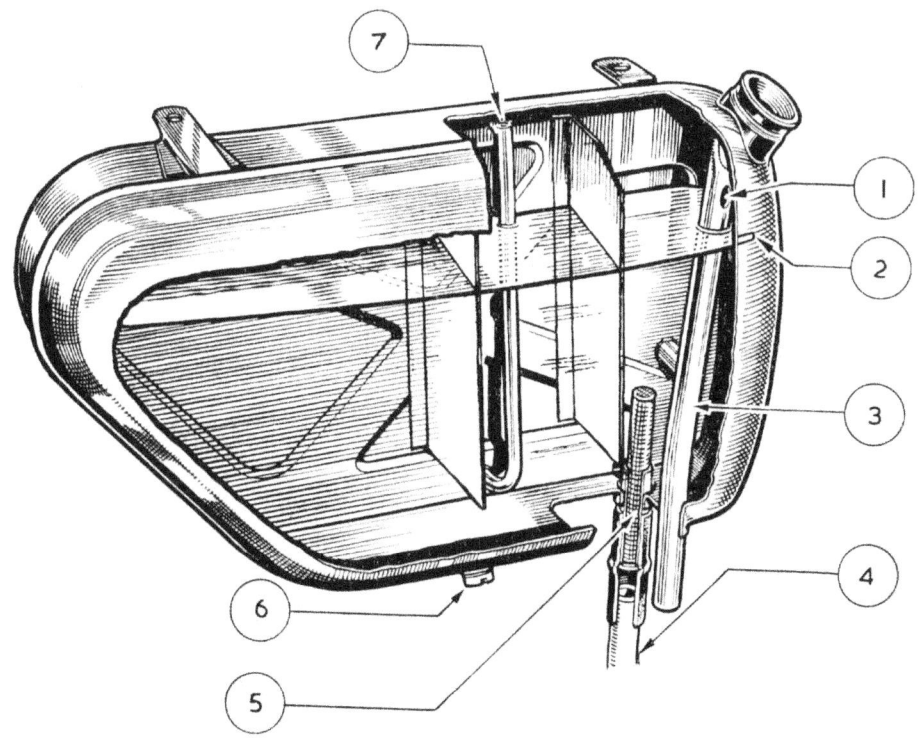

1 OUTLET IN OIL RETURN PIPE.
2 LEVEL INDICATOR LINE.
3 OIL RETURN PIPE.
4 OIL FEED PIPE.
5 OIL FEED GAUZE FILTER.
6 DRAIN PLUG.
7 VENT PIPE.

Illustration 4

Interior view of the oil tank showing the metal strainer mounted on the entry end of the feed pipe union, the return flow pipe from the engine to tank via the small spout, located so that it can be inspected by removing the tank filler cap, and air vent pipe, provided to ensure freedom from air-locks.

ENGINE OIL CIRCULATION

Oil, from the oil tank, is fed by gravity, through a coarse mesh metal filter, via an external pipe, to the suction side of the delivery pump, from whence it is discharged, under pressure, to a large and easily detachable felt filter that is housed in the crankcase.

After passing through the felt filter the main supply is directed to the crankshaft centre bearing and thence, through passages in the crankshaft, to each big-end, the splash from which provides adequate cylinder lubrication.

A metered by-pass provides an oil supply to the overhead rockers and push rod ball ends which then drains into the camshaft tunnels where upon reaching a pre-determined level the surplus overflows into the timing gear case. The four drilled oilways in the cylinder heads are also intentionally metered.

A predetermined level of oil is allowed to build up in the timing case to ensure adequate lubrication of the gears, and also in the camshaft tunnels, to ensure adequate lubrication of the cams and cam levers. Upon reaching these determined levels, the surplus overflows into the crankcase, and so to the sump.

The return pump collects all surplus oil from the crankcase sump and returns it, *via* another external pipe, to the oil tank. (See illustration 4.)

The stream of oil flowing into the tank is instantly visible upon removal of the tank filler cap.

THE OIL TANK

The level of oil in the supply tank should never be allowed to fall below the low level mark and, upon replenishment, should not be higher than the upper mark line, at which level the oil content is $4\frac{1}{2}$ pints.

After the first 500 miles, again at 1,000 miles, and subsequently at 5,000 mile intervals, it is recommended that the oil tank is drained, the oil filter cleaned in petrol and the tank replenished with new oil.

THE OIL FILTERS

There are three filters for the oil.

(A) The metal filter located in the feed pipe in the bottom of the oil tank.

This is a thimble shaped filter of coarse metal mesh inserted, from the exterior, in the short metal feed pipe located in the bottom of the oil tank. It has an open end finished with a turned over metal ring, which, upon the fitting of the tubular rubber sleeve connecting the oil feed pipe to the end of the rigid feed pipe to the engine, is gripped by the rubber sleeve, thereby preventing it from moving from its correct location.

(B) The felt fabric filter located in a chamber in the front part of the crankcase and parallel to the exhaust camshaft.

This is a cylindrical filter made of close grain felt that is supported by a tubular wire cage.

On the inner end is fitted a steel cup which effectively seals that end of the cylindrical filter. This cup is a push on fit.

In the outer end is inserted an aluminium plug, or valve, which acts as a relief valve, allowing the oil to escape if, for any reason, it cannot percolate through the felt fabric. In normal conditions this valve does not operate but, if for example, the cleaning of the filter had been neglected to such an extent that it was so clogged the oil could not pass through it in the volume supplied by the pump, then the valve would lift to give immediate temporary, or permanent, relief, as may be necessary.

(C) The magnetic filter in the crankcase oil sump.

CLEANING OIL FILTERS

To remove and clean the feed pipe metal filter :

Drain Tank.

Release the engine end of the oil feed pipe. (This leads from the rear outlet in the base of the oil tank to the forward banjo connection on the timing side of the crankcase.) Then remove the oil feed pipe by withdrawing the rubber connecting sleeve from the metal feed pipe protruding from the bottom of the oil tank.

The metal filter may come away with the rubber sleeve, in which case there is no need to disturb it. On the other hand it may remain in the oil tank bottom pipe, in which case it may be withdrawn by grasping the ringed open end and pulling away.

After removal the filter should be cleaned in petrol and allowed to dry before re-fitting.

Reverse the above procedure to **re-fit** the filter and pipes.

1 NON-RETURN VALVE ASSEMBLY ORDER.
2 BALL AND SCREWED PLUG 013332.
3 NON-RETURN VALVE COMPLETE 016179.

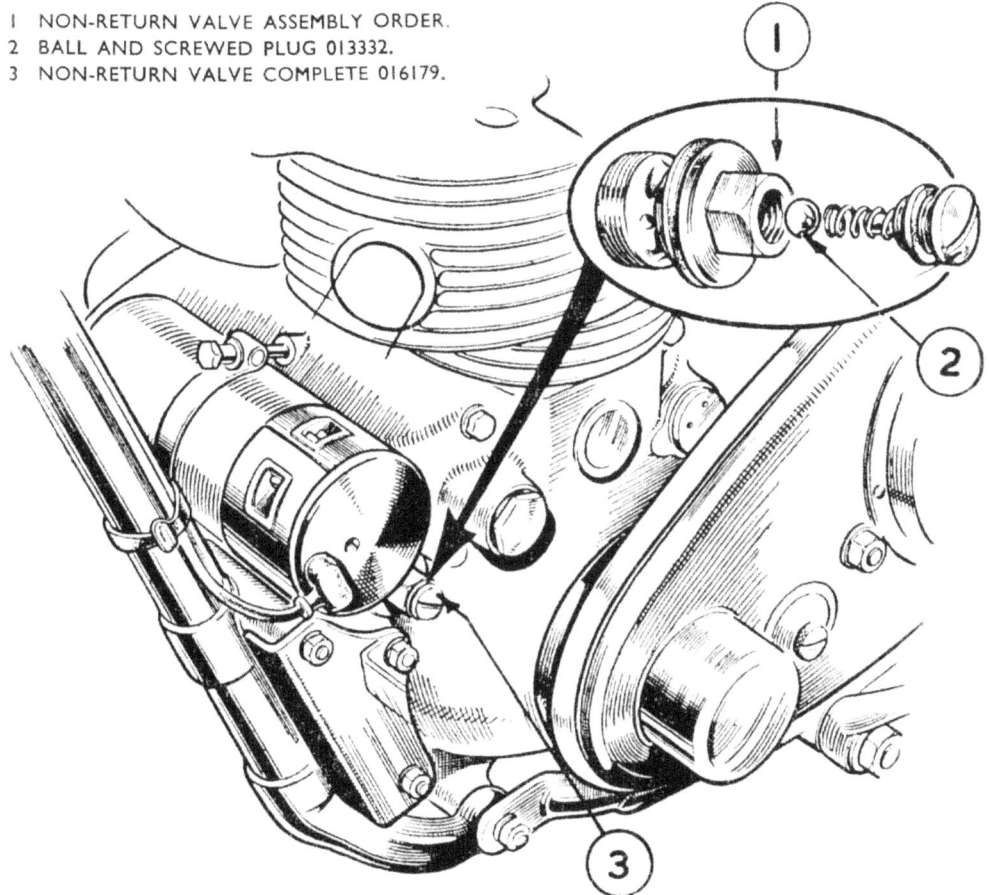

Illustration 5

**Location and exploded view of oil non-return valve.
Remove the valve complete to gain access to oil filter.**

Body 016179 screws into the housing for the oil felt filter. This body contains the oil non-return ball valve, and the complete assembly, as shown in the small inset picture, must be removed to obtain access to the oil felt filter. The screwed plug 013332 must be removed in order to apply the oil pressure gauge mentioned on **page 18**.

To remove and clean the felt crankcase filter :

Unscrew and remove the non return valve complete (016179) (See illustration 5). Withdraw the spring which removal of the non return valve will expose also withdraw the aluminium cap into which this spring is recessed.

This will expose the felt fabric filter which can be withdrawn by inserting a finger in the open end. In the other end of the filter is a steel cup which should be pulled away from the filter.

The filter should be cleaned in petrol and allowed to dry before re-insertion.

The housing tunnel for the filter should also be thoroughly cleaned out with a fluff-free rag moistened in petrol.

Reverse the above procedure to re-fit the felt filter and, when doing so, do not forget to replace the steel cup on the open end of the filter before inserting it in its housing tunnel.

To remove the magnetic filter located in the crankcase :

Incorporated with the crankcase drain plug is a powerful magnetic filter. To remove the filter merely unscrew the plug.

As the metal particles will adhere very strongly to the magnet they must be forcibly removed by wiping the magnet with a greased rag. The grease will help to retain the metal particles on the rag. Keep the magnet away from iron filings, etc., that may litter the bench, and do not bring the magnet into contact with large pieces of iron and steel, such as a bench vice, for this will impair the efficiency of the magnet and consequently its action as a filter.

OIL PRESSURE GAUGE (Workshop service only)

Upon the removal of screwed plug 013332 (see Illustration 5) a suitable oil pressure gauge can be applied to enable a check to be made of oil pump efficiency and operation, subsequent to an overhaul or dismantling.

The pressure gauge should be graduated in pounds and must have a shank threaded ·518 inch by 19 T.P.I. ($\frac{1}{4}$ B.S.P.). We can supply a suitable gauge, graduated to 250 lbs. The Part Number is B4108.

The gauge should be screwed into the valve body 016179, and the pressure checked when the engine is hot, that is, has reached its normal running temperature.

When the oil is warm and thin, the recorded pressure at idling speed should be between 20 to 40 lbs., rising somewhat when the engine revolutions are increased.

As indicated, the important check is at idling speed, and, if the mentioned pressures are obtained, the oil delivery pump is operating as intended.

NOTE—Beware loss of non return valve spring and ball which flow of oil may dislodge upon removal of screwed plug 013332.

GEAR BOX LUBRICATION

Use one of the grades of Oils specified. In no circumstances must heavy grease be used.

Lubricant is inserted through the filler cap orifice mounted on top edge of kick-starter case cover.

The gearbox must not be entirely filled with oil. An excess will cause leakage. Check the level every 1,000 miles and top-up if necessary.

A screwed drain plug in gear box shell, low down at rear, facilitates gear box flushing and change of lubricant.

An oil level plug, adjacent to K.S spindle, indicates maximum permissible oil level (content 1 pint).

CHAIN LUBRICATION

Front driving chain runs in an oil bath. (Front chaincase). Use engine oil. Maintain level to height of the inspection cap opening.

Oil in front chaincase also lubricates the engine shock absorber. Transmission harshness generally indicates level of oil in chaincase is too low.

Remove chaincase inspection cap each week, inspect level of oil, top up as necessary.

To remove inspection cap:—
Unscrew knurled screw about four turns.
Slide cap sideways till the back plate can be slipped through the opening, and take away the complete cap assembly.

When replacing inspection cap, centralise cork washer and then fully tighten knurled screw. Essential this is kept tight otherwise cap assembly will be lost.
Rear driving chain should be removed occasionally for lubrication particularly under Winter conditions.

Clean chain in paraffin, allow to drain and wipe. Then immerse in one of the greases recommended, heated to just fluid state. Leave in soak for at least ten minutes while maintaining grease fluidity. Then hang to drain off surplus and replace.
Engine oil is a poor substitute for one of the recommended greases and if used the chain should be allowed to soak for several hours to ensure penetration to all joints, hanging to drain off surplus before refitting.

See chain removal and refitting instructions Page 43.

HUB LUBRICATION
Keep hubs packed with grease. This prevents entry of water and dirt. Grease nipple accessible through hole in side hub disc. Inject small quantity of grease. Excessive grease may impair efficiency of brakes.

BRAKE DRUM BEARING
The independent ball bearing upon which the rear brake drum is mounted, is packed with grease upon assembly and requires no further attention for a considerable time.
During a general overhaul however it is recommended that the bearing is dismantled and re-packed with fresh hub grease.

BRAKE EXPANDER LUBRICATION
Grease nipple on each brake expander bush. (One on each brake cover plate). Use grease sparingly. Excessive grease may impair efficiency of brakes.

BRAKE ROD JOINT LUBRICATION
A few drops of engine oil on each brake rod yoke end pin and on the threaded portion of brake rod. (One pin on yoke each end of brake rod and on bottom of foot brake cable).

BRAKE PEDAL LUBRICATION
Grease nipple in heel of foot brake pedal.

SPEEDOMETER LUBRICATION
One grease nipple on top of speedometer gear box attached to right side of rear wheel spindle. (No other part of the speedometer requires lubrication).

STEERING HEAD BEARING LUBRICATION
One grease nipple on Front Frame Head Lug and another on right hand side of Handlebar Lug.

CONTROL CABLE LUBRICATION
To ensure free smooth action the clutch and throttle cables are fitted with a conveniently situated grease nipple. Use engine oil and hold the grease gun as near vertical as possible (spout downward) to obtain efficient ejection of oil, the gun being primarily intended for grease. Lubricate at the first sign of stiff or jerky action.

CONTROL LEVER LUBRICATION
Occasionally a drop of engine oil on all moving parts of the handlebar control levers.
If twist grip is too stiff : remove two screws binding the two halves of the clip. This releases the grip which may be pulled off the handlebar. Smear handlebar, the drum on which the inner wire is wound and the friction spring on the half clip with grease and replace.

REAR FORK HINGE
Heavy Gear Oil. (See pages 20 and 50.) **SAE-140.**

LUBRICATION CHART

The figures in diamond frames refer to parts located on the left hand side of the machine and those in circles refer to parts located on the right hand side.

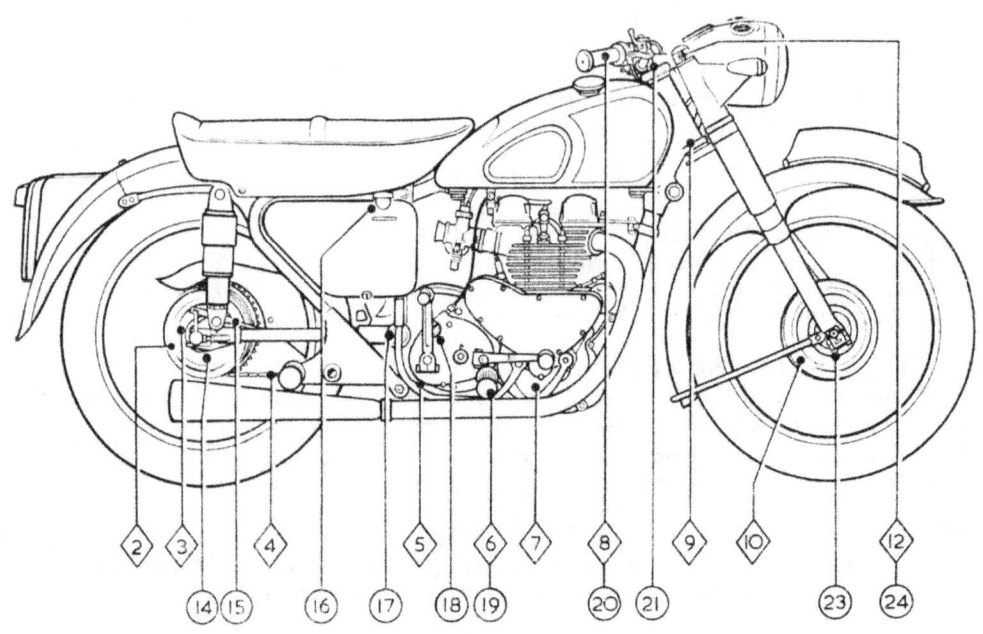

Illustration 6

Lubrication Chart

Engine Oil Locations
- 16 MAIN OIL TANK.
- 7 FRONT CHAINCASE.
- 8/20 } CONTROL LEVER MOVING PARTS.
- 2 BRAKE ROD JOINTS.
- 6/19 } CENTRE AND PROP STAND HINGE PINS

Hydraulic Fluid Locations
- 12/24 } FRONT TELEDRAULIC FORKS.

Heavy Engine Oil Location
- 18 GEAR BOX.

Grease Locations
- 23 FRONT HUB.
- 14 REAR HUB.
- 21 STEERING HEAD TOP BEARING.
- 9 STEERING HEAD BOTTOM BEARING.
- 15 SPEEDOMETER GEAR BOX.
- 10 FRONT BRAKE EXPANDER.
- 3 REAR BRAKE EXPANDER.
- 5 BRAKE PEDAL SPINDLE.

Heavy Gear Oil Location SAE-140
- 17 REAR FORK HINGE.

Molten Grease Location
- 4 REAR CHAIN.

When buying oils and greases it is advisable to specify the **Brand** as well as the grade and, as an additional precaution, to only buy in sealed containers or from branded cabinets.

MAINTENANCE

PERIODICAL MAINTENANCE

Regular maintenance attention to lubrication and certain adjustments must be made to ensure unfailing reliability and satisfactory service. This necessary attention is detailed below and owners are strongly recommended to carefully follow these suggestions and to make a regular practice of doing so from the first.

The reference numbers, in brackets, refer to the locations specified on the Lubrication Chart, illustration 6, page 20.

DAILY

Oil tank	Inspect oil level (16) and top-up to top line level if necessary. Check oil circulation.
Petrol tank	Check level and re-fill if necessary.

WEEKLY

Oil tank	Check level and re-fill to top line level if necessary. (16).
Tyres	Check pressures and inflate if necessary.

EVERY 500 MILES

Oil tank	Drain at first 500 miles and re-fill to top line level with new oil, and clean filter. (16).
Gear Box	Drain at first 500 miles and refill (18) 1 pint.
Chaincase	Check level of oil when machine is standing vertically on level ground when level of oil should not be less than $\frac{3}{16}$" below bottom edge of inspection orifice. (7). Fill up to orifice if level is low.
Battery	Inspect each cell for level of electrolyte and top up with distilled water if necessary. (See pages 69 and 70). Level of electrolyte should just be over top of plates. Beware of overfilling.

EVERY 1,000 MILES

Oil tank	Drain at first 1,000 miles and re-fill with new oil. (16).
Rear chain	In wet weather remove and soak in molten grease. See page 13. (4)
Gear box	Add 2 fluid ounces of specified oil. (18).
Hubs	Inject small amount of grease. (14–23).
Expanders	Inject small amount of grease. (3–10).
Steering head	Inject small amount of grease. (9–21).
Small parts	Smear all moving parts with engine oil and wipe off surplus. (2-6-8-19-20).

EVERY 2,000 to 5,000 MILES (according to road conditions.)

Air Filter	(If fitted) clean and re-oil filter element.

EVERY 3,000 MILES

Rear chain	In dry weather remove and soak in molten grease. (4).
Brake pedal	Inject small amount of grease. (5).
Speedometer	Inject small amount of grease into speedometer gear box. (15).
Magneto	Clean contact breaker points and re-set if necessary.
Plugs	Clean sparking plugs and re-set points as necessary. When refitting reverse respective positions.
Steering head	Test steering head for up and down movement and adjust if necessary.
Bolts and nuts	Check all nuts and bolts for tightness and tighten if necessary but beware of over-tightening.
Rockers	Check O.H.V. rocker adjustment and correct if necessary.

EVERY 5,000 MILES

Oil tank	Drain and re-fill with new oil. (16). If machine is only used for short runs renew oil every three months instead of mileage interval.
Filters	Clean metal mesh filter in oil tank (illustration 4), and felt fabric filter in crankcase.
Magneto	Clean and adjust as detailed in Electrical section.
Dynamo	Clean as detailed in Electrical section.
Front fork	Check each side of front fork for hydraulic fluid content and, if necessary, top up. (12–24). Insufficient oil content is indicated by abnormally lively action.
Rear legs	Check each leg for hydraulic fluid content and, if necessary, top up. Insufficient oil content is indicated by abnormally lively action. (Dealers' Service only).
Carburetter	Remove carburetter float chamber side cover and clean interior. Also detach petrol pipe banjo and clean gauze strainer.

EVERY 10,000 MILES

Magneto and **Dynamo**	Get a **Lucas Service Station** to dismantle, clean, lubricate and generally service.
Air Filter	(If fitted) renew filter element.

ENGINE SERVICE

TO ADJUST OVERHEAD ROCKERS (Tappet clearance)

Using key bar 018055 remove screws securing a rocker cover. (It is desirable to deal only with one cover at a time).

Lift off the cover, exposing the rocker.

Using single ended spanner 015264, slightly slack off the nut of the bolt clamping the disc headed end of the rocker spindle. (See note below).

Then slowly revolve the engine, by means of the kick-starter pedal, till well past the position at which the valve closes and then proceed to revolve the rocker spindle until the correct clearance is obtained, whereupon, re-tighten the locking nut and replace the cover. (Inspect gasket under rocker cover and, if damaged, replace with new.)

The correct rocker clearance, with cold engine, is .006" for both inlet and exhaust.

It is best to ensure that each piston, in turn, is at the top of its firing stroke when adjusting rocker clearances. The method of obtaining that position is explained in the paragraph dealing with **Timing the Ignition**. This piston position is essential to ensure the cam levers are well clear of the cam quietening curves when adjusting rocker clearance.

It should, perhaps, be explained here that these quietening curves, as they are called, are actually slight inclines from the base circles of the cams to the foot of each hump and their object is to slowly take up the clearance between the cam levers and valve push rods as the valves open and close thus reducing noise.

NOTE—If the rocker spindle clamping bolt nut is unscrewed to an unnecessary extent the rocker spindle will then move sideways, under the influence of the spring washer, and then the thrust washer at the end of the rocker spindle may drop out of exact location and, unless noticed and re-positioned, damage to the flanged end of the rocker spindle may result upon re-tightening the clamping bolt nut. Care to avoid this is necessary. (See illustration 7.)

1. PLAIN WASHER-MENTIONED ABOVE
2. SPRING WASHER
3. PLAIN WASHER
4. ROCKER
5. CYLINDER HEAD
6. ROCKER CLEARANCE ·006
7. VALVE SPRING CAP
8. CLAMPING BOLT NUT
9. CLAMPING BOLT WASHER
10. CLAMPING BOLT
11. CUTAWAY ON ROCKER SPINDLE
12. ECCENTRIC ROCKER SPINDLE

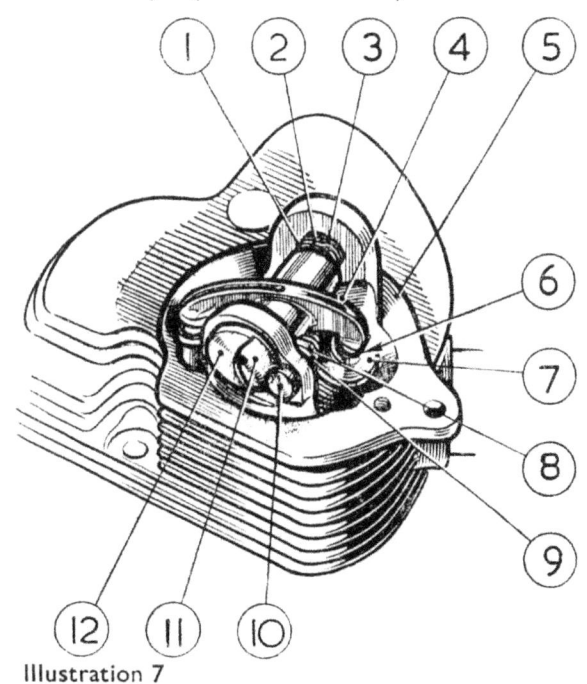

Illustration 7

Rocker Adjustment

ACCESS

For all service work to the upper part of the engine, other than adjustment of the rockers, it is necessary, in order to obtain accessibility, to first remove the petrol tank. The two petrol taps facilitate this operation by removing the need to drain the tank of petrol.

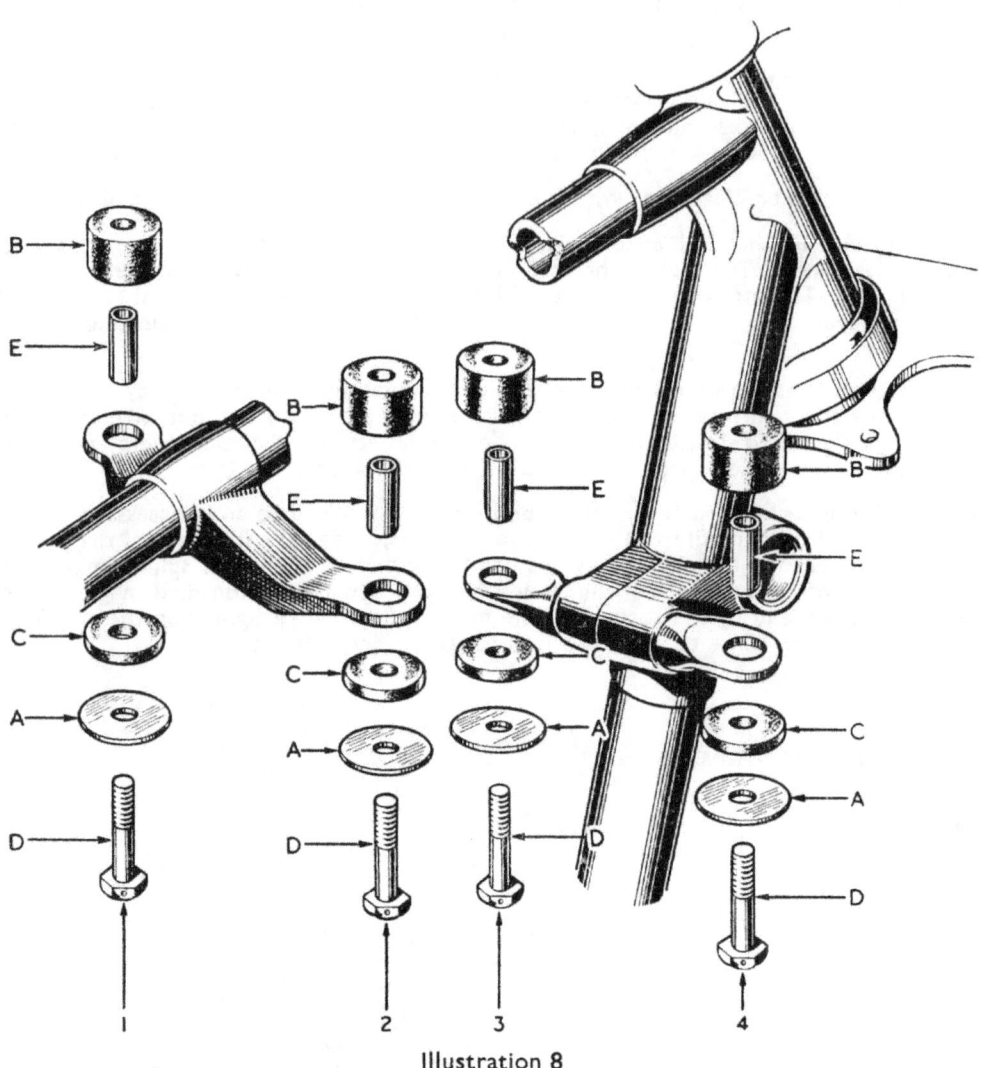

Illustration 8

Details and order of assembly, of the fuel tank fixing bolts and components

			Part Number	
A	METAL WASHER	... ...	014999	1¼" diameter.
B	THICK RUBBER PAD	... ...	014995	⅝" high.
C	THIN RUBBER PAD	... ...	014996	7/16" high.
D	TANK FIXING BOLT	... ...	014997	1¼" × 5/16" × 26.
E	SLEEVE FOR FIXING BOLT	... ...	014998	13/16" long.

TO REMOVE THE PETROL TANK

Remove the twin seat.

Close both petrol taps and remove the cap nut securing each petrol pipe banjo connector. Use two spanners, one to hold the tap and the other to unscrew the cap nut.

Beware losing the fibre washers (4 in all) fitted one each side of each banjo connection.

Cut the wires interlacing the four fixing bolts.

Unscrew the tank fixing bolts and the tank is then free to be taken away.

NOTE—The disposition of the various rubber and metal washers should be specially observed so that they may be correctly replaced.

TO REPLACE THE PETROL TANK

Proceed in reverse order to removal. Firmly screw home the four fixing bolts and interlace them, in pairs, with 22 gauge copper wire.

DECARBONISATION

Instead of the usual stipulated mileage interval between periods of decarbonisation it is recommended that this is undertaken only when the need for same becomes apparent because of excessive pinking, loss of power or generally reduced performance. When undertaken, unless it is thought necessary to inspect the pistons and rings, the cylinder barrels are best left undisturbed. The various stages in decarbonisation are described below.

TO REMOVE CYLINDER HEADS FOR DECARBONISATION

To ensure the various parts of each head are not intermixed it is recommended that only one head is removed at a time.

Remove the petrol tank, as already described.

Remove the rocker box covers, as already described.

Remove the sparking plugs.

Remove the exhaust pipes and silencers (no need to separate pipes and silencers) by taking away nuts and washers holding pipes to stays and silencers to rear frame, pulling silencer end of each assembly outwards far enough to allow fixing studs to disengage and then pulling each assembly forwards till disengaged from the cylinder head.

Remove air filter (if fitted).

Remove carburetter by taking away the two fixing bolts and withdrawing to the rear. Lay carburetter aside.

Remove inlet manifold by taking away the four fixing nuts and washers and withdrawing to the rear. Take care not to damage the gaskets between manifold and heads or rubber ring insert.

Remove cylinder head steady plate (secured by 3 bolts and nuts).

Remove heads by using box spanner 015213 to remove the four domed nuts that retain each head.

After removal invert each head to dislodge the spacers under the domed nuts and lay aside to await re-assembly.

The cylinder head gaskets will generally adhere to the tops of the barrels but care must be taken not to damage them.

TO REMOVE THE VALVES

Remove rockers.

Assuming that a valve spring compressor is not available :

Prepare a block of wood about 2" cube, lay same on a bench, place cylinder head over it so that the heads of both valves are supported on the block.

Apply pressure to each valve spring cap, in turn, to sufficiently compress the springs to permit the extraction of the split collet. The collets are a taper fit in the valve spring collar and it may be necessary to give the collar a sharp tap to release them. (A stout screwdriver is a handy tool with which to apply the pressure).

Lift away valve spring collar, springs and spring seat from each valve.

Lift head off the wood block and valves will drop out.

TO REMOVE VALVE GUIDES

Apply gentle heat to cylinder head and press upward guide to be removed just sufficiently to permit removal of external circlip. Then thoroughly clean protruding top end of guide re-heat and press downward to extract.

Re-heat when replacing.

REMOVING CARBON DEPOSIT

Do not use a sharp implement for removing carbon deposit from the interior of the aluminium cylinder head and the piston crown. A blunt piece of soft brass will be found quite suitable and the use of such will obviate the risk of making deep scratches. Care is necessary to avoid damaging the inserted valve seatings and in no circumstances should any abrasive material, such as emery cloth, be used for cleaning and polishing.

VALVE GRINDING

Before commencing valve grinding, carefully examine the face of each valve and, if any are found to be deeply pitted, have them refaced. (Most garages have suitable equipment for that purpose). Any attempt to remove deep pit marks by grinding will inevitably cause undue and undesirable widening of the seats.

As a rule, inlet valves require very little attention and one light application of fine grinding paste should be sufficient to restore an even matt finish to both valve face and seat. The exhaust valves may require two, or even three, applications but, as already mentioned, excessive grinding is both unnecessary and harmful.

The grinding is accomplished by smearing a thin layer of fine grinding paste (obtainable ready for use at any garage) on the valve face and then, after inserting the valve in the head, partially revolve, forwards and backwards, while applying light finger pressure to the head, raising the valve off its seat and turning to another position after every few movements. (Never revolve the valve continuously in one direction).

The grinding may be considered to be satisfactorily completed when a continuous matt ring is observed on both valve face and seat.

After grinding, all traces of abrasive must be carefully washed off with petrol and a piece of rag, moistened in petrol, should be pulled through the bore of each valve guide to remove any abrasive that may have collected.

NOTE—A piece of oil resisting rubber tube having a bore of $\frac{1}{4}"$ slipped over the valve end will be found a suitable device for revolving the valves during grinding in. This is not included in the standard tool kit. The Part number is 011381.

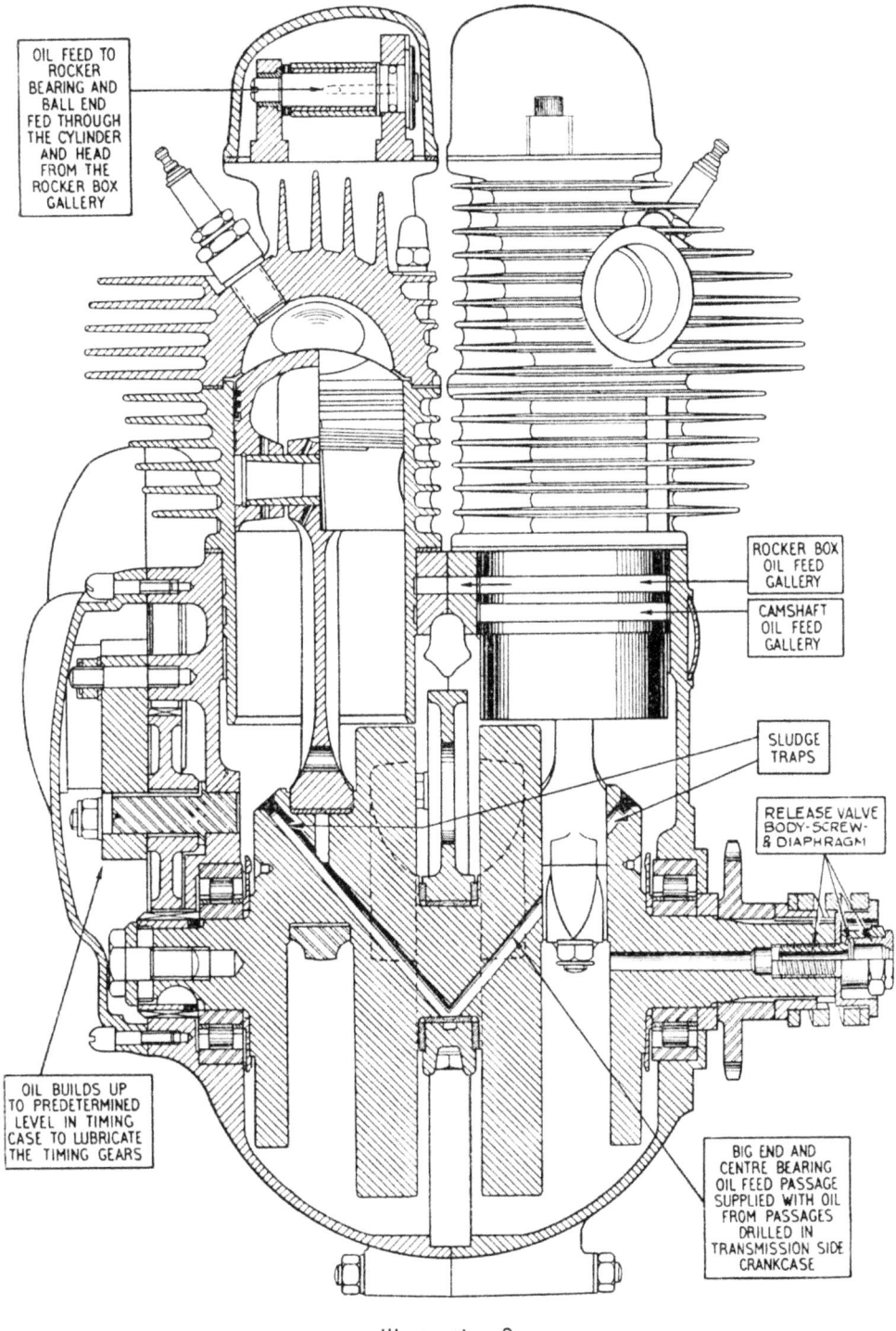

Illustration 9

Cross section of engine showing oil galleries, oil passages, and release valve.

REMOVING CYLINDER BARRELS AND PISTONS

> Unless it is desired to inspect the pistons and rings, during decarbonisation, they are, as already advised, best left undisturbed.

Having removed the cylinder heads **withdraw the cylinder barrels** by :

Lift away the four push rods, identify them for re-fitting and lay aside.

Dealing with one barrel at a time, exert upward pressure on a barrel, slightly rocking to and fro while doing so, and steady the piston with one hand as it emerges from the barrel.

Cover the crankcase throat with clean rag to prevent the entry of foreign matter.

To remove a piston

Using 011188 circlip pliers, contract one of the gudgeon pin circlips and, with a rotary motion, gently withdraw the circlip from its housing. The gudgeon pin may then be pushed out of the piston which action frees the piston from the connecting rod. (Being a parallel, floating fit in the piston and connecting rod small end it is immaterial from which side the gudgeon pin is withdrawn.)

NOTE—It may be necessary to apply a little heat to the piston to permit free gudgeon pin removal and replacement.

Rings may be removed from a piston by peeling off or by introducing behind them three thin and narrow metal strips, equally spaced round the piston, and then sliding them off, taking care not to scratch the piston.

Carefully examine the contact edge of each piston ring and replace any which do not show a bright surface over the whole circumference.

FITTING PISTONS AND CYLINDER BARRELS

Pistons to be free of carbon on their crowns and all piston ring grooves to be clean. Piston rings to be clean and on pistons.

Fit a piston to its connecting rod by : Smear gudgeon pin with clean engine oil.

Place piston over connecting rod so that the slotted side faces to the front of the machine, introduce gudgeon pin to piston and pass through connecting rod, press right home against the circlip still in situ. Then again, using pliers 011188, contract the other circlip, introduce same into its groove in the piston, using a rotary movement. Make quite certain that the circlip lies snugly in its groove because failure to do so will inevitably lead to serious damage.

(See " NOTE " above).

Before fitting the cylinders, make sure they are clean and examine the base washers and renew same if not perfect.

To fit a new cylinder base washer : first clean off the old washer and all traces of jointing compound. Then smear one side of the new washer with jointing compound and, when that is nearly dry (" tacky ") apply to the cylinder.

Place rings on piston, scraper first, then the two compression rings. On all models the top compression ring is chromium plated. These chrome plated rings have a slightly tapered exterior and when new are clearly marked with the word TOP on one side to indicate assembly position. After use this word tends to become indiscernible, but over a large mileage the assembly position can be determined by brightness of the edge contacting cylinder wall. This bright edge is the lower one. When as the result of wear, contact with the cylinder wall appears uniform over the whole width of the ring, it is then immaterial which way round it is refitted.

Space the piston rings so that the gaps are 120° to each other, smear piston and rings and bore of barrel with clean engine oil and, supporting the piston with one hand, gently pass over the barrel, compressing each piston ring with the fingers, as it enters the barrel.

Press the cylinder barrel right down into the throat of the crankcase.

Fit the second piston, gudgeon pin, rings and barrel in a like manner.

Revolve the engine till the pistons are at the top of their strokes and then, with a clean rag, wipe off all surplus oil. All is now ready to re-fit the cylinder heads.

TO RE-FIT THE CYLINDER HEADS

Clean the valve stems and the bores of the valve guides with rag moistened with petrol, make sure all other parts are clean, then smear each valve stem with clean engine oil and proceed to re-fit the valve stems by reversing the procedure taken to dismantle them.

Insert the four valve push rods Into their original positions and, after making sure that the cylinder head gaskets are undamaged and in position, proceed to fit the two heads and leave the two sets of four cylinder head retaining nuts finger tight.

Now re-fit the inlet manifold, making sure the two paper gaskets are undamaged, and leave the four retaining nuts only just tight enough to ensure correct alignment.

Next, fully tighten down the four retaining nuts on each head, treating each, diagonally, bit by bit, till all are fully down.

Then, fully tighten the inlet manifold retaining nuts and re-fit the carburetter.

Next, carefully check each rocker clearance, as previously described, and re-set if necessary. (The correct rocker clearance with cold engine is .006" for inlet and exhaust).

The gaskets under each rocker cover should be inspected and, if not sound, should be replaced after which the rocker covers can be refitted.

Next re-fit the cylinder head steady plate and securely tighten the three fixing bolts.

NOTE—Before re-fitting carburetter make sure the rubber ring in manifold joint face is in position and undamaged.

VALVE TIMING

Inlet valve opens   35° before top dead centre
Inlet valve closes   65° after bottom dead centre
Exhaust valve opens 65° before bottom dead centre
Exhaust valve closes 35° after top dead centre

(Check valve timing with .012" rocker clearance)

Upon removing the timing gear cover (secured by 10 screws and 1 nut) and the pump plate assembly it will be observed the valve timing gears are marked to facilitate correct assembly.

One tooth of the mainshaft small pinion is marked with one centre punch dot and a tooth gap of the idle pinion, into which it meshes, is similarly marked. With these two marks coinciding it will be seen that a tooth gap on each side of the intermediate pinion is marked with two centre punch dots which also coincide with a similarly marked tooth on each of the camshaft driving gear wheels.

During assembly it is only necessary to mesh the gears with these various marks coinciding to ensure correct valve timing.

The dynamo and magneto drive pinions are not marked. The dynamo does not need "timing" and if, for any reason, the magneto timing has been disturbed, it is re-set as described later.

Removal of gears

When completely dismantling the engine there is no necessity to remove the small timing pinion from the crankshaft before splitting the crankcase because the complete crankshaft can be taken away with the pinion still in position.

If, however, it is desired to remove the pinion without completely dismantling the engine a special extractor is required (part number 015273). This consists of a nut, threaded externally and internally. The external threads enable it to be screwed into the threaded centre of the pinion and the internal threads accommodate a specially designed and hardened bolt which, upon screwing down, pulls off the pinion. This same tool is used for the removal of the magneto gear.

The intermediate gear needs no extractor.

The gears on the two camshafts (secured by nuts having left-hand threads) have to be mechanically withdrawn and each has two holes drilled and threaded to accommodate the two bolts of a bridge type extractor (part number 015374) which has a central bolt threaded in the bridge. The two outside bolts are screwed into the holes in the gears whereupon application of the centre bolt being screwed into the bridge bears on the end of the shaft thereby causing the gear to be withdrawn.

The gear on the dynamo needs no extractor because the dynamo, complete with gear assembled, is easily and quickly removed from the engine and the subsequent removal of the gear from the dynamo shaft is a simple workshop operation.

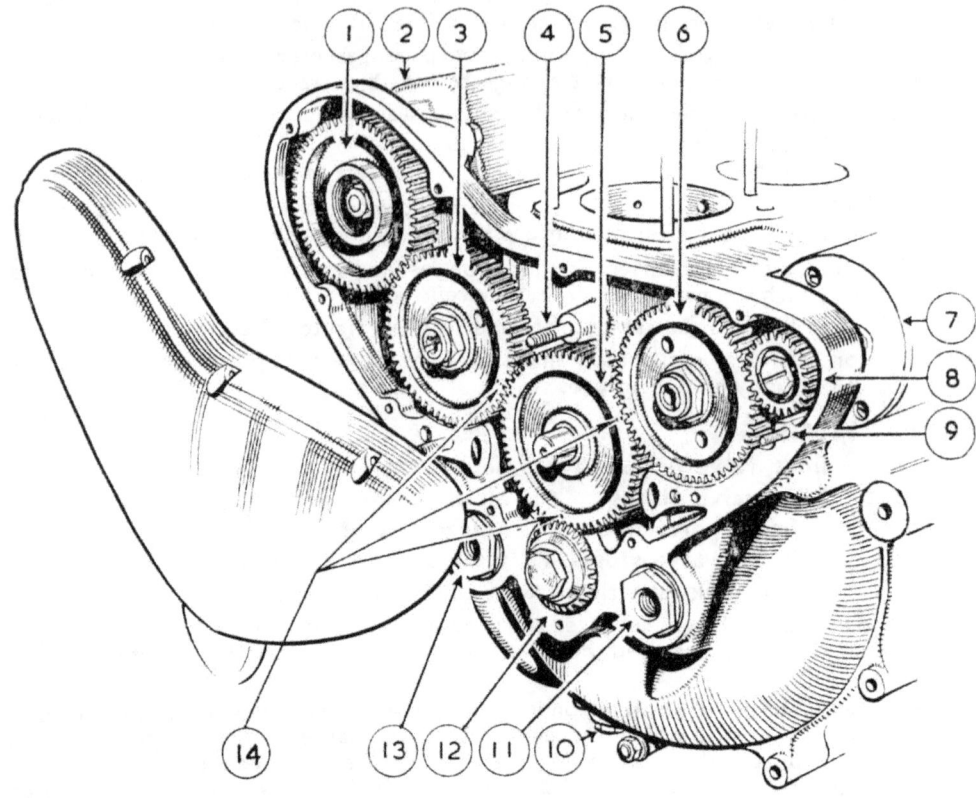

Illustration 10

Valve timing gear

See page 82 for particulars of special timing disc graduated in degrees.

1. GEAR WHEEL ON MAGNETO ARMATURE SHAFT.
2. MAGNETO.
3. GEAR WHEEL ON INLET CAMSHAFT.
4. ONE OF THE THREE STUDS RETAINING THE OIL PUMPS ASSEMBLY.
5. INTERMEDIATE (OR IDLE) GEAR.
6. GEAR WHEEL ON EXHAUST CAMSHAFT.
7. DYNAMO.
8. GEAR WHEEL ON DYNAMO ARMATURE SHAFT.
9. STUD, IN DYNAMO BODY AND PASSING THROUGH CRANKCASE AND TIMING GEAR COVER.
10. CRANKCASE DRAIN PLUG.
11. ADAPTOR TO ACCOMMODATE OIL FEED PIPE BANJO PIN.
12. TIMING PINION ON CRANKSHAFT.
13. ADAPTOR TO ACCOMMODATE OIL RETURN PIPE BANJO PIN.
14. MARKS TO SET TIMING.

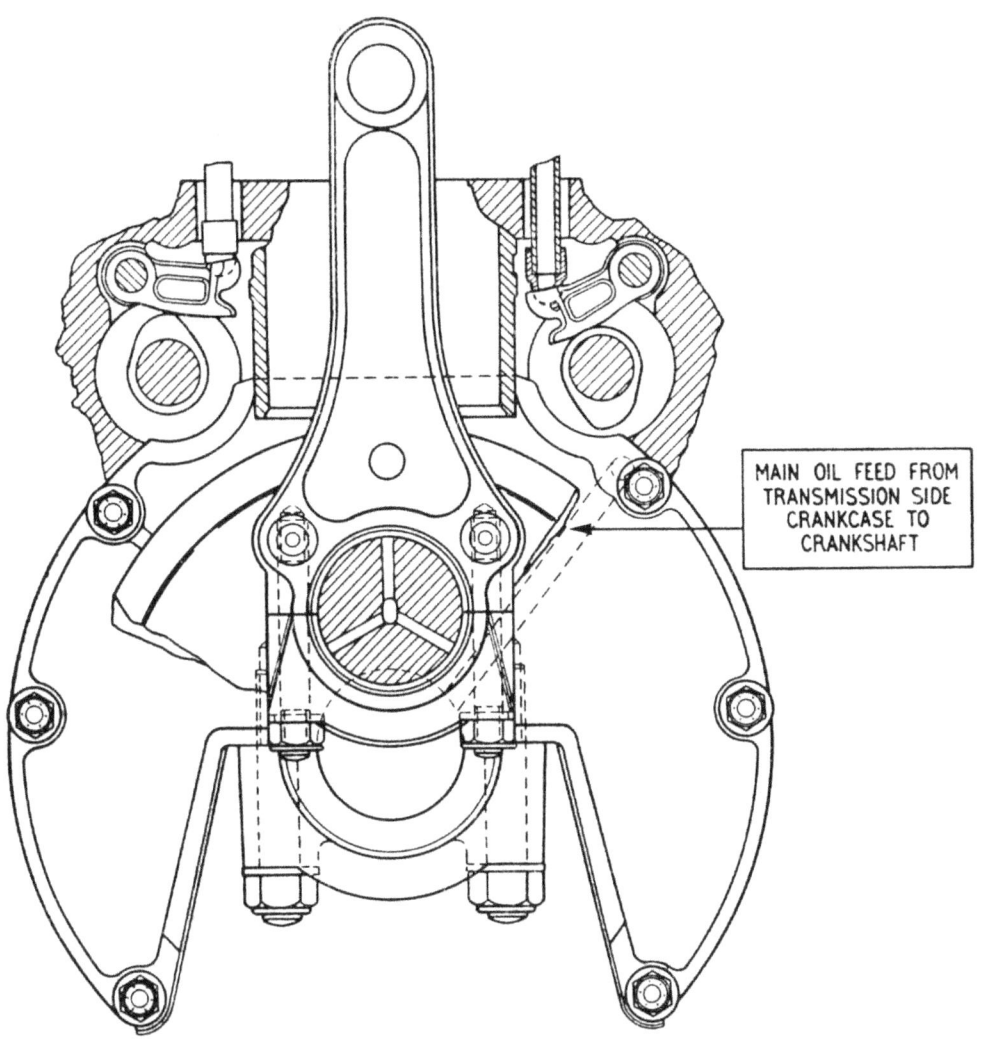

Illustration 11

**Mounting for centre bearing for crankshaft, and
a connecting rod with big-end bearing**

TO RE-TIME THE IGNITION

Before proceeding to time the ignition it is advisable first to check the contact breaker point gap, which should be from .010" to .012", and correct it if necessary.

Having loosened the nut securing the magneto driving pinion, release same from the tapered end of the magneto shaft by means of a special extractor, as described on **page 29**. Remove the inlet rocker cover from the off-side cylinder head.

Remove the sparking plug from the off-side cylinder.

Insert a small rod into the sparking plug hole and, feeling the piston with the end of this rod, carefully turn the engine in its normal direction of rotation until the piston is exactly at the top of the stroke after the inlet valve has closed.

Hold the rod as vertical as the angular sparking plug hole will permit, make a mark on same exactly coinciding with the top edge of the sparking plug hole boss. Then withdraw the rod and make another mark exactly $\frac{3}{8}$" higher up. Re-insert the rod and turn the engine backward until the higher mark coincides with the top edge of the sparking plug hole boss.

Place the ignition control lever in the fully advanced position.

Next, taking care not to disturb the piston position, turn the magneto in a clockwise direction (looking at the contact breaker end of the magneto) until the contact breaker points are just about to separate by reason of the fibre block on the bell crank lever commencing to mount the lower cam hump.

The exact point of separation is best found by inserting between the contact points a strip of thin tissue paper when the separation point can be determined by the paper just being released with a light pull.

Having obtained this position, press the magneto driving gear on to its taper with the fingers and lightly tighten the securing nut.

It is next advisable to re-check the setting by again turning the engine to the position at which the piston is $\frac{3}{8}''$ before the top of the firing stroke, re-inserting tissue paper between the contact points and confirming that same can be released with a light pull.

Upon being satisfied that the setting is correct securely tighten down the nut fixing the magneto driving gear.

Thoroughly clean off all traces of jointing compound from face edges of the timing cover and crankcase and then smear both faces with new jointing compound, which leave till tacky and then re-fit the cover to the crankcase. ("Wellseal" recommended.)

The whole operation of timing the ignition will be found quite simple if the foregoing instructions are carefully followed.

NOTE—The sparking plug High Tension cable for the off-side cylinder is that connected to the rear pick-up on the magneto.

TO DISMANTLE AND REFIT CRANKCASE RELEASE VALVE IN CRANKSHAFT (see Illustration 9)

Upon removal of the outer portion of front chaincase as described elsewhere, the release valve will be observed on the end of the engine shaft.

The larger hexagon, is the release valve body, which also secures the shock absorber spring cap.

The smaller hexagon is the release valve screw, which retains the spring and diaphragm.

To inspect release valve and ensure correct re-assembly it is essential to remove the valve body from the engine shaft, then the valve screw can be removed.

When re-fitting diaphragm, hold the valve body vertical with large hole uppermost, and correctly locate spring when the valve screw is assembled.

REMOVING SPARKING PLUG

Always exercise the greatest care to avoid thread seizure when removing a sparking plug. If any resistance is felt, apply paraffin. Before replacing plug, it is desirable to coat the thread with "Oil Dag" or Graphite paste. This will guard against seizure upon subsequent removal.

CARBURETTER SERVICE

The information given in this section includes all that will normally be required by the average rider. For further details, particularly those connected with racing and the use of special fuels, we refer the enquirer to the manufacturers of the carburetter, **Amal Ltd., Holford Road, Witton, Birmingham, 6.**

Our **Spare Parts Department** does not stock every part of the carburetter but confines its stock to those parts that, from time to time, may be required. Those parts include floats and float needles, jet taper needles, pilot jets, main jets, needle jets and washers.

CARBURETTER FUNCTION

The petrol level is maintained by a float and needle valve and, in no circumstances, should any alteration be made to these parts. In the event of a leaky float, or a worn needle valve, the part should be replaced with new. (Do not attempt to grind a needle to its seat).

The petrol supply to the engine is controlled, firstly, by the main jet and, secondly, by means of a taper needle (see illustration 12) which is attached to the throttle valve and operates in a tubular extension of the main jet.

The main jet controls the mixture from three-quarters to full throttle, the adjustable taper needle from three-quarters down to one-quarter throttle, the cut-away portion of the intake side of the throttle valve from one-quarter down to about one-eighth throttle, and a pilot jet, having an independently adjusted air supply, takes care of the idling from one-eighth throttle down to the almost closed position. These various stages of control must be kept in mind when any adjustment is contemplated. (See illustration 12, for location of the pilot jet air adjustment screw). The pilot jet unlike on earlier models is now detachable for cleaning.

The size of the main jet should not be altered save for some very good reason. See " DATA " for details of standard sizes of jet, throttle valve, and jet taper needle. With the standard setting it is possible to use nearly full air in all conditions, except, perhaps, when the engine is pulling hard up hill or is on full throttle, when some benefit may be obtained by slightly closing the air control.

Weak mixture is always indicated by popping, or spitting, at the air intake.

A rich mixture usually causes bumpy, or jerky, running and, in cases of extreme richness, is accompanied by the emission of black smoke from the exhaust.

CARBURETTER ADJUSTMENT

With the taper needle projection, main jet size, and type of throttle slide specified (See Page 6) correct carburation except at idling speed is assured.

In the event of difficulty being experienced look for cause under heading Useful Information (Pages 74 and 75.)

To check for correct idling mixture, first run the engine until it is just warm but not hot when with the throttle nearly closed and air fully open it should fire evenly and slowly. If it fails to do so, first of all make certain that the sparking plug is clean and the point setting correct. Having done this and idling is still uneven try resetting the pilot jet air screw.

Adjustment of this air screw is not unduly sensitive and it should be possible to obtain the correct setting for even firing in a few seconds.

In the event of even firing at idling speed being unobtainable by adjustment of the air screw look for obstruction in the pilot jet.

Having obtained even firing all that remains is to adjust if necessary the position of the throttle stop screw until the desired idling speed is obtained.

TWIST GRIP ADJUSTMENT

A screw is provided in one of the halves of the twist grip body to regulate the spring tension on the grip rotating sleeve. This screw, which is locked by a nut, must be screwed into the body to increase the tension.

The most desirable state of adjustment is that when the grip is quite free and easy to operate but, at the same time, will stay in the position in which it is placed.

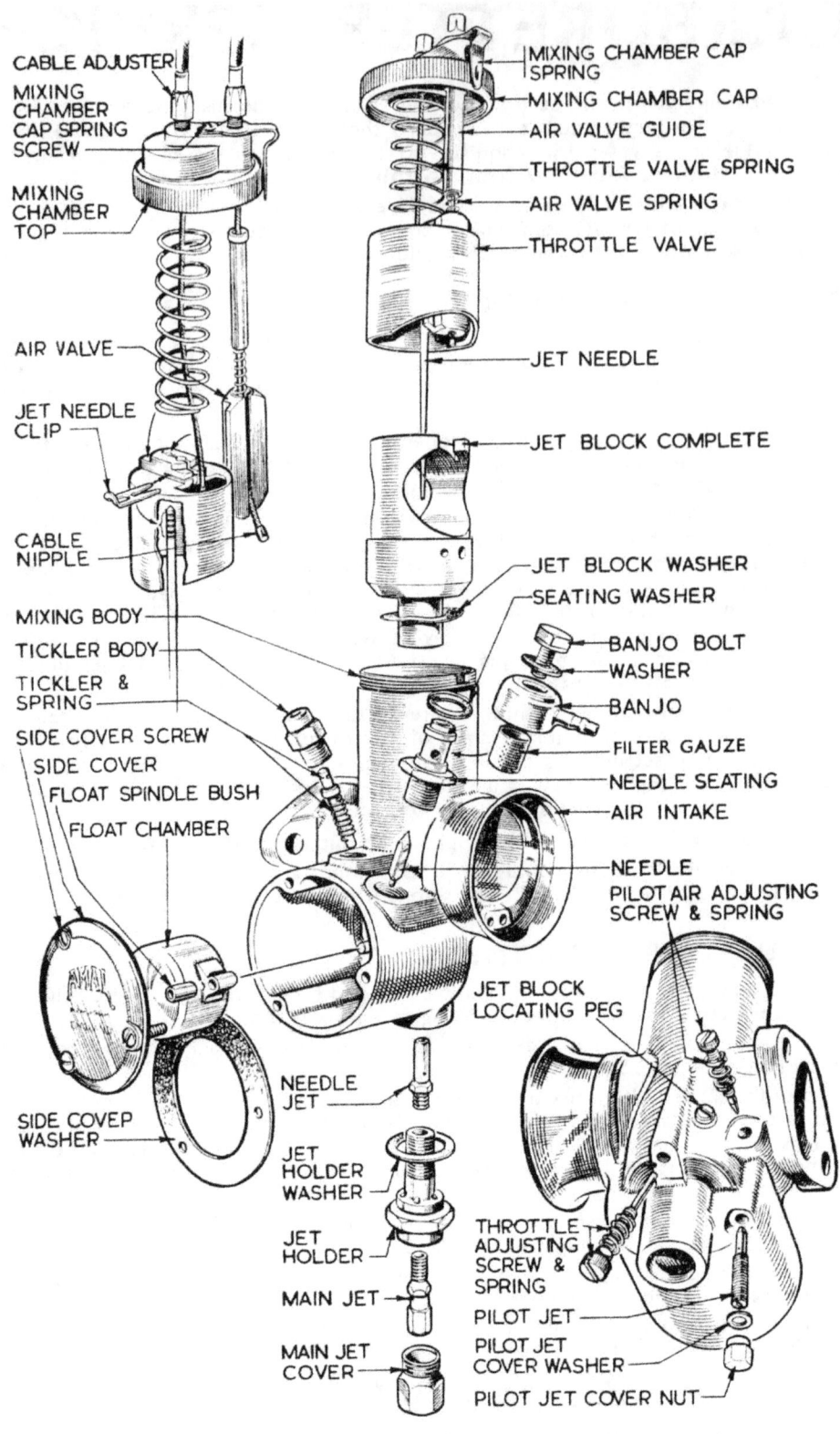

Illustration 12

Carburetter details in assembly order

TWIST GRIP ADJUSTMENT CONT.

The complete twist grip can be moved on the handlebar by slackening the two screws that clamp together the two halves of the body. The most desirable position is that in which the throttle cable makes the cleanest and most straight path to the under-side of the petrol tank.

Smooth throttle operation is assured by the provision of a cable oil nipple. At the first signs of jerky action a little engine oil should be injected applying the gun as near vertical as possible (nozzle downward).

AIR FILTER

In locations, such as the United Kingdom, where the roads and atmosphere are particularly free from dust, it is not considered necessary to have an air filter fitted to the carburetter, but in countries where the atmosphere contains a very heavy dust content, an air filter is essential in order to prevent abrasive wear.

The filter available (optional extra) for the conditions mentioned above is of the " Oil Wetted " type, and this requires periodical servicing.

When servicing the air filter, withdraw the filter element. Thoroughly wash this in petrol, paraffin or other suitable solvent and allow to dry. Then re-oil, using one of the light oils (SAE-20), enumerated in the final table on page 13, and allow to drain before replacing in the filter case. Clean at intervals of 2,500 to 5,000 miles according to road conditions, and renew the element every 10,000 miles.

TO REMOVE THE AIR FILTER ELEMENT

Pull the rubber hose off the carburetter air intake.

Remove the frame cover and pull off the hose end from the air filter.

Remove the bolts securing the filter to the oil tank and withdraw the entire filter unit.

The filter element is held in its cage by bolts and nuts and lock washers. After cleaning, replace the filter. When the hose is replaced on the filter make sure that it is properly located. The end of the hose is split along the edge of the lip, and the neck of the filter unit slips into this groove.

CARBURETTER TUNING INFORMATION

Poor idling may be due to :
    Air leaks. Either at junction of carburetter and inlet manifold, or by reason of badly worn inlet valve stems or guides.
    Faulty engine valve seatings.
    Sparking plug faulty, or its points set too closely.
    Ignition advanced too much.
    Contact breaker points dirty, pitted, loose, or set too closely.
    High-tension wire defective.
    Pilot jet not operating correctly. Partially choked or incorrect air supply.
    Rockers adjusted too closely.

Heavy petrol consumption may be due to :
    Late ignition setting.
    Bad air leaks. Probably at carburetter or manifold joints.
    Weakened valve springs.
    Leaky float. (Causing flooding).
    Taper needle extension insufficient.
    Poor compression, due to worn piston rings or defective valve seatings. (Test compression with throttle wide open).

TRANSMISSION SERVICE

THE GEAR BOX

The gear box provides four speeds and has a positive foot change, operated by the right foot and a kick-starter.

It is retained to the frame by being clamped between the two engine rear plates by two bolts. The bottom fixing bolt acts as a pivot. The top fixing bolt passes through the gear box top lug and the rear plates, which are slotted, thereby allowing a swinging fore and aft movement of the gear box to enable the front driving chain to be adjusted. That movement is controlled by an adjusting bolt (marked 1 in illustration 15) secured in an eye bolt (marked 2 in illustration 15) and locked in the required position by a nut (marked 3 in illustration 15).

Illustration 13 clearly shows the general internal gearbox layout, the simple gear selection and kickstarter mechanism. It will be seen that movement of the foot change lever causes movement of the cam barrel through the medium of an ingenious trip fork to which the lever is attached.

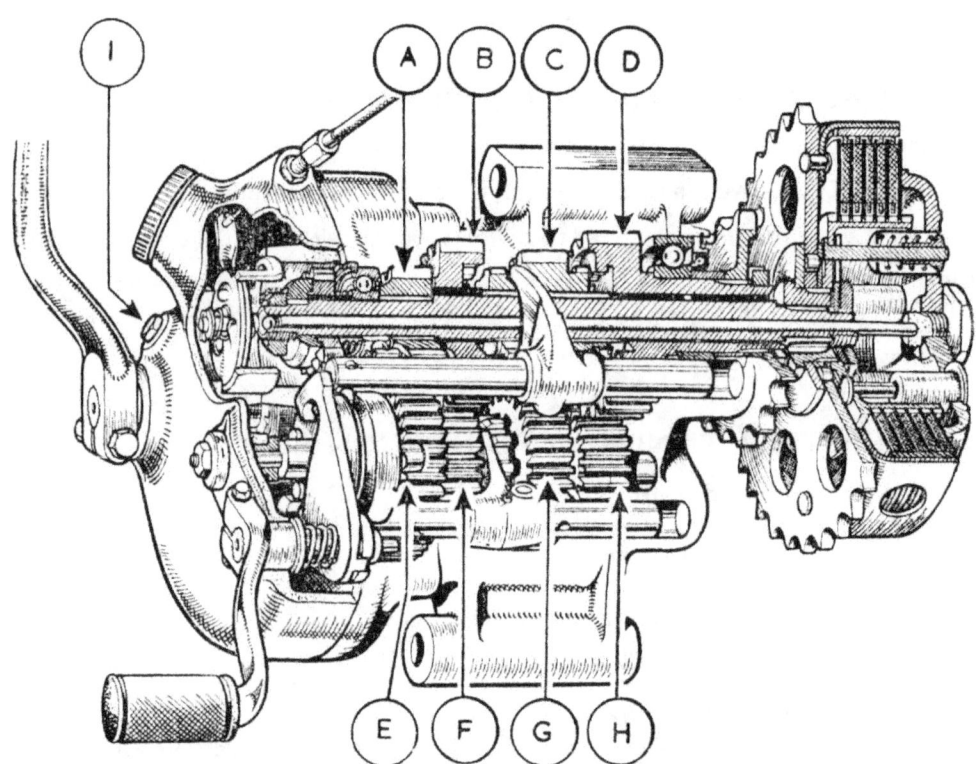

A   LOW GEAR ON MAINSHAFT.
B   THIRD GEAR ON MAINSHAFT.
C   SECOND GEAR ON MAINSHAFT.
D   MAIN DRIVING GEAR.
E   LOW GEAR ON LAYSHAFT.
F   THIRD GEAR ON LAYSHAFT.
G   SECOND GEAR ON LAYSHAFT.
H   SMALL PINION ON LAYSHAFT.
I   OIL LEVEL PLUG.

Section through gearbox showing gears and clutch with actuating mechanism

Illustration 13

This cam movement actuates the sliding gear striker forks causing movement of the sliding gears which engage the stationary gears by dogs. As each gear is selected it is held in engagement by means of a spring loaded conical ended plunger operating in depressions on the end of the cam barrel.

The trip mechanism referred to allows the foot change lever to return to its normal position, upon foot pressure being released, in readiness for the next change of gear. Downward direction of movement causes engagement of higher gears and upward movement with the toes causes a lower gear to become engaged.

As mentioned elsewhere an external marked disc shows at a glance which gear (or neutral), is engaged.

The unusual method of clutch operation should be noted, the necessary thrust rod movement to free being obtained through the medium of three balls operating on inclined planes. (See illustration 14.)

Operation of the clutch handlebar lever moves clutch operating lever B causing inward movement of the thrust rod by reason of the three balls mounting the inclined planes in which they are located. The resulting inward movement of the clutch thrust rod forces out the pressure plate, normally maintained in contact with the friction plates by the springs E, thereby allowing the engine to drive the clutch sprocket D without imparting drive to the mainshaft C.

Consequently no power is transmitted to the rear wheel, the clutch is said to be " out " or " free." Upon releasing the clutch handlebar lever the clutch operating lever returns to its normal position by the pressure of the spring forcing the balls down these inclined planes thereby allowing the spring pressure through the medium of the pressure plate to be transferred to the friction plates which causes the gear box mainshaft to revolve and impart driving power to the rear wheel.

TO REMOVE KICK-STARTER CASE COVER FOR EXPOSURE OF K.S., GEAR CHANGE, AND INTERNAL CLUTCH ACTUATING MECHANISM

Remove oil drain plug and drain off oil contents of the gear box.

Remove the large oil filler plug and slack off the clutch cable adjuster sufficiently to permit the cable end to be detached from the slotted end of the internal clutch operating lever which is exposed by the removal of filler cap.

Unscrew the clutch cable adjuster until it is free from the K.S. case cover and withdraw the cable nipple through the adjuster hole.

Remove the nut and small spiral spring securing small gear indicator disc from the cam barrel spindle.

Next remove the five cheese head screws by which the K.S. case cover is secured to the gear box end plate.

Withdraw the cover about $\frac{1}{2}$ inch, holding the K.S. pedal firmly while doing so.

Now swing the K.S. crank round until it can be tied to the foot change lever. This prevents the K.S. return spring unwinding and facilitates re-assembly.

The entire cover can now be removed.

Re-assemble in exactly reverse order, taking care to avoid damage to the paper joint gasket.

Fill to correct level with one of the recommended oils and lastly refit the gear indicator disc and adjust its position to give correct indication of gears.

NOTE—The position of the various cheese head screws securing the K.S. case cover are as follows :—

In the top position, screw measuring $3\frac{1}{8}$ inches under head.

In the bottom position, screw measuring $2\frac{7}{8}$ inches under head.

In the rear position, screw measuring $\frac{7}{8}$ inch under head.

In the front position, top screw measuring $1\frac{1}{8}$ inches under head.

In the front position, bottom screw measuring $1\frac{3}{8}$ inches under head.

TO REMOVE GEAR BOX END PLATE FOR EXAMINATION OF GEARS

Remove K.S. case cover as already described.

Remove split pin securing both gear striker shaft pins and withdraw the pins and also the cam barrel in which they operate together, with the spring ball ended plunger which engages depressions on the underside of the cam barrel.

Remove the mainshaft end nut and draw off the K.S. ratchet driver, pinion, spring and bush upon which the pinion is mounted.

Remove the three cheese head screws by which the end plate is secured to the gear box shell and the end plate is then free to be withdrawn leaving the gears and gear striker shafts in situ.

Take care to avoid losing the steel ball fitted in the end of the mainshaft and interposed between the clutch actuating lever and the clutch thrust rod.

TO RE-ASSEMBLE

If gears have been disturbed insert them in their proper order with slider shafts in correct location and apply end plate with paper joint gasket in position.

Re-fit the three cheese head screws and firmly tighten down with a stout screwdriver. Then insert ball ended plunger and spring and apply the gear selection cam barrel with any one of the depressions on its underside engaging with the ball end of the spring loaded plunger.

Next insert the selector shaft pins and secure each in position with its split pin.

Complete the assembly in reverse order of dismantling ascertaining, before applying the K.S. case cover, that the ball is inserted in the end of the mainshaft.

Fill to correct level with one of the recommended oils and lastly re-fit the gear indicator disc and adjust its position to give correct indication of gears.

TO REMOVE FRONT CHAINCASE AND CLUTCH ASSEMBLY

To remove outer half of front chaincase

Remove left side exhaust pipe and silencer (the pipe with its silencer is taken away as a unit).

Remove the left side footrest arm.

Place tray under chaincase to catch oil.

Remove screw binding chaincase metal band at its rear.

Remove metal band and endless rubber band.

Remove nut and washer, in centre of chaincase front.

Take away outer half of chaincase.

TO REMOVE FRONT DRIVING CHAIN, SHOCK ABSORBER & CLUTCH

Engage top gear, apply the rear brake and unscrew engine shock absorber retaining bolt.

Unscrew the five nuts retaining the five clutch springs.

Take away the clutch spring pressure plate with the clutch springs and clutch spring cups.

Remove front chain connecting link and take away chain.

Withdraw shock absorber assembly consisting of cap, spring, cam and sprocket.

Flatten the turned up edge of the lock plate under the clutch centre retaining nut.

Engage top gear, apply the rear brake, and unscrew the nut retaining the clutch centre to the gear box main shaft sleeve.

Lift away the plain and lock washers under the retaining nut.

Remove the remainder of the clutch assembly by pulling it away, as one unit, from the gear box main shaft. Take care not to lose any of the twenty-four clutch sprocket bearing rollers which will be displaced during withdrawal. (The clutch centre is a sliding fit on the splined main shaft sleeve and an extractor should not be required).

TO REMOVE BACK HALF OF CHAINCASE

Flatten turned up ends of tab lock washers under the three bolts retaining the back half of the chaincase to the boss of the crankcase and remove the three bolts and the lock washers.

Remove the wide nut on the centre fixing bolt and also the washer under it.

Back half of front chaincase is now free to be lifted away.

TO RE-FIT THE FRONT CHAINCASE AND CLUTCH

Check truth of faces of both chaincase halves. (See note at end of these instructions.)

Fit back half of front chaincase by:

Place on face of crankcase boss and back of chaincase some liquid jointing compound, and leave till tacky. ("Wellseal" recommended.)

Ensure the spacer is in position on the centre bolt. This is located between the engine plate and the chaincase.

Place in position rear half of front chaincase.

Fit to crankcase boss the three lock washers and bolts retaining case to boss.

Fully tighten the three bolts and turn up the tabs of the three lock washers.

Fit spacer nut (inside chaincase, $\frac{7}{8}''$ long) and washer to the centre fixing bolt and fully tighten.

Fit engine shock absorber by:

Ensure the spacing collar, which fits between crankcase roller bearing and the back of the engine sprocket, is in position on the driving side flywheel axle.

Then place in position, on the flywheel axle, in the order specified, the engine sprocket, the shock absorber cam, the spring and cap washer and, finally, the shock absorber retaining bolt. Do not attempt to fully tighten the bolt.

Fit the clutch centre and sprocket by:

Place on the gear box main shaft splined sleeve the thicker of the two clutch sprocket roller bearing retaining washers.

Place on the gear box main shaft splined sleeve the clutch sprocket roller bearing ring.

With grease, stick in place on the bearing ring the twenty-four clutch sprocket bearing rollers.

Introduce clutch sprocket over the rollers.

Place on the gear box main shaft splined sleeve the thin clutch bearing retaining washer.

Push on the splined end of the gear box main shaft splined sleeve the clutch centre.

Fit the lock plate plain washer and nut that retain the clutch centre but do not attempt to fully tighten the nut.

Fit the front chain and lock centre nut by:

Replace the front driving chain. (Connecting link adjacent to engine sprocket on bottom run is most convenient position). Ensure the spring connecting link is fitted so that the closed end of the spring clip faces the direction of rotation.

Engage top gear, apply the rear brake and then fully tighten the nut that retains the clutch centre to the gear box main shaft.

Finally, turn up one edge of the lock plate so that it is firmly against one of the faces of the nut.

Fit the clutch plates and springs by:

Slide into position, in the clutch case attached to the clutch sprocket, one of the steel plain clutch plates.

Slide into position a clutch friction plate (plate with fabric inserts) and follow with a steel plain plate, then another friction plate and so on, alternatively, till all plates are fitted. (Six plain and five friction plates).

Drop into the spring pressure plate the five cups for the clutch springs.

Show up the spring pressure plate and insert, over the studs, the five clutch springs, retaining each one a few turns, as fitted, with a clutch spring adjusting nut.

Fully tighten the five clutch spring adjusting nuts using end of spanner part number 017254.

Slacken back, four complete turns, each clutch spring adjusting nut.
Engage top gear, apply the rear brake and then fully tighten the engine shock absorber retaining bolt.
Check front driving chain for adjustment.
Check clutch operating lever for correct free movement as detailed elsewhere.

Fit outer half of front chaincase by :
Ensure faces of both halves of chaincase are clean.
Ensure the rubber and metal bands are clean and undamaged.
After carefully positioning the outer half so that its exterior edge exactly coincides with that of the inner half, apply the endless rubber band.
Fit the metal band, starting at the front end of the chaincase and drawing together the two free ends with the fingers of one hand while with the other hand insert the binding screw.
Whilst slowly tightening this binding screw apply at the same time light taps all round the band exterior using a small rubber mallet.
These light taps will cause the metal band to creep on the rubber to ensure an even all-round pressure.
Remove the inspection cap from the chaincase and pour in engine oil to the level of the bottom edge of the inspection cap orifice and then replace the cap.
Replace the left side footrest arm.
Replace and fully tighten the nut on the left side of the footrest rod.
Replace the exhaust pipe and silencer unit.

NOTE—If, after replacing a front chaincase, it is found not to be oil tight, the general reason is distortion of the two joint faces or incorrect position of the rubber band. These faces must be undamaged and, on test, should closely fit to a surface plate. They must also be absolutely clean before replacement and the edges must be in exact register, one with the other. Any distortion caused by accidental impact must be remedied before refitting.
If any doubt exists, **CHECK** for **DISTORTION BEFORE ASSEMBLY.**

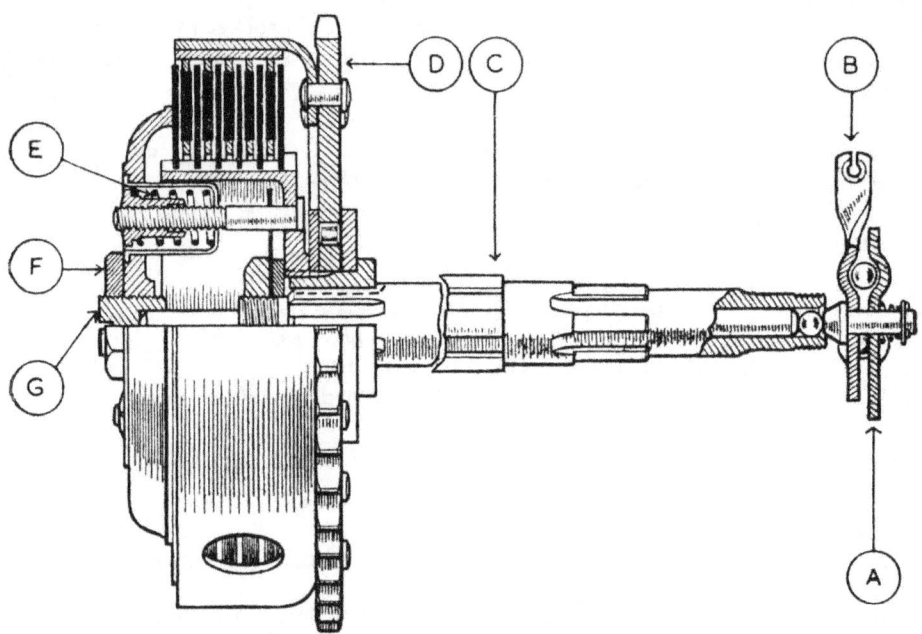

A FIXED CLUTCH INTERNAL ACTUATING PLATE.
B CLUTCH INTERNAL OPERATING LEVER.
C GEAR BOX MAINSHAFT.
D CLUTCH SPROCKET.
E CLUTCH SPRING.
F LOCK NUT FOR CLUTCH ROD THRUST CUP.
G THRUST CUP (in clutch pressure plate) FOR CLUTCH ROD.

Clutch, gear box main shaft and clutch operating mechanism

Illustration 14

CLUTCH SPRING ADJUSTMENT

If clutch slip occurs the most probable cause is either incorrect cable adjustment or absence of free movement of the internal clutch lever. If both are found to be correct the clutch spring adjusting nuts may require adjustment.

To obtain access to clutch spring adjusting nuts, remove the domed clutch cover (secured by eight screws).

With the slotted driver provided on one of the thin spanners in the tool kit, screw each nut, in turn, fully home, then unscrew exactly four complete turns.

Before replacing the domed clutch cover, test for slip by starting up the engine, engaging top gear, and applying the rear brake when it should be possible to pull up the engine on full throttle without slip occurring.

If to cure slip it is found necessary to further tighten the adjusting nuts this is a clear indication that either the clutch springs have lost their tension, the inserts are so worn that they require renewal or that they have become impregnated with oil.

In the two former instances renewals are necessary, but if oil is the cause of slip this may be rectified by soaking the plates in petrol and allowing to dry off. If inserts are glazed roughen with sand paper.

CLUTCH OPERATING MECHANISM ADJUSTMENT

Correct adjustment of the clutch operating mechanism is of the utmost importance and the following instructions must be carefully observed.

In order to understand the method of clutch withdrawal a study of illustrations 14 and 15 should be made. See also paragraphs 7 and 8, Page 36 (Transmission Service).

To enable the clutch to function satisfactorily $\frac{1}{8}''$ to $\frac{3}{16}''$ free movement of the operating cable is essential. This is checked by lifting the outer casing of the clutch cable at the position where it enters the screwed adjuster on the kick starter case cover. If the adjustment is correct it should be possible to freely move the casing up and down with the fingers $\frac{1}{8}''$ to $\frac{3}{16}''$.

If the free movement is excessive causing clutch drag or noisy gear changing, adjustment should be made as follows.

Release the clutch cable adjuster lock nut and then screw in the adjuster as far as it will go to ensure that the operating lever B (illustration 14) is in its normal position.

Now turn to the opposite side of the cycle and remove the domed clutch cover secured by eight screws.

Then using the sparking plug box key supplied in tool kit, loosen lock nut F.

Then with a screw driver gently screw in the thrust cup G until contact with the thrust rod can be felt, after which unscrew exactly one half turn and then securely retighten the lock nut F taking care to observe that the screwed thrust cup does not also turn while doing so.

Replace the clutch cover and then make the final adjustment by unscrewing the cable adjuster until the recommended free movement of the casing is obtained after which retighten the cable adjuster lock nut.

As a result of wear of the clutch friction plate inserts after prolonged use, the plates tend to close up towards each other. This will have the effect of reducing the free movement in the operating mechanism referred to above.

Clutch slip resulting from lack of free movement will rapidly ruin the inserts and may generate sufficient heat to soften the clutch springs. Therefore should clutch slip develop an immediate check of free movement must be made.

In this case after slacking off the cable adjuster, unscrew the cup G a turn or two and then gently screw in until contact with the thrust rod is felt, after which as already detailed it should be unscrewed exactly one half turn before retightening the lock nut F. Lastly adjust the cable for the specified free movement.

To remove a clutch control cable

Remove the oil filler cap from the kick-starter case cover.

Screw right home the clutch cable adjuster that is located in the top of the kick-starter case cover.

Disengage, from the operating lever, the clutch cable inner wire by operating through the oil filler cap opening.

Completely unscrew the clutch cable adjuster.

Disengage, from the handlebar operating control lever, the clutch inner wire.

Pull cable, by its lower end, till removed from the machine, easing it through the frame cable clips while doing so.

To replace a clutch control cable
Reverse the above instructions and, finally, adjust as detailed earlier.

FRONT CHAIN ADJUSTMENT
Refer to Illustration 15
Remove engine plate cover.
Slacken the nut of bolt (5).
Slacken the nut (3).
Screw bolt (1) clockwise to take up slack in the chain.
Remove inspection cap from chaincase and check tension by applying upward pressure, with finger, to the chain.
The correct amount of whip is $\frac{3}{8}$ inch.
Check the adjustment in several positions and adjust for the tightest point.
When the correct adjustment has been obtained, tighten nuts (3) and (5), replace covers.
If the chain is tight, screw the bolt (1) in an anti-clockwise direction.
Pull on the rear chain to move the gearbox and slacken the primary chain.

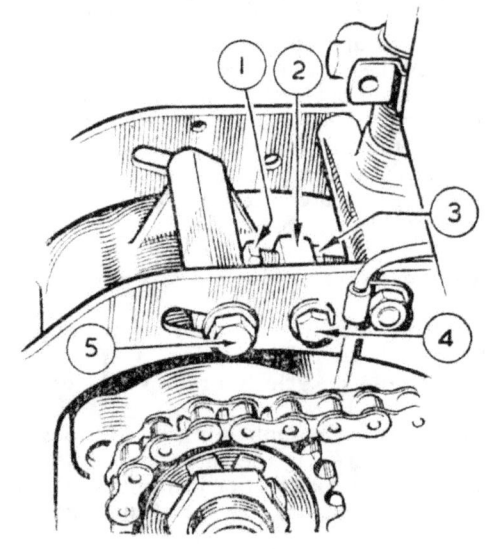

Illustration 15

Front chain adjustment

1. ADJUSTING BOLT.   3. ADJUSTING BOLT LOCK NUT.   5. ENGINE PLATE BOLT.

REAR CHAIN ADJUSTMENT
To obtain rear chain adjustment the rear wheel is bodily moved in the rear frame fork ends, which are slotted for the purpose. Adjusting screws with lock nuts are provided on the forward side of each slotted end.

To adjust the chain place cycle on the stand and slightly slacken the spindle end nut and also slightly slacken the brake drum dummy splindle locknut the hexagon of which is adjacent to the spindle end nut. Then slacken back the adjuster screw lock nut on each side and unscrew each adjuster bolt in turn to exactly the same extent until the correct chain tension is obtained. While on the stand the chain whip should be $1\frac{1}{8}''$ (see note below). Then fully retighten spindle nuts and also the adjuster screw locknuts. Chain whip must always be checked midway between the two sprockets and the rear wheel should always be turned to obtain the position of least slackness. This is because chains rarely wear evenly and there is usually one position at which the chain is tighter than at any other. It is at this position that the adjustment check should be made.

NOTE—The chain adjustment specified while cycle is on the stand is reduced to $\frac{1}{2}''$ when the wheel is on the ground and the rider seated. This is due to chain sprocket centres varying slightly as the result of movement of the rear swinging arm.

NOTES ON REAR CHAIN ADJUSTMENT

Before tightening the rear chain always first check front chain adjustment and if attention is necessary adjust the front chain first. This is because adjustment of the front chain disturbs that of the rear chain.

Therefore after making adjustment to the tension of the front chain always afterwards check that of the rear chain.

It should also be noted that adjusting the rear chain will disturb rear brake adjustment which should therefore always be checked subsequently.

REMOVING AND REFITTING REAR CHAIN

To protect the rear chain from mud and water it is very closely shrouded by the chain guard and removing the chain without first detaching the chain guard can present considerable difficulty. A simple procedure however is as follows.

First obtain a piece of thin string about ten feet long.

With cycle on the stand turn the rear wheel until the chain connecting link is at a position near the rear sprocket and remove the connecting link.

Now pass the string through the centre hole of the end link of the top run, draw the two ends of the string level and tie together.

Then pull the bottom run of the chain backwards with one hand while keeping the string taut at the rear end with the other hand.

As the end of the top run of the chain disengages with the gear box sprocket it will leave the string attached lying one strand each side of the sprocket teeth.

When the chain is well clear cut the string on one side only at a point about one foot from where it is looped through the chain link.

Leave the string then in situ awaiting chain refitting.

To refit the chain.

Pass the longer cut end of the string through the centre hole of the end chain link and then tie the two loose ends of the string together.

Then pull the string from the rear end at the same time guiding the chain up to engage with the gear box sprocket.

Continue pulling until the chain encircles the rear wheel sprocket when remove the string and refit the connecting link taking care while doing so to attach the spring clip with its closed end facing the direction of rotation.

ENGINE SHOCK ABSORBER

The engine shock absorber is a spring device for smoothing out the engine impulses.

The engine sprocket is a free fit on the driving side axle. It has, integral with it, a face cam that engages with a similar face cam ("shock absorber cam") which is keyed to the driving side flywheel axle by splines. A spring keeps the shock absorber cam in close engagement with the cam on the sprocket, and, the shock absorber cam being driven by the engine, over-rides the sprocket cam under the influence of the engine impulses. The shock absorber spring is compressed by the over-riding of the cams, thereby absorbing the shocks.

It is essential the faces of the cams are adequately lubricated otherwise the shock absorbing action will be nullified and this is automatically taken care of, providing the level of the oil in the front chaincase is maintained according to the instructions given in the "Lubrication Section." This bolt also houses the crankcase breather valve.

The shock absorber spring is retained by a cap washer and a retaining bolt which must be fully tightened.

Behind the engine sprocket (between the sprocket and the crankshaft roller bearing) is a spacing collar which is a sliding fit on the driving side flywheel axle and in no circumstances must this be omitted.

NOTE—At the first sign of transmission harshness examine front chaincase for correct oil level, and dismantle and lubricate the shock absorber parts if the harshness continues. For access to the shock absorber parts it is necessary to remove the outer half of the front chaincase.

The order of assembly of the engine shock absorber is

1. The spacing collar between the crankshaft roller bearing and the engine sprocket.
2. The engine sprocket.
3. The shock absorber cam.
4. The shock absorber spring.
5. The cap washer.
6. The retaining bolt incorporating crankcase breather.

FORK & FRAME SERVICE

STEERING HEAD ADJUSTMENT

The steering head frame races are of the floating self-aligning type and have spherical seats. Therefore they do not fit tightly in the head lug.

Occasionally test the steering head for correct adjustment by exerting pressure upwards from the extreme ends of the handlebars.

It is particularly important that the adjustment is tested after the first one hundred miles because of the initial settling down that always occurs in that period.

Should any shake be apparent, adjust the steering head bearings.

Adjust steering head bearings by:

Jack up the front of the machine so that all weight is taken off the front wheel. (A box under each footrest serves that purpose).

Slacken the two fork crown pinch screws.

Slacken the domed nut at top of the steering column.

Screw down the nut underneath the domed nut a little at a time (using adjustable spanner 017249) and, while doing so, test the head assembly for slackness by placing the fingers over the gap between handlebar lug and frame top lug, at the same time exerting upward pressure by lifting from the front edge of the front mudguard. Tested in this manner the slightest slackness is discernable.

Continue to tighten the lower adjusting nut until no perceptible movement can be felt and yet the steering head is perfectly free to turn, then tighten down the domed nut in order to lock the adjustment.

Securely tighten the two fork crown pinch screws (this is very important.)

Remove packing from under footrest.

FRONT FORKS (TELEDRAULIC)

Owing to the unusual construction of the " **TELEDRAULIC** " fork it is desirable to understand what happens in use and, in order to clearly follow the descriptions and subsequent assembly and adjustment instructions, reference to Illustrations 16 and 17 will be necessary.

As will be seen from the general arrangement drawing, Illustration 17, the main members of the forks are two long tubes. These are of heavy gauge and are externally ground to very fine limits. These fork main, inner, tubes are firmly fixed to the handlebar clip lug by the top bolts 021830 and are clamped to the fork crown by the clamping screws. Upon the external of these tubes are mounted the springs and sliding members, to which latter the front wheel, mudguards and front stand are fixed.

The telescopic action of the sliders, combined with the hydraulic dampers, described later, explain the word " **Teledraulic,**" coined for the description of the fork.

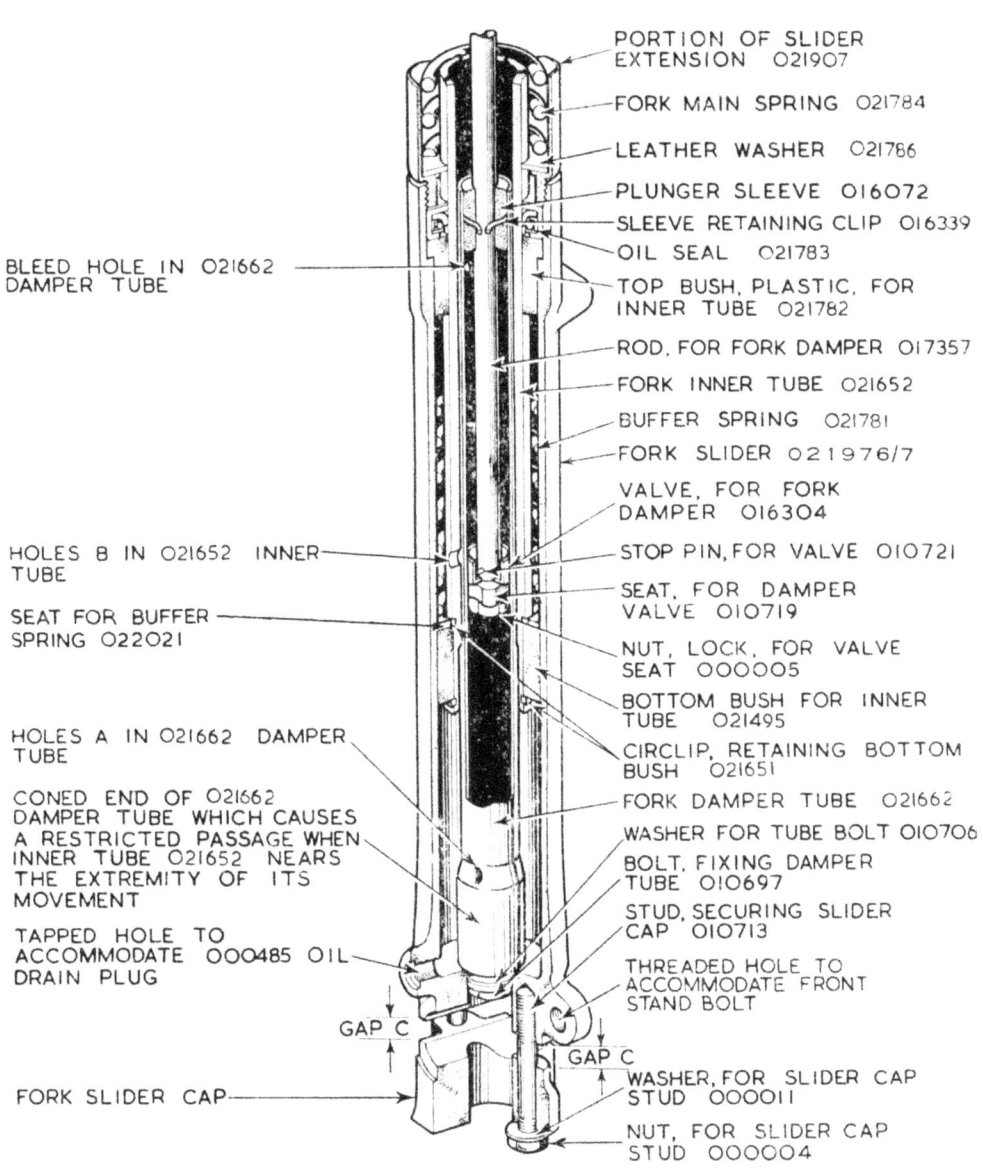

Illustration 16

Introduced in early 1941 for use under strenuous war conditions by all the allied armies, it remains unaltered, except in detail, to this day, and copied practically universally. The hydraulic dampers operate in tubular members located inside the main tubes. As will be seen the aluminium sliding members operate upon steel bushes attached to the bottom ends of the main tubes and also upon bakelite bushes, secured to the top end of the sliders themselves. Above these bushes, an oil seal is fitted, the object of which is to prevent leakage of oil from below into the main spring chamber. The normal level of oil is well above the bottom extremity of the main inner tubes and bearing this in mind, it is at once clear that upward movement of the sliders resulting from impact with road bumps in addition to meeting resistance from the main springs also causes oil to be ejected by the close fitting steel bushes. This oil is forced upward through the open ends of the main inner tubes and also through the holes A (Illustration 16) in the bottom of the damper tubes, then past the damper disc valve which the passing oil raises off its seat. As the oil level rises inside the main inner tubes, air trapped is compressed, thereby forming an air buffer acting as auxiliary to the main springs. This displacement of oil upon impact imposes a certain amount of damper effect, the extent of which increases with the violence of the shock, or in other words, the bigger the bump the greater the damping effect. Upon the recoil movement, the damper disc valve returns to its seat and the oil trapped between this valve and the plunger sleeve above has no other source of escape but past this sleeve and the adjacent small metered bleed hole. This intentionally restricted passage causes a considerable damper effect to the recoil action. It will thus be gathered that on the shock movement of the fork, slight damper action occurs, with a greatly increased damper action on the reverse movement, both actions automatically increasing in effect the more violent the movement. Before concluding this description, it should be mentioned that upon a very violent impact, as a result of which the main springs are almost fully compressed, the damping of the upward movement of the sliders is intentionally increased by the automatically greatly restricted passage for the displaced oil, brought about by the lower ends of the main tubes encircling the tapered enlarged ends of the damper tubes as the sliders near the limit of their upward movement. Thus bottoming is prevented, no matter how violent the impact. For ordinary purposes the recommended oil content is $6\frac{1}{2}$ ozs. (184·6 c.c.) each leg of one of the S.A.E. 20 oils specified. To deal with heavier loads than normal, the oil content may be increased to a permissible maximum of 10 fluid ozs. (284 c.c.) per leg. To increase damping oil of heavier grade may be used. It will be found, however, that for normal purposes the recommended grade and quantity of oil will give the most comfortable ride.

FRONT FORK "TOPPING UP"

No part of the **TELEDRAULIC** Front Fork requires individual lubrication, but it is advisable to check the oil content, once every five thousand miles. The normal content as already stated, is $6\frac{1}{2}$ fluid ounces (184·6 c.c.) each side.

Support motor cycle vertically with weight on both wheels. A steady under each footrest is the best method.

Remove the rubber grommet and unscrew the top bolts. These are on level with handlebars and attached to them are the damper rods. Have a graduated measure of not less than 10 fluid ozs. capacity available in which to catch and measure the oil. Remove the drain plug from the bottom of a slider and catch the oil which drains out. Then reinsert drain plug and work the top plugs to which damper rods are attached up and down (pumping action), making upward strokes as violent as possible but using only fingers to do so. This pumping action is to eject any oil trapped in the damper tubes above the damper disc valve. Wait two minutes and again remove drain plug. Repeat the action until no further oil can be drained off when, if the fork had the correct oil content, about 6 fluid ozs. (170·4 c.c.) will have been drained off. If less, add to make this quantity, or reduce if an excess quantity has been drained off. Next refit drain plug and carefully pour into the top of the tube being checked exactly 6 fluid ozs. (170·4 c.c.) after which the top plug may be replaced.

NOTE—Although the normal oil content of each side is specified as $6\frac{1}{2}$ fluid ozs., it is not possible to drain all the oil via the drain plug. This explains the lesser quantity of 6 fluid ozs. (170·4 c.c.) referred to above. However, if the fork is at any time completely dismantled and then reassembled in a dry state, it should be noted that in that event the correct quantity of oil to add to each leg is $6\frac{1}{2}$ fluid ozs. (184·6 c.c.).

TO REMOVE THE COMPLETE FRONT FORK ASSEMBLY

Support the machine with the front wheel clear of the ground. (A box, of suitable height, under each footrest is the best method.)

Remove the front wheel as described in Wheel Section.

Remove the front mudguard and stay.

Slacken the screw on head lamp top, gently prise out the rim and reflector assembly, detach with a slight rotary and lifting movement the cap to which head lamp wires are attached and take away rim and reflector assembly.

Gently ease back the rubber sleeves covering the pilot lamp wire snap connectors and pull latter apart.

Disconnect the driving cable from the speedometer head and draw same down through fork crown.

Remove the nuts on the tubular bolts through which the pilot lamp wires pass, which enables the pilot lamps to be taken away, leaving the head lamp shell, etc., free to be gently suspended by the wiring loom.

Remove the two nuts securing speedometer head and take same away.

Remove the handlebar half clip and lay the handlebars, complete with controls, upon a pad on top of the petrol tank.

Detach the front brake cable from the forks. (First remove the slotted yoke end and then completely unscrew the cable adjuster.)

Remove the rubber grommett and unscrew the top bolt on each inner tube, raise same and slacken the lock nuts securing the damper rods attached. Then, before removing the top bolts, attach a piece of wire about 18 inches long underneath each damper rod lock nut, to enable the damper rods to be raised for reassembly.

Remove domed nut at top of steering column.

Remove lock nut on steering column.

Use a soft mallet to tap upward the handlebar lug until it disengages with the fork stem (steering column) and main tubes. The fork assembly can then be withdrawn. (Take care to avoid loss of any of the 56 steering head steel balls.)

To re-fit a complete front fork assembly

Secure, with grease, 28 balls in fork crown ball race.

Secure, with grease, 28 balls in main frame top ball race.

Proceed to fit fork assembly by reversing the instructions given above to dismantle, carefully retightening the damper rod locknuts before inserting the hexagonal headed plugs to which they are attached.

TO REMOVE A FORK SLIDER (either side) (Dealers' service only)

Support the motor cycle with the front wheel clear of the ground, and unscrew the tubular slider extension from the slider which it is intended to remove. Special articulated clamp tool required. (Available in workshop tools.)

Next remove the front wheel, front stay and mudguard as detailed above. Then with a thin tubular box key, remove the bolt securing the damper tube. The hexagonal head of the bolt is sunk in the upper half of the wheel spindle clamp. Place a receptacle underneath to catch the oil which will drain out upon removing the bolt, and take care of the fibre washer located under the head. A sharp jerk downward should now enable the slider to be withdrawn, but should difficulty be experienced, apply a little heat to the enlarged top end of the slider. This will cause sufficient expansion to release the oil seal which is normally a snug push-in fit, in the top of the slider. The re-assembly is carried out in exactly the reverse order, again if necessary applying a little heat to enable the oil seal to be pushed down into the slider top before screwing in the slider extension. After completion, the oil which has escaped **MUST** be returned via the top. (See Front Fork " Topping up.")

TO REMOVE A FORK INNER TUBE ASSEMBLY (either side) (Dealers' service only)

Remove the rubber grommet, then with the spanner 018667 unscrew the top bolt of the inner tube it is intended to remove. The damper rod will now be partially withdrawn. Slacken the lock nut by which the damper rod is secured to the top bolt, unscrew the bolt and allow the damper rod to fall. It is not necessary to remove the adaptor. Next proceed to remove the slider as already detailed, except do not disturb the bolt securing the damper tube. This damper tube and protruding rod can be removed intact with the slider. Now loosen the fork crown clamping screw when it should be possible to draw the entire inner tube assembly down through the crown lug. Upon re-assembly, the inner tube is first pushed home as far as possible by hand and then pulled right home by screwing down the top hexagonal plug. With this plug tightened down, then proceed to tighten the crown clamping screw, after which the hexagonal plug may be removed and a piece of wire passed down through the inner tube. Loop the bottom end of this wire underneath the damper rod lock nut. The slider is then carefully pushed upward while at the same time pulling on the wire until the top end of the damper rod projects sufficiently to permit the screwed plug to be attached and secured with the lock nut, after which the wire may be removed. It may be found necessary to apply a little heat to enable the oil seal to be pressed home with the fingers before screwing on the tubular extension.

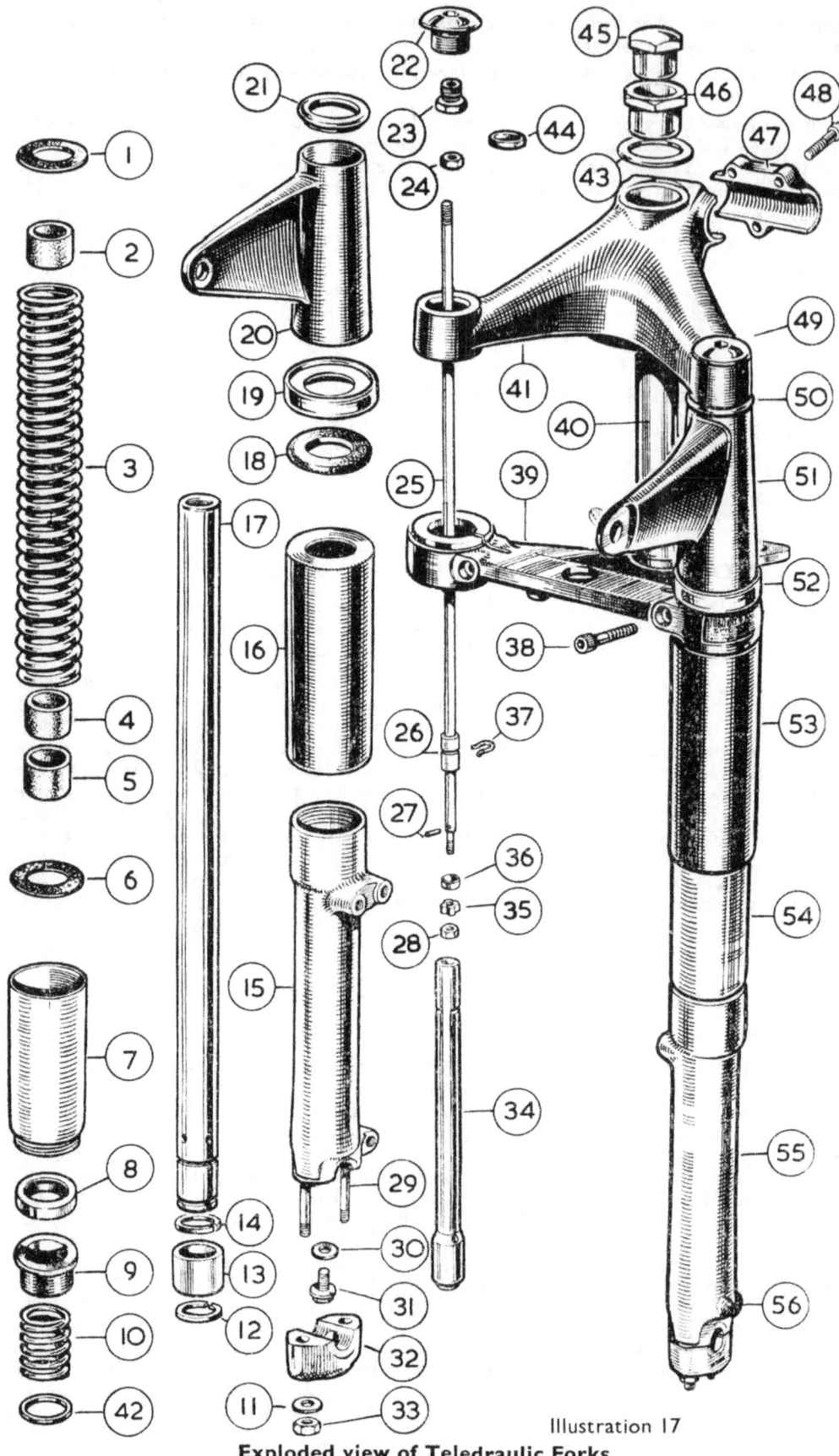

Illustration 17
Exploded view of Teledraulic Forks

REF. NO.	DESCRIPTION
1	WASHER, LEATHER, FOR FORK SPRING TOP SEATING.
2	BUFFER, RUBBER, FOR FORK INNER TUBE.
3	SPRING, MAIN, FOR FRONT FORK.
4	BUFFER, RUBBER, FOR FORK INNER TUBE.
5	BUFFER, RUBBER, FOR FORK INNER TUBE.
6	WASHER, LEATHER, FOR FORK SPRING BOTTOM SEATING.
7	EXTENSION, FOR FORK SLIDER.
8	OIL SEAL, FOR FORK INNER TUBE.
9	BUSH, TOP, PLASTIC, FOR INNER TUBE.
10	SPRING, BUFFER, FOR FRONT FORK.
11	WASHER, PLAIN, FOR FORK SLIDER CAP SECURING STUD.
12	CIRCLIP, LOCATING FORK INNER TUBE BOTTOM BUSH.
13	BUSH, BOTTOM, STEEL, FOR FORK INNER TUBE.
14	CIRCLIP, LOCATING, FORK INNER TUBE BOTTOM BUSH.
15	SLIDER, FOR FORK, WITH STUDS (RIGHT SIDE).
16	TUBE, FORK COVER, BOTTOM.
17	TUBE, FORK, INNER.
18	RUBBER RING FOR TOP COVER TUBE HOUSING RING.
19	HOUSING RING, TOP COVER TUBE.
20	TUBE, FORK COVER, TOP, RIGHT, WITH LAMP LUG.
21	SPIGOT RING TOP COVER TUBE.
22	BOLT, TOP, FOR FORK INNER TUBE.
23	ADAPTOR.
24	NUT, LOCK, FOR TOP END OF DAMPER ROD.
25	ROD, FOR FORK DAMPER.
26	SLEEVE, PLUNGER, ON FORK DAMPER ROD.
27	PIN, STOP, FOR FORK DAMPER VALVE.
28	NUT, LOCK, FOR DAMPER VALVE SEAT.
29	STUD, SECURING CAP TO FORK SLIDER.
30	WASHER, FIBRE, FOR DAMPER TUBE BOLT.
31	BOLT, FIXING DAMPER TUBE TO SLIDER.
32	CAP, FOR FORK SLIDER.
33	NUT, FOR FORK SLIDER CAP SECURING STUD.
34	TUBE, FOR FORK DAMPER.
35	SEAT, FOR FORK DAMPER VALVE.
36	VALVE, FOR FORK DAMPER.
37	CLIP RETAINING DAMPER ROD SLEEVE.
38	SCREW, PINCH, FOR FORK CROWN.
39	FORK CROWN. } NOT SOLD SEPARATELY.
40	STEM, FOR FORK CROWN.
41	LUG, FOR HANDLEBAR AND STEERING HEAD.
42	COLLAR FOR BUFFER SPRING.
43	WASHER FOR FORK STEM ADJUSTING NUT.
44	RING, RUBBER, SEALING, FOR INNER TUBE TOP BOLT.
45	NUT, LOCK, FOR FORK STEM.
46	NUT, ADJUSTING, FOR FORK STEM.
47	CLIP (HALF ONLY), FOR HANDLEBAR LUG.
48	SCREW, PINCH, FOR HANDLEBAR CLIP.
49	BOLT, TOP, FOR FORK INNER TUBE.
50	SPIGOT RING TOP COVER TUBE.
51	TUBE, FORK COVER, TOP, LEFT, WITH LAMP LUG.
52	HOUSING RING TOP COVER TUBE.
53	TUBE, FORK COVER, BOTTOM.
54	EXTENSION, FOR FORK SLIDER.
55	SLIDER FOR FORK WITH STUDS (LEFT SIDE).
56	SCREW, PLUG, WITH FIBRE WASHER, FOR FORK SLIDER OIL DRAIN HOLE.

REAR SUSPENSION

The rear wheel is mounted in a fork that is hinged just behind the gear box. The hinge has robust plain bearings lubricated from a reservoir of 1½ fluid ounces (42.6 c.c.) of heavy gear oil which is sufficient to last almost indefinitely. Provision is, however, made for replenishment should same be required. A small screw will be observed in the right-hand end cap of the hinge bearing, upon removal of this screw, oil can be injected into the reservoir, the screw orifice operating as a level control.

On a new machine, or after replenishment, oil may leak from this bearing. This is of no consequence and the leakage will cease after a few hundred miles have been covered.

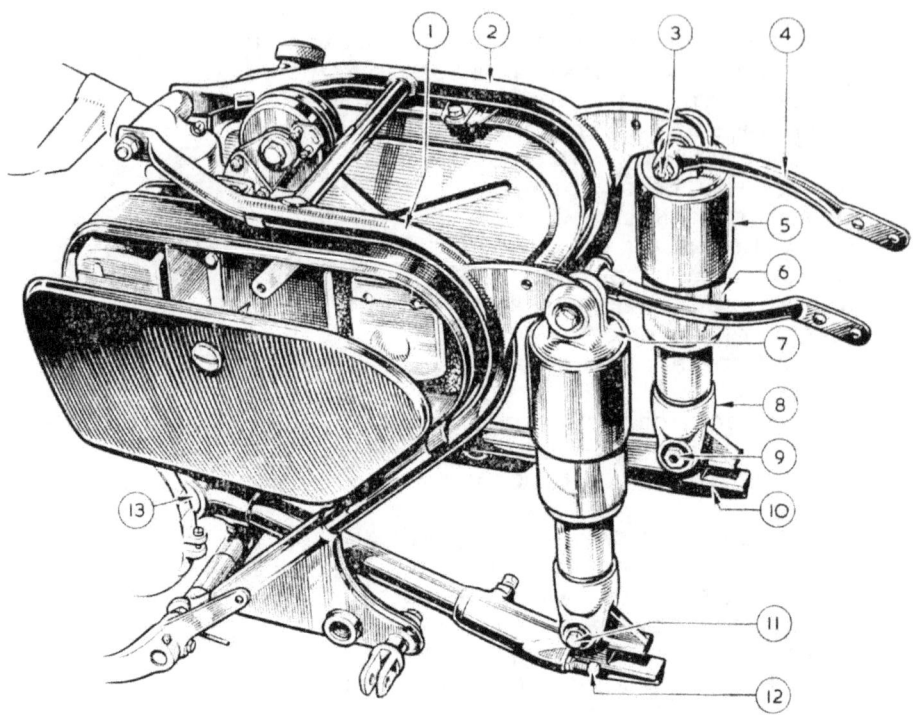

Illustration 18

Rear sprung frame and "TELEDRAULIC" legs

1. MAIN FRAME LEFT LOOP.
2. MAIN FRAME RIGHT LOOP.
3. TOP PIVOT BOLT AND NUT.
4. TUBULAR MUDGUARD SUPPORT.
5. TOP COVER TUBE.
6. BOTTOM COVER TUBE.
7. TOP PIVOT BODY.
8. BOTTOM PIVOT BODY.
9. BOTTOM PIVOT NUT.
10. FORK END.
11. BOTTOM PIVOT BOLT.
12. CHAIN ADJUSTER.
13. FORK HINGE BEARING.

The rear wheel fork is suspended on springs located in the two "**TELEDRAULIC**" legs joining the rear of the fork to the main frame rear loops, and the spring action is damped by hydraulic dampers identical in design to those used in the "**TELEDRAULIC**" **Front Fork Assembly.**

The hydraulic fluid used is one of the grades of oil specified in the Lubrication Section for use in the "**TELEDRAULIC**" Front Forks.

The recommended quantity for each leg is 85 c.c. or a trifle under 3 fluid ozs. of S.A.E. 20 grade of one of the brands specified. For abnormal loads, the next heavier S.A.E. grade may be used, but unlike the front fork, recoil damping as well as maximum load capacity is increased by this alteration of grade alone, and under no circumstances should the oil content of each leg exceed 90 c.c. or roughly 3⅛ fluid ozs. Unless serious doubt exists as to correct functioning of the rear legs, owners are advised to leave well alone. Should the need arise, however, the oil content of each leg should be separately checked as follows:

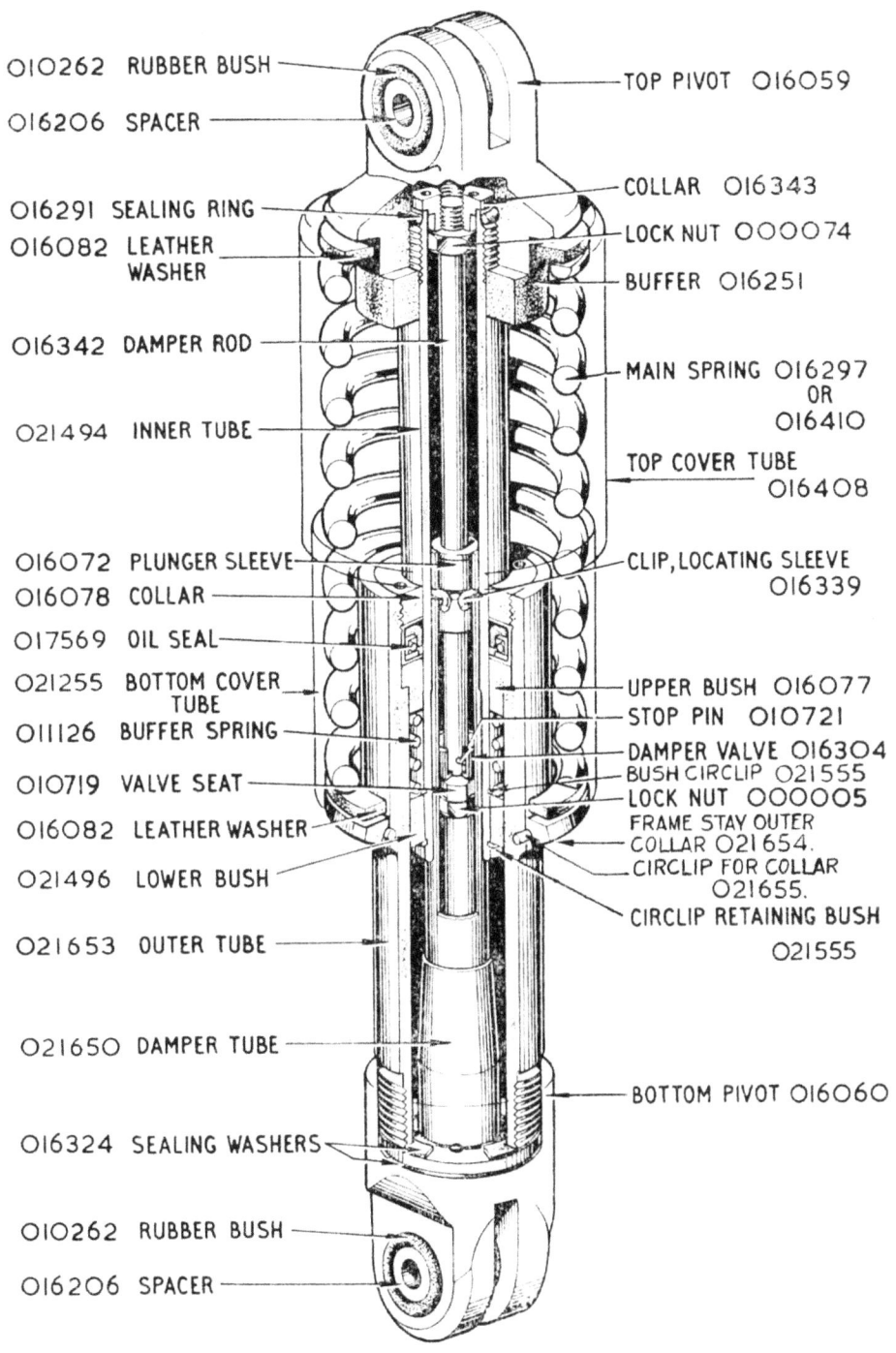

Illustration 19

"Ghost" view of "TELEDRAULIC" leg

To check oil content of " TELEDRAULIC " leg and top-up :

Dealing with one leg at a time, remove top securing bolt, taking care to observe the location of the spacing washers on it. Remove bottom securing bolt and take away the leg.

Using a suitable clamp encircling the outer tube adjacent to the bottom pivot lug, grip in a vice and loosen the pivot lug.

Then holding leg vertically, bottom end uppermost, carefully remove the loosened pivot lug, and gripping the exposed end of the damper tube with the fingers, raise and lower several times (pumping action) after which pour the oil contents into a graduated measure.

It may be necessary to repeat the pumping action to eject oil from underneath the damper valve, and finally the open end of tube should be supported above the measure and left to drain for several minutes.

If the leg contained the correct amount of oil, 75 c.c. ($2\frac{5}{8}$ ozs.) should have been drained out into the graduated measure, leaving 10 c.c. ($\frac{1}{3}$ oz.) which cannot be withdrawn.

All that now remains is to pour carefully back into the leg exactly 75 c.c. ($2\frac{5}{8}$ ozs.) of oil, after which the pivot lug may again be screwed on and securely tightened down to prevent oil leakage when the leg is re-fitted, after which the other leg may be dealt with in a similar manner.

NOTE.—Shortage of oil is evidenced by very lively action.

PROP STAND

The prop stand hinges on a bolt which passes through a lug brazed to the frame and screws into the jaw of the stand leg. It is then locked by a nut and split pin. Care in tightening this bolt is necessary to avoid pinching, and it is essential to observe after securely tightening the lock nut that the stand is perfectly free. Smear the hinge bolt with engine oil before replacing it.

CENTRE STAND

The centre stand is mounted on a bolt set across the bottom rear of the main frame and is removed by taking off a nut of the centre bolt and pushing bolt through the frame. During removal and replacement the stand should be in a horizontal position in order to take off as much of the tension off the return spring as is possible.

TO REMOVE OIL TANK

Remove the twinseat.

Remove the frame cover. It is held in position by two large knurled and slotted screws.

Remove the oil tank drain plug and empty the tank.

Disconnect the oil feed and return pipes from the bottom of the tank by sliding the rubber connectors down the pipes.

The tank is held in position by four brackets and nuts and bolts, two at the top, one at the front, and one at the back.

Remove the nuts, bolts and washers, lift the tank away from the frame a few inches, and disconnect the vent pipe. The tank is now free. To refit, reverse the foregoing instructions.

TO REMOVE THE REAR CHAIN GUARD

Remove the rear wheel. (See Wheel Section).

Remove the bolt retaining the front end of the chain guard to the rear fork.

Remove the bolt retaining the rear end of the chain guard to the rear fork. (There is one spacer on this bolt, between the two sides of guard.)

WHEELS AND BRAKES

TO REMOVE FRONT WHEEL

Place machine on centre stand.

Remove the split pin, and pin, retaining yoke end of front brake cable to the brake expander lever.

Remove bolt retaining brake anchor stay to brake cover plate.

Slacken the nut on the left-hand end of front wheel spindle.

Remove the four nuts retaining the caps to the fork sliders, which will permit the removal of the two caps and, putting pressure on the front wheel (in order to decrease the effective height of the wheel spindle) the wheel can be withdrawn towards the front.

NOTE—The two caps **MUST** be re-fitted in same order and position as originally. Therefore, lay them aside so that the order and position of assembly will be correctly made.

TO RE-FIT FRONT WHEEL

Holding the left side cap on the wheel spindle, offer wheel up so as to engage the cap with its securing studs. Then apply fixing nuts and washers but only loosely tighten.

NOTE—To pass the wheel spindle into position it may be necessary to apply pressure to flatten the tyre so as to enable the spindle to pass the forward fixing studs.

Next fit the right side cap and again only loosely tighten the securing nuts. Now attach the brake anchor arm and refit the yoke end pin.

Next fully tighten the nuts securing the left side cap, taking care to keep the gap fore and aft approximately equal. Then tighten the left side spindle nut and lastly the nuts securing the right side cap.

Should any fork stiffness be apparent after refixing the front wheel, loosen the nuts securing the right side cap and after working the fork up and down violently, retighten. This action will ensure that the wheel clamp occupies its natural position on the spindle end on which it is intentionally not positioned.

TO REMOVE QUICKLY DETACHABLE REAR WHEEL

Place the machine on the centre stand. Loosen the bolt in the rear most position on each tubular member to which the detachable rear portion of the mudguard is secured. Also slacken off the two bolts securing the two portions of mudguard together. Disconnect the snap connectors of the rear lamp wire when the rear portion of mudguard is free to be taken away.

Disconnect speedometer drive by unscrewing the cable gland nut and withdrawing drive cable end from the speedometer gear box. Then remove the wheel spindle end nut and washer and withdraw spindle together with distance collar which will fall as spindle is withdrawn. The wheel is now free to be removed.

In refitting it will be found best to offer up the wheel, insert spindle without the distance collar and after engaging the driving pegs hold wheel in situ, withdraw the spindle and insert the distance collar.

Upon tightening the spindle end nut make certain the collar end of the spindle is in contact with the chain adjusting screw to ensure correct wheel alignment. Also see that the speedometer gear box is positioned correctly.

WHEEL BEARINGS AND ADJUSTMENT

The wheel bearings are of taper roller type. See illustrations. The outer cups for the rollers are pressed into the hub shell. They have a fixed location one side and an adjustable location on the other. The fixed location is provided by a circlip in a groove cut in one end of the hub shell, while the adjustable location is regulated by a screwed ring that is threaded into the opposite end of the hub and the position of which can be locked by an encircling nut.

On each wheel the adjusting ring is located on the right-hand side.

It is rarely necessary to make adjustment to wheel bearings. It is most important they are not adjusted too tightly as this would quickly ruin them. There must always be a slight amount of end play. This should be about .002", which represents a just perceptible rim rock.

A service method of ensuring correct adjustment is:

Slacken the lock nut.

Tighten the adjusting ring until all slackness has been taken up.

Slacken back the adjusting ring exactly one-half turn.

Tighten the lock nut, making sure that, when doing so, the adjusting ring does not creep round, and the cover disc positioned to permit grease gun application to the nipple.

TO DISMANTLE FRONT WHEEL BEARINGS

Refer to Illustration 21, page 55.

Remove wheel from machine.

Remove nut securing brake cover plate, withdraw cover plate with brake shoes, etc.

Then remove brake cover positioning nut and washer.

Then turn to the right hand side of wheel, remove adjusting ring lock nut and lift off cover disc.

Then completely unscrew the adjusting ring.

Now carefully apply pressure to the threaded end of the wheel spindle which will eject from the opposite end of the hub, the washer (7) oil seal (8) and oil seal cup (9) together with the bearing outer ring (6). The wheel spindle with its two sets of rollers in cages may now be lifted out leaving in situ only the fixed bearing ring together with the oil seal, washer and cup for that side bearing.

If it is desired to remove these pressure is first applied to the visible washer, by which the assembly is forced inward sufficiently to permit extraction of the retaining circlip after which through the medium of a mandrel or a piece of tubing of external diameter a trifle smaller than the hub bore apply pressure to the inner edge of the fixed bearing ring so that it is forced out of the hub end. As it emerges it will push out the end washer (2) the oil seal (3) and the oil seal encircling collar (4) and the inner washer (5).

To refit reverse the above procedure remembering that after bearing ring (6) washer (5) spacer (4) oil seal (3) and washer (2) have been inserted, to refit the circlip (1) snugly in its groove and to then apply pressure to the inner edge of the bearing ring to force the assembly tightly back against the retaining circlip.

Finally position the disc when tightening the adjusting ring lock nut so that access to the grease nipple is possible.

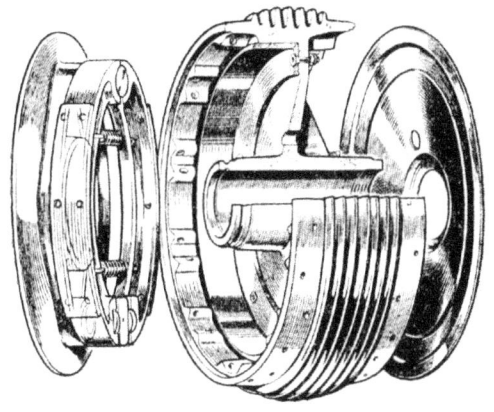
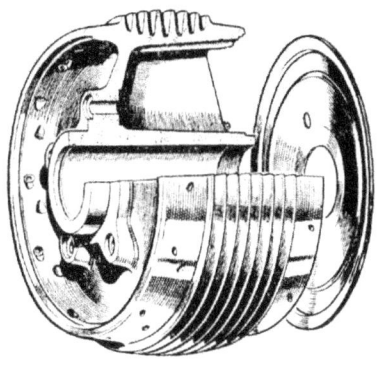

Front and rear hubs

Illustration 20

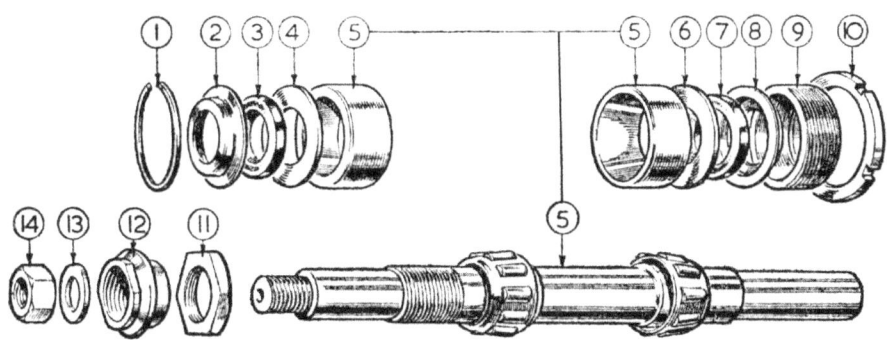

1. CIRCLIP.
2. OIL SEAL CUP.
3. OIL SEAL.
4. WASHER RETAINING SEAL.
5. WHEEL SPINDLE COMPLETE.
6. WASHER RETAINING SEAL.
7. OIL SEAL.
8. OIL SEAL CUP.
9. ADJUSTING RING.
10. ADJUSTING RING LOCKNUT.
11. NUT LOCATING BRAKE COVER PLATE.
12. NUT SECURING BRAKE COVER PLATE.
13. SPINDLE END WASHER.
14. SPINDLE END NUT.

Front wheel bearings

Illustration 21

TO DISMANTLE REAR WHEEL BEARINGS
Refer to Illustration 22, page 57.

With wheel still in situ first of all slacken the nut (16) securing the speedometer drive gear box. Then remove the wheel from cycle when the above nut should be removed and the speedometer gear box withdrawn.

Next, slacken the adjuster sleeve lock nut (13) and completely unscrew the adjuster sleeve (14) which will come away together with the sleeve upon which speedometer drive is mounted and also the cover disc. Then withdraw the washer (3) the oil seal (4) and the oil seal cup (5).

Now turn to the brake side of wheel and using a short bar of $\frac{7}{8}''$ external diameter apply pressure to the end of the projecting sleeve, which pressure will force out wheel bearing ring (7) together with the two taper roller bearings (7) and the spacing sleeve (8), leaving in situ only the bearing ring on the brake side together with oil seal, washers and retaining circlip.

If it is desired to remove this spacer bearing ring pressure must be applied to the cup washer immediately under the circlip until it is possible to extract the circlip. The outer cup washer (5) the oil seal (4) and the spacer (6), etc., are then free to be withdrawn. The bearing ring may then be forced out of the end of the hub bore by applying pressure to its inner edge through the medium of a bar or tube of suitable diameter passed through the hub bore.

Re-assembly is carried out in exactly reverse order, care being necessary after pressing in the brake side bearing ring sufficiently far to permit fitting the circlip, to then force the ring back until cup washer (5) is tightly in contact with the retaining circlip before proceeding with further assembly.

Final adjustment of the bearings should allow the slightest possible degree of end play and when correctly adjusted just perceptible rim rock upon refitting the wheel should be observable.

NOTE—Upon tightening the adjusting ring nut (13) the cover disc must be positioned to permit application of the gun to the grease nipple, the hole in disc being provided for that purpose.

FRONT BRAKE COVER PLATE

It is most important the front brake cover plate is correctly positioned.

It is retained to the front wheel spindle by an inside nut (part number 021931) and an outside nut (part number 018171).

The inside nut must be positioned so that, when the cover plate is applied, the outer face of the latter lies flush with the hub shell edge.

The outside nut is fitted so that its hexagonal side is against the brake cover plate.

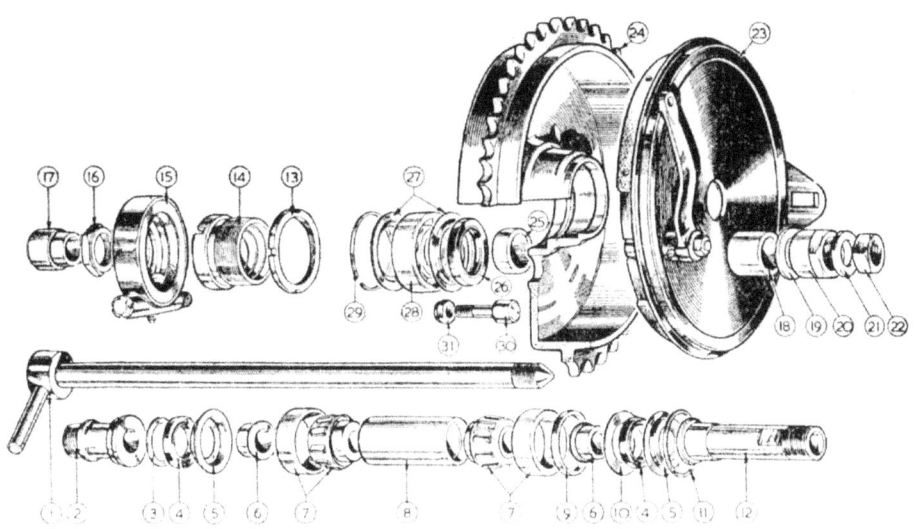

Rear brake and wheel bearings

Illustration 22

1. WITHDRAWABLE WHEEL SPINDLE
2. SPEEDOMETER GEAR BOX SLEEVE.
3. RING RETAINING OIL SEAL (Small).
4. OIL SEAL.
5. CUP FOR OIL SEAL.
6. OIL SEAL DISTANCE PIECE.
7. TAPER ROLLER BEARING COMPLETE.
8. SPACER BETWEEN BEARINGS.
9. BEARING SPACING COLLAR (Brake Side).
10. RING RETAINING OIL SEAL (Large).
11. CIRCLIP.
12. BRAKE DRUM DUMMY SPINDLE.
13. LOCK NUT FOR ADJUSTING RING.
14. ADJUSTING RING.
15. SPEEDOMETER GEAR BOX COMPLETE.
16. SPEEDOMETER GEAR BOX FIXING NUT
17. SPACER FOR WITHDRAWABLE SPINDLE.
18. OUTER SPACER FOR BRAKE COVER PLATE.
19. WASHER FOR COVER PLATE FIXING NUT.
20. BRAKE COVER PLATE FIXING NUT.
21. SPINDLE END WASHER.
22. SPINDLE END NUT.
23. BRAKE COVER PLATE COMPLETE.
24. REAR BRAKE DRUM.
25. INNER SPACER FOR BRAKE COVER PLATE.
26. BRAKE DRUM BEARING OIL SEAL.
27. BRAKE DRUM OIL SEAL WASHERS.
28. BRAKE DRUM BALL BEARING.
29. CIRCLIP RETAINING BEARING.
30. DRIVING PEG (5 Off).
31. NUT SECURING DRIVING PEG (5 Off).

BRAKE DRUMS

The front wheel brake drum is a shrunk in fit in the hub shell (assembled under heat) and secured additionally by five screws.

The rear brake drum is mounted on a separate ball bearing and the drive to rear wheel is by means of five studs projecting from the hub face which engage with holes in the drum back face, thereby permitting removal of the rear wheel with the brake drum still in situ.

BRAKE SHOES

The front and rear brake shoes, springs and expanders are interchangeable. The two shoes in each brake are **NOT** identical, they are "handed."

One end of each shoe bears on a fulcrum fixed in the brake cover plate. The other end accommodates a detachable thrust pin. By inserting washers under a thrust pin its effective height can be increased, thereby compensating for wear on the brake linings.

BRAKE SHOE ADJUSTMENT

Brake adjustment, to compensate for lining wear, is normally made by means of a finger adjuster on the rear brake rod and a cable adjuster for the front brake cable.

After a very considerable mileage this continual adjustment causes the brake cam to occupy a position whereby the available leverage is considerably reduced and, as a result, the brake loses efficiency. See illustrations 24 and 25.

To overcome this a hardened headed thrust pin is fitted to each shoe to enable a packing washer to be fitted under the head as, and when, required. Eight of these washers (000174) are provided in the tool kit. When wear of the brake linings is taken up in this manner it is then necessary to unscrew considerably the adjusting nut on the rear brake rod, or screw in the cable adjuster of the front brake cable, and afterwards adjust the brake, as described afterwards.

When a brake cover plate has been disturbed, it is advisable, upon re-assembly, to centralise the shoes in the brake drum to ensure equal pressure to each. In the case of the front wheel this is best done before re-fitting the wheel to the machine, but in the case of the rear wheel it is best done after re-fitting.

If brake shoes tend to squeak, when the brake is applied it is generally an indication the brake shoes are not centralised in the drum.

Centralise brake shoes by:

Ensure the nut securing the cover plate to the wheel spindle and also the fulcrum stud nut (front only) are slightly slacked off.

Place on the brake expander lever a tubular spanner (to increase the leverage), and, while maintaining pressure on the tubular spanner (to expand fully the brake shoes), fully tighten the spindle nut binding the cover plate to the spindle and also the nut on fulcrum stud.

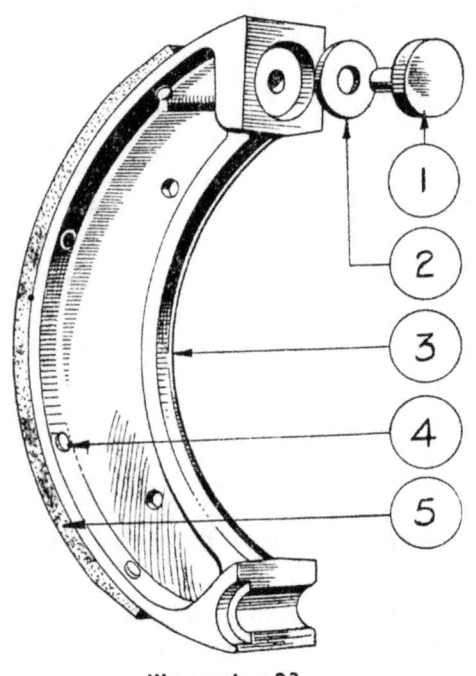

(1) Brake shoe thrust pin.
(2) Thrust pin packing washer.
(3) Brake shoe.
(4) Rivet, securing brake shoe lining.
(5) Brake Shoe Lining.

Illustration 23

FRONT BRAKE ADJUSTMENT

Major adjustment of the front brake shoes is made on the brake thrust pins, by fitting packing washers under the pins, as already described.

Minor adjustment of the front brake shoes is made by altering the position of the brake cable adjuster on the fork assembly. Unscrew the adjuster to "take up" the front brake.

The adjuster is locked in position by a nut.

Adjust front brake by :

Place machine on centre stand.

Slacken lock nut on cable adjuster.

Unscrew the cable adjuster till, by rotating the front wheel, it can be felt the brake shoes are just touching the brake drum.

Then screw back the adjuster two complete turns and tighten the lock nut.

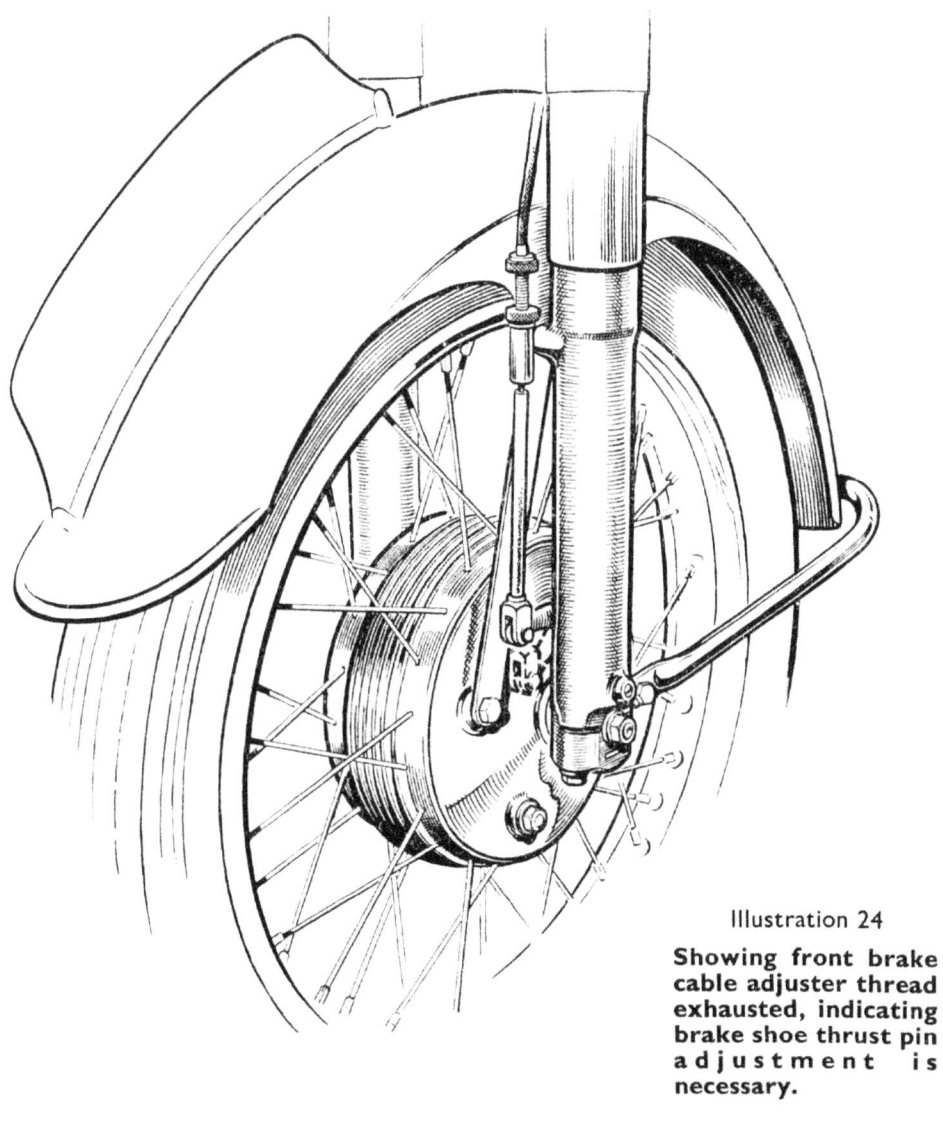

Illustration 24

Showing front brake cable adjuster thread exhausted, indicating brake shoe thrust pin adjustment is necessary.

REAR BRAKE ADJUSTMENT

Major adjustment of the rear brake shoes is made on the brake thrust pins, by fitting packing washers under the pins, as already described.

Minor adjustment of the rear brake shoes is made by altering the position, on the brake rod, of the knurled adjusting nut. Screw the nut further on the rod to " take up " the rear brake.

Adjust rear brake by :

Place machine on centre stand.

Screw further on the brake rod the knurled adjusting nut till, by rotating the wheel, it can be felt the brake shoes are just touching the brake drum.

Then unscrew the adjusting nut two complete turns. (The adjusting nut is automatically locked in position in virtue of the two projecting noses on it engaging in accommodating slots cut in the clip which connects the brake rod and brake expander lever and being retained in that position by the spring which encircles the rear end of the brake rod).

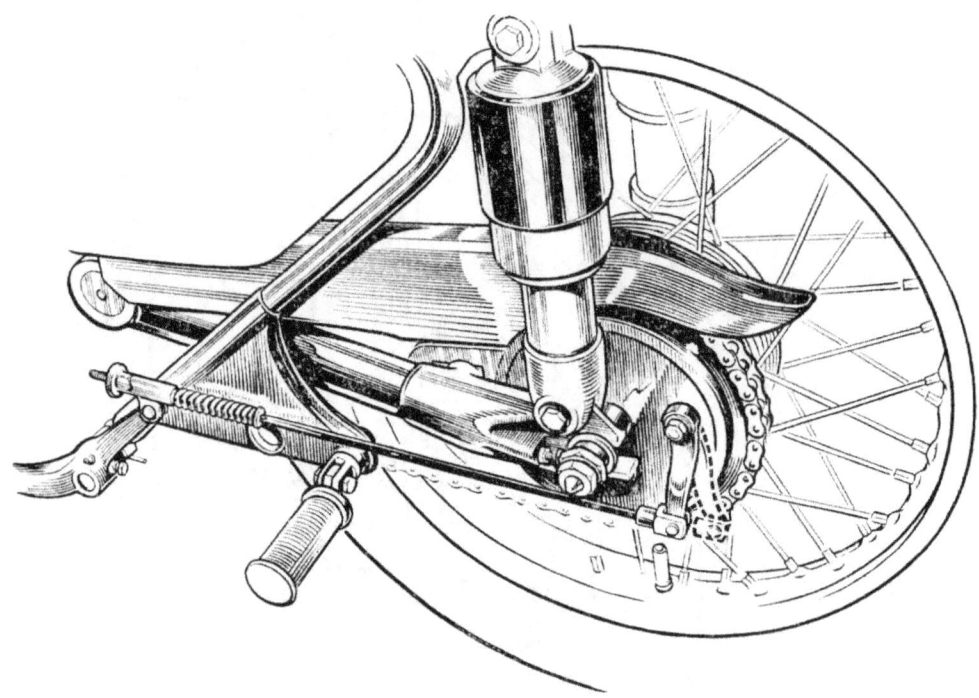

Illustration 25

Showing brake rod adjustment exhausted, indicating the need for brake thrust pin adjustment.

BRAKE PEDAL ADJUSTMENT
Refer to Illustration 26.

The Pedal is located by a spring-loaded sprag which lies between the stop on the pedal and the leg of hair pin spring.

To adjust the position of the pedal: slacken the spindle nut on the right hand side of the machine; move the pedal to the desired position; hold the pedal in this position and tighten the spindle nut.

The most suitable position for normal use is, with the brake " OFF", for the pedal just to be clear of the footrest rubber.

After altering the pedal position, check the rear brake adjustment.

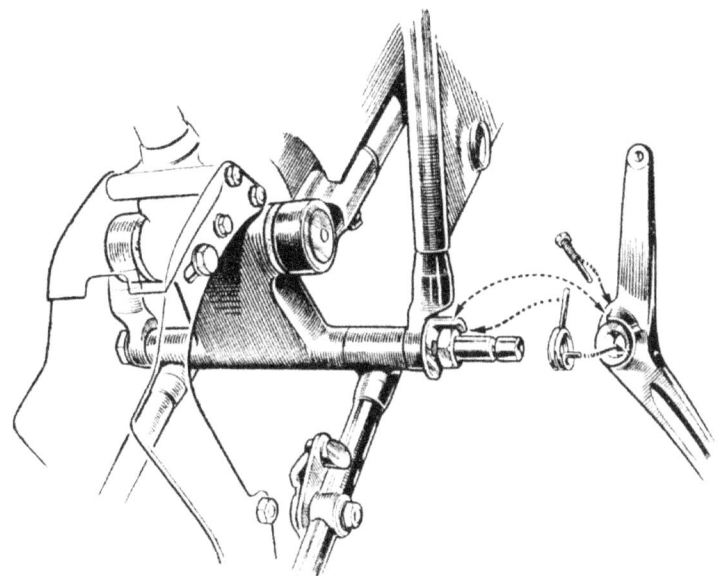

Pedal Position Adjustment
Illustration 26

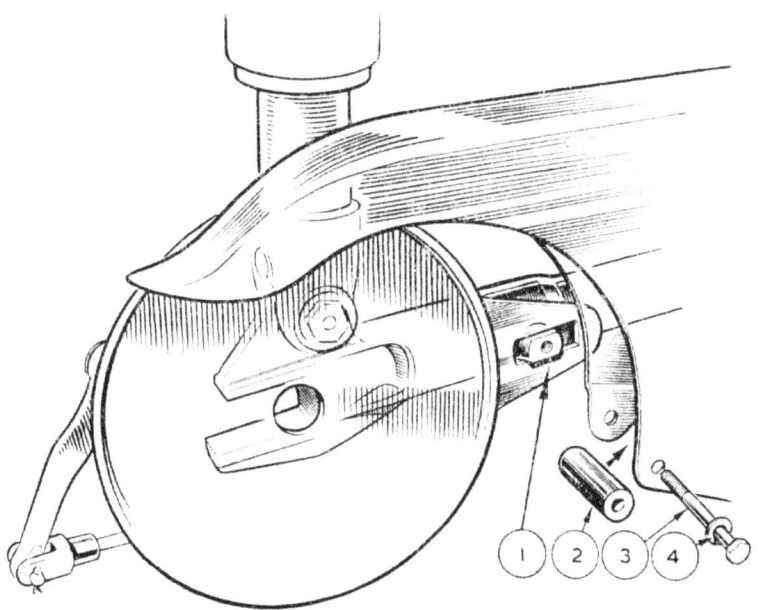

Brake Anchorage   Illustration 27

1 BRAKE ANCHORAGE BOSS.   3 FIXING BOLT.
2 SPACER.   4 WASHER.

TYRES AND SERVICE

Obtaining satisfactory life and service from the tyres is largely a matter within the user's control because the first essential is correct inflation. Check tyre pressures with a low pressure gauge at least once a week. Inflate as may be necessary.

Avoid unnecessary, or "stunt," acceleration and fierce braking, which wear out tyres by causing wheel spin and skid.

Do not drive in tram lines. It is dangerous, especially when wet, and the uprising edges of worn rails will damage the tyres.

Remove flints, etc., that become embedded in the tread and, if any oil gets on the tyres or spokes, clean it off with petrol.

Make sure the front and rear wheels are in track. When the wheel alignment is correct, a piece of thin string stretched taut across both wheels, about four inches from, and parallel to, the ground, should just touch each tyre at both sides of the wheel centres.

Alternatively, a straight wooden batten, about seven feet long, is handy to use for checking wheel alignment. This should be applied, as in the case of string, parallel to and about four inches from the ground.

Always check the rear chain adjustment, and the rear brake adjustment, after making an alteration to the rear wheel position.

NOTE.—Above remarks on wheel alignment apply only to similar width tyres back and front.

On Models with larger rear tyre than front observe equal gap each side of latter when checking.

TYRE REMOVAL

It is not essential to remove a wheel from the machine to repair a puncture but it will usually be found desirable and more convenient to do so.

Take off outer cover and remove inner tube by :

Remove cap from tyre valve.

Remove nut from tyre valve.

Remove the "inside" from tyre valve. This allows inner tube to deflate. Most valve caps have a reduced and slotted top to engage with the valve "inside" in order to unscrew it.

Push edge of cover, that is diametrically opposite to the valve, **RIGHT INTO WELL OF RIM** and, using tyre levers 017007, pick up edge of cover **NEAR VALVE** so that it comes off over the edge of the rim.

Work off the remaining edge of the cover till it is clear of the rim. This is quite easy and there is no reason to use force.

Push upwards **valve stem** through its hole in the rim, and the inner tube is then free to be taken away.

Remove cover from rim by pushing it right into well of rim and, diametrically opposite, picking it up with the tyre lever and then working it off all the way round.

TYRE FITTING

Re-fit inner tube and outer cover by:

Place one edge of cover right into well of rim, with the three white dots on the cover side **adjacent to the valve hole,** and, commencing diametrically opposite, and using the hands only, work the cover over the edge of the rim.

Replace the valve " inside " and slightly inflate the inner tube. (Do not distend the tube).

Fit the valve into its hole in the rim and replace its nut, only screwing it on the valve stem about half an inch.

Tuck in the inner tube so that it lies snugly in the cover. Ensure it is not twisted.

Smear some soapy water round the free edge of the cover. This is a great help in fitting and in ensuring the cover centralises itself on the rim and should always be employed if at all possible.

Introduce the free edge of the cover into the rim at the spot diametrically opposite to the valve. Get this edge right into the well of the rim and then, by working round the cover, equally on either side of the valve position, the cover will slip into place without excessive exertion, fitting the part nearest to the valve last of all.

Slightly inflate the inner tube and inspect for the inner tube being trapped between the outside edge of the cover and the rim at the spots where the valve is located.

Half inflate tyre, spin wheel and test for trueness because it is essential the pattern of the tread runs evenly and the cover must be manipulated till that occurs. This **centralisation** of the **cover is most important.**

Inflate to required pressure.

Screw fully home the nut on the valve.

Replace the valve cap.

TYRE PRESSURES

The following are correct minimum inflation pressures for specified loads per tyre :

Load per tyre,	200 lb.	Pressure	16 lb.	per square inch
do.	240 lb.	do.	18 lb.	do.
do.	280 lb.	do.	20 lb.	do.
do.	350 lb.	do.	24 lb.	do.
do.	400 lb.	do.	28 lb.	do.
do.	440 lb.	do.	32 lb.	do.

The best method of ascertaining the correct pressure is to actually weigh the loads on the front and rear tyres. This should be done on a weighbridge and is a service that can usually be provided by British Railways at a Goods Depot or by a Corporation at its Depot.

When the weights are known the table above can then be used.

As a rough guide it may be stated that, with a rider of average weight and with normal equipment, solo, the **pressures should be 18 lb. for the front tyre and 22 lb. for the rear.**

ELECTRICAL SERVICE

ELECTRICAL EQUIPMENT

LUCAS electrical equipment is fitted and this comprises three independent electrical circuits, as follows :

(1) **IGNITION**—Magneto, High-tension wires, Sparking plugs and Cut-out switch.

(2) **CHARGING**—Dynamo Automatic Voltage Control Unit and Battery.

(3) **LIGHTING AND ACCESSORIES**—Lamps, Horn, Switches and wiring.

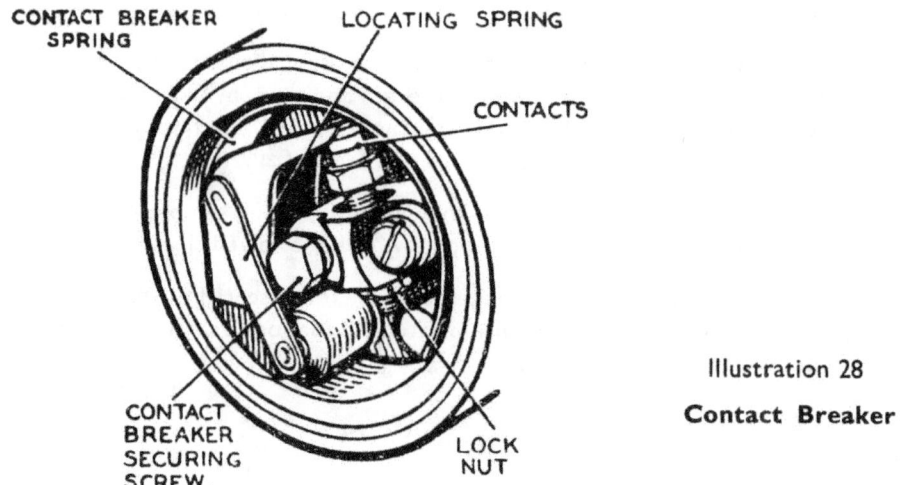

Illustration 28

Contact Breaker

IGNITION

A LUCAS type **K2F** magneto is fitted. The replacement part number is 42230-A and the part number of the complete contact breaker is 470534.

Lubrication and adjustment is required every 3,000 miles, cleaning is required every 5,000 miles and every 10,000 miles the complete unit should be handed to a **Lucas Service Station** for dismantling, replacement of worn parts, cleaning and lubrication.

Lubrication every 3,000 miles

(a) The cam is supplied with lubricant from a felt pad contained in a pocket in the contact breaker housing. A small hole in the cam fitted with a wick, enables the oil to find its way on to the surface of the cam. Remove the contact breaker cover and turn over the engine until the hole in the cam can be clearly seen and then carefully add a few drops of thin machine oil. (The hole is located in the lowermost part of the cam ring). Do not allow any oil to get on the contact points.

(b) The contact breaker rocker arm also requires lubrication and the complete contact breaker must be removed for this purpose. Take out the hexagon headed screw from the centre of the contact breaker and pull the contact breaker off the tapered shaft on which it fits. Then push aside the rocker arm retaining spring, prise the rocker arm off its bearing and lightly smear the bearing with clean engine oil. When replacing the contact breaker, take care to ensure that the projecting key, on the tapered portion of the contact breaker base, engages with the keyway cut in the magneto spindle, otherwise the timing of the magneto will be upset. Tighten the hexagon-headed screw with care; it must not be too slack, nor must undue force be used.

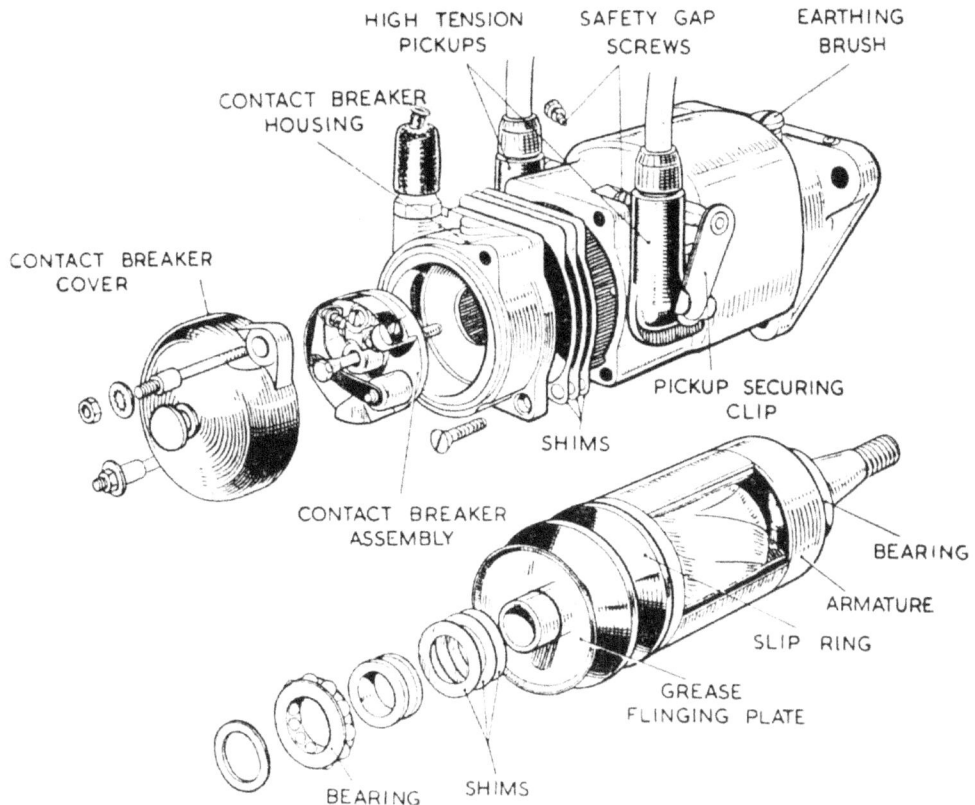

Illustration 29

Dismantled components of magneto

Adjustment every 3,000 miles

Remove the contact breaker cover and turn the engine until the contact points are fully opened. Check the gap with a gauge having a thickness of .012" (Spanner 015023 has a gauge of this thickness as an integral part of it). If the setting is correct the gauge should be a sliding fit, but if the gap varies appreciably from the gauge it should be adjusted.

Keep the engine in the position to give maximum opening of the contact points, slacken the lock nut on the fixed contact point and turn the contact screw, by its hexagon head (use spanner 015023) until the gap is set to the gauge. Finally, tighten the lock nut and re-check the setting.

Cleaning every 5,000 to 6,000 miles

Take off the contact breaker cover and remove the contact breaker. If the contact points are burned or blackened, clean them with a fine carborundum stone or with very fine emery cloth, and afterwards wipe away any dust or dirt with a petrol moistened cloth. After replacing the contact breaker check the point gap and, if necessary, re-set it.

Remove the high tension pick-ups (held by swinging spring clips), wipe clean and polish with a fine dry cloth. The high tension pick-up brush must move freely in its holder.

If it is dirty, clean with a cloth moistened with petrol. If the brush is worn to within $\frac{1}{8}$" of the shoulder it must be renewed. Treat both pick-ups and their brushes.

While the pick-ups are removed, clean the slip ring track and flanges by holding a soft cloth on the ring by means of a suitably shaped piece of wood, while the engine is slowly turned.

If, on inspection, the high tension cable shows signs of perishing or cracking, it must be replaced by a suitable length of 7 mm. rubber covered ignition wire.

SPARKING PLUG

The K.L.G. Type FE80 " Corundite " Plug is fitted to all models.

It has a thread of 14 mm. and the reach is $\frac{3}{4}$". The point gap is ·020-·022". Check the point gaps every time the engine is decarbonised and, if necessary, re-set the points.

See the plug is fitted with its external seating washer.

Coat the thread with "Oil Dag" or Graphite paste. (See page 32).

Firmly tighten the plug by using the standard box spanner and tommy bar (Part No. 017252.) All that is required is a GAS-TIGHT joint. Therefore do not over tighten, which will **not** make a gas-tight joint more gas-tight, but can, and possibly will, distort and damage the body of the plug.

Set the gaps to ·020-·022". NEVER TRY TO MOVE THE CENTRAL ELECTRODE. To widen, or narrow, the gap between the electrodes, only move the earth (side electrodes). Check the gaps first with a gap gauge. If they are too wide, tap the earth (side electrodes) towards the central electrodes using preferably a small copper drift and light hammer. Check the gaps between each tap and stop when the gauge is a nice sliding fit between the central electrode and the three earth side electrodes.

If the gaps are too small to start with, gently lever the earth electrodes away from the centre electrode, using a small screwdriver, and then tap them back as described above. Avoid damaging the centre electrode and do not attempt to move the electrodes apart by forcing anything between them.

For maximum efficiency, plugs should be cleaned at every 3,000 miles. To take the plug to pieces for cleaning, unscrew the gland nut by holding the smaller hexagon on the gland nut upside down in a vice and then using the box spanner to unscrew the larger hexagon on the body.

Then lift away the central electrode assembly which should be washed in petrol or paraffin. Then, using fairly coarse glass paper, remove the carbon deposit and wash again.

The central firing point should be cleaned with fine emery cloth. The inside of the body should be scraped clean with a knife and finally rinsed in petrol.

There is an internal washer, between the insulator and its seating in the body. On re-assembly lightly smear this with thin oil and then screw up the gland nut sufficiently tight to give a gas-tight joint.

Finally adjust the gap to ·020"—·022".

Illustration 30

Magneto removal and fitting

The magneto is "spigot fitting" and is retained to the crankcase by two studs and one bolt.

To remove the magneto it is necessary to:

Take away the timing gear cover.

Withdraw the driving gear from the magneto shaft. (Already described in the Engine Section).

Disconnect the high tension wires from the sparking plugs.

Disconnect the ignition control cable.

Remove the nuts from the two studs and one bolt that secure the magneto body to the crankcase and the unit is free to be taken away.

The re-fitting is done by the above procedure reversed and the method of timing has already been described in the Engine Maintenance Section.

DYNAMO

A LUCAS type E3L-L1-0 dynamo is fitted. It is anti-clockwise in rotation. The cutting in speed is 1,050—1,200 r.p.m. at 6.5 volts and at 1,850 to 2,000 revolutions per minute it gives an output of 8.5 amps at 7 volts. The positive brush is earthed. The two exterior terminals are marked "D" and "F," indicating the respective terminals for the Positive and Field wires that lead to similarly marked terminals on the Regulator Unit.

Inspect commutator and brush gear every 5,000 to 6,000 miles (Maker's Recommendation.)

Remove the dynamo (see page 68 for instructions.)

Remove the cover band to inspect commutator and brush gear.

The brushes are held in contact with the commutator by means of springs. Move each brush, see they are free to slide in their holders, if dirty, or if sticking, remove and clean with a cloth moistened with petrol. Take care to replace brushes in their original positions, otherwise they will not "bed" properly on the commutator.

If, after long service, the brushes have become worn to such an extent that the brush flexible wire is exposed on the running face, or if the brushes do not make good contact with the commutator, they must be replaced by genuine LUCAS brushes.

The commutator must be free from any trace of oil or dirt and should have a highly polished appearance. Clean a dirty, or blackened, commutator by pressing a fine dry cloth against it while the engine is slowly turned over by means of the kick-starter. (It is an advantage to remove the sparking plugs before doing this). If the commutator is very dirty, moisten the cloth with petrol.

At every 10,000 miles, the complete dynamo should be handed to a **Lucas Service Station** for dismantling, replacement of worn parts, cleaning and lubrication.

Electrical breakdown of the dynamo is most unusual and therefore before assuming this unit is defective, it should be tested as follows:

Check that the dynamo, regulator and battery are correctly connected.

Test Dynamo in position by:

(a) Remove the two wires from the dynamo terminals and connect the two terminals with a short length of wire.

(b) Start the engine and set to run at normal idling speed.

(c) Connect the negative lead of a moving coil voltmeter (calibrated not less than 0 to 10 volts) to either of the two dynamo terminals and connect the positive lead to a good earth point on the dynamo or engine.

(d) Gradually increase the engine speed, when the voltmeter reading should rapidly rise and without fluctuation.

> Do not allow the voltmeter reading to rise above 10 volts.
>
> Do not race the engine in an attempt to increase the voltage. It is sufficient to run up the engine to a speed of 1,000 r.p.m.
>
> If the above reading is obtained the dynamo is in order.
>
> If there is no reading, check the brush gear.
>
> If there is a low reading of approximately $\frac{1}{2}$ volt, the field winding may be at fault.
>
> If there is a low reading of approximately $1\frac{1}{2}$ to 2 volts, the armature winding may be at fault.

If the tests, mentioned above, clearly indicate the dynamo is not charging, it is then desirable to remove the dynamo from the machine in order to make further tests and repairs or replacements.

To remove and re-fit dynamo

The dynamo rests on a cradle forming part of the crankcase and is retained by a band having an adjustable clamping action and one stud passing through timing gear case. It is rotated by a gear meshing with the timing gear wheel on the exhaust cam shaft.

Upon merely slackening the clamping strap and removing the sleeve nut on the outside of timing cover, the dynamo, complete with its driving gear, can be withdrawn from the crankcase. The two wires from dynamo to regulator unit are retained by an insulated bridge secured by one screw and, upon removing that screw, the bridge, with the two cables, can be taken away from the dynamo.

A.V.C. UNIT

Although the voltage regulator and the cut-out are combined structurally, they are electrically separate.

The regulator is set to maintain a pre-determined generator voltage at all speeds and regulates the output of the dynamo to the battery according to the state of charge of the battery. The charge rate is at its maximum when the battery is discharged, automatically tapering off to a minimum as the battery becomes charged and its voltage rises.

Normally, during day-time running, when the battery is in good condition, the dynamo gives only a trickle charge, so that the ammeter reading will seldom exceed 1 to 2 amperes, *i.e.* :- Half to one division of scale.

The cut-out is an automatic switch which is connected between the dynamo and the battery. When the engine is running fast enough to cause the voltage of the dynamo to exceed that of the battery the cut-out allows the battery to be charged by the dynamo. On the other hand, when the engine speed is low, or the engine is stationary, the cut-out disconnects the battery from the dynamo, thereby preventing current flowing back from the battery to the dynamo, a proceeding that would soon cause the battery to become completely discharged.

The regulator and cut-out are accurately set during manufacture and the cover protecting them is therefore sealed. If, under normal running conditions, it is found that the battery is continually in a low state of charge, or is being constantly overcharged, then the regulator setting should be checked by a qualified electrician and, if necessary, re-set. Whenever possible, this should be carried out by a Lucas Service Depot or Agent.

TO REMOVE A.V.C. UNIT

The A.V.C. unit is held in sponge rubber and housed in a partition at the rear top corner of the tool box. To remove it, open the box lid, grasp the unit between the fingers and thumb of one hand, and gently and firmly pull it out of the rubber envelope.

The four terminals of the A.V.C. Unit are plainly marked by the letters F.A.D.E. Wires from F and D go to similarly marked terminals on the dynamo. The A terminal is connected to one of the ammeter terminals and the E terminal is " earthed."

We specially warn against unskilled meddling with the settings of the regulator and the cut-out contacts.

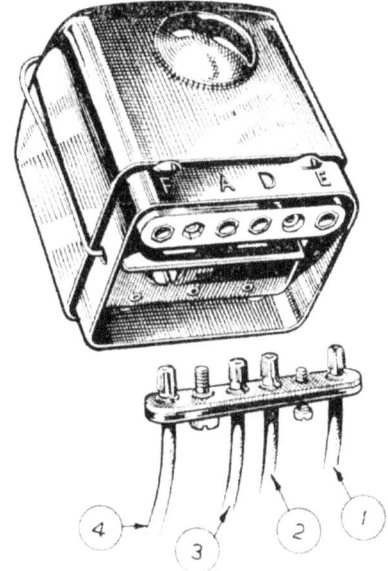

1 TO EARTH.
2 TO TERMINAL D ON DYNAMO.
3 TO TERMINAL 3 ON SWITCH.
4 TO TERMINAL F ON DYNAMO.

Illustration 31

Connections to regulator and cut-out unit

BATTERY

The battery fitted is LUCAS type   This is a lead-acid battery in which the electrolyte is in free liquid form. The voltage is 6 and the capacity is 12 ampere hours.

BATTERY REMOVAL

The battery is housed in the front portion of the tool box and retained in position on its platform by a stout rubber strap.

To remove the battery, release the strap by grasping the metal loop attached to its lower end, pull downwards until the strap and loop are freed from the retaining clip at the base of the platform, and allow the strap to go slack. The battery can now be lifted out.

Once every fourteen days, remove the battery, lift off the cover and brush away any dirt that may have accumulated. Remove the three vent plugs and check the electrolyte level and the specific gravity.

> NOTE—**NEVER** bring a naked light near a battery when the vent plugs have been removed, or when the battery is being charged, as the gas given off by the electrolyte is highly explosive.

The specific gravity of the electrolyte indicates the state of charge of the battery. With a fully charged battery the specific gravity of the electrolyte should be 1·280 to 1·300. Check the gravity by means of a hydrometer, and if it is below 1·150 the battery should be charged as soon as possible by the normal running of the motor cycle. If this cannot be arranged, the battery should be charged from an external source.

If the level of the electrolyte is so low that a hydrometer reading cannot be taken, no attempt should be made to take a reading after adding distilled water until the battery has been on charge for at least 30 minutes.

NEVER transfer the electrolyte from one cell to another.

NEVER leave a battery in a discharged condition. It must be put on charge as soon as possible.

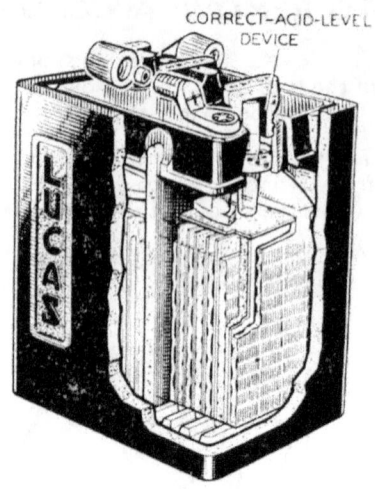

Illustration 32
Lucas Battery

Check if the electrolyte in each cell is level with the top of the separators. Top-up, is necessary, with distilled water. Do not allow the distilled water to come into contact with metals—always only use a glass or earthenware container and funnel. See filling instructions on underside of battery lid. Beware excessive filling.

If a battery is found to need an excessive amount of topping up, steps should be taken to find out the reason. For example, the battery may be receiving an excessive charge, in which case the regulator setting may need adjustment. If one cell in particular needs topping up more than another, it is likely the case, or container, is cracked, in which event the battery must be replaced and arrangements made to clean up the battery carrier.

Metal parts should be well cleaned and, if possible, washed, with a solution of ammonia, or bicarbonate of soda, in water.

Vent plugs should be kept clean and air passages in them kept free. Re-fix vent plugs tightly.

Keep the battery, and surrounding parts, particularly the tops of the cells, clean and dry. Brush away any sand, dust or road slush.

Battery electrolyte, which contains sulphuric acid in a diluted form, is destructive to practically everything except rubber, lead, glass or earthenware. Therefore, rags used to clean battery tops, etc., should be thrown away afterwards. If put back in the tool box they will cause the tools to rust.

Assuming the temperature of the electrolyte is about 60° F. a test with a hydrometer quickly shows the state of charge, as under :
    Reading 1.280 to 1.300 indicates fully charged.
    Reading about 1.210 indicates half discharged.
    Reading below 1.150 indicates fully discharged.

If the electrolyte exceeds this, ·002 must be added to the hydrometer reading for each 5° F. rise to give the specific gravity at 60° F. Similarly, ·002 must be subtracted from the hydrometer reading for every 5° F. below 60° F.

LIGHTING AND ACCESSORIES

Headlamp

A LUCAS headlamp is fitted and snugly mounted, on each side is a neat torpedo shaped pilot lamp. These pilot lamps and also the head lamp are secured to the front fork arms by means of tubular bolts through which a wire passes to each pilot lamp. The headlamp bulb has two filaments one of which provides the main driving beam and the other a dipped beam brought into operation as required by the dipping switch on the left handlebar. The headlamp reflector and glass are made up as one assembly and are in consequence not sold separately as spares. The main bulb is of the pre-focus type and the design of its holder is such that the bulb is correctly positioned in the reflector. No focussing is therefore necessary when a replacement bulb is fitted. See Controls page 9 for switch functions.

To remove headlamp rim and light unit

Slacken the screw on the top of the lamp body at the front, pull the rim outward from the top and, as the front comes away, lower slightly to disengage the bottom tag from the lamp shell. Twist the back cap in an anti-clockwise direction and pull it off, the bulb can then be removed. The light unit is secured to the rim by means of spring clips. These can be disengaged from the turned up inner edge of the rim by pressing with a screwdriver blade and, at the same time, working away from the edge.

1 SPEEDOMETER.
2 SPEEDOMETER, LAMP.
3 SPEEDOMETER, SEALING RING.
4 AMMETER.
5 LAMPS, CONTROL SWITCH.
6 HEADLAMP SHELL.
7 PILOT LAMP.
8 LAMP CONNECTOR.
9 HEADLAMP BULB.
10 GLASS, REFLECTOR AND BULB HOLDER. SEALED UNIT.
11 NUT AND WASHER, FIXING PILOT LAMP.
12 SPEEDOMETER SECURING BRACKET.
13 NUT AND WASHER FOR 12.
14 PILOT LAMP SEALING RING.
15 PILOT LAMP GLASS.
16 PILOT LAMP RIM.
17 PILOT LAMP BULB.
18 PILOT LAMP SECURING CLIP.
19 PILOT LAMP SHELL.
20 PILOT LAMP RUBBER SEAL.
21 SPEEDOMETER TRIP RESET KNOB.
22 DRIVING CABLE CONNECTOR UNION.

Illustration 33

To replace headlamp rim and light unit

Lay the light unit in the rim so that the location block on the unit back engages with the forked bracket on the rim. Replace, by springing in, the spring clips so that they are evenly spaced around the rim.

To replace the back cap engage the projections on the inside of the back cap with the slots in the holder, press on and secure by twisting it to the right.

Engage bottom tag on lamp rim with the small slit in the shell and gently force the top of the rim back into the shell, after which re-tighten the locking screw on the top of the lamp body.

Access to the pilot lamps interior for bulb removal is obtained by removing the screw at the rear end and gently pulling forward on the glass rim.

Rear lamp

A LUCAS rear lamp is fitted. The body, with bulb holder, is secured to the rear number plate. (Convertible to stop light at option.)

Details of lamp bulbs are given in "**DATA**."

Horn

The horn push switch, situated on the right handlebar.

Fuses

There are no detachable fuses in LUCAS motor cycle electrical equipment.

Snap wire connector

The LUCAS snap connector, as shown in illustration 34, is made up of four components. Two are tubular sleeves, having pointed extremities, and which are soldered to the ends of the two wires to be connected. The third part is the centre split ferrule, into which the two sleeves snap and the fourth component is a rubber sleeve which covers the whole connector. That rubber sleeve serves the dual purpose of insulating the various metal parts and also preventing same from separation as the result of vibration.

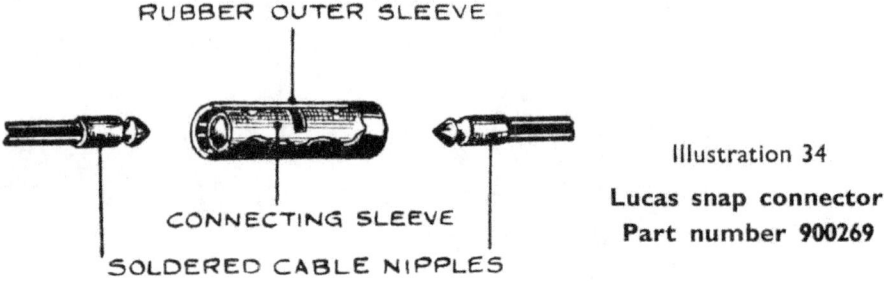

Illustration 34

Lucas snap connector
Part number 900269

One snap connector is used in the rear lamp wire and another is used in the wire connecting the regulator unit to the output side of the ammeter in the head lamp.

Two more are used in the headlamp interior (pilot lamp wires).

Terminals

All models have the POSITIVE battery terminal connected to "EARTH".

The earth wires (two—one from regulator, the other from terminal of battery) and the high-tension wires (two—one on sparking plug end of each wire from magneto to sparking plug) have terminals of the solid sleeve type having an eye at the extreme end. To make such a connection, it is necessary to bare the end of the wire for $\frac{3}{8}''$, pass the terminal over the wire so that the bared end fully enters the reduced core of the terminal and then flatten that part by either pinching in a vice or by hammering.

The two earth wires, mentioned above, are connected to the " earth " by securing them to the seat lug nut (which is situated just under the saddle) by means of a washer and a screw. It is essential that the connections are kept clean and the screw must be kept fully tight.

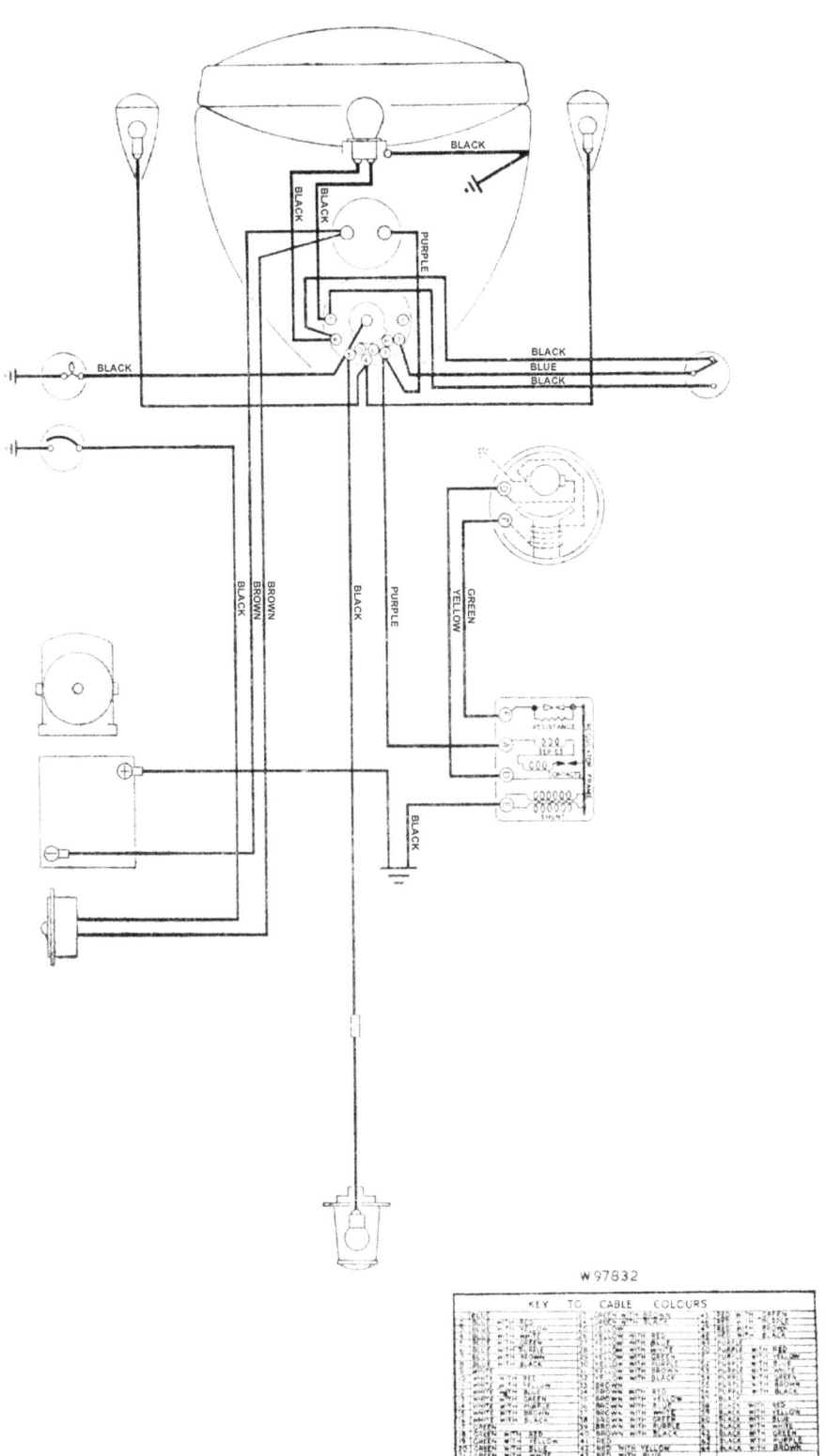

Illustration 35

Wiring diagram

USEFUL INFORMATION

In the following five paragraphs are particulars of failures and troubles that can occur, together with the probable reasons. These troubles are arranged in the order of their probability.

TRACING TROUBLES

Engine fails to start, or is difficult to start, may be due to :
Water on high-tension pick-ups.
Moisture on sparking plugs.
Oiled up, or fouled, sparking plugs.
Throttle opening too large.
Pilot jet choked.
Air lever in open position or bad air leak at carburetter joints.
Lack of fuel because of insufficient flooding.
Lack of fuel because of pipe, or tap, obstruction.
Excessive flooding of carburetter (with hot engine only).
Stuck up engine valve.
Weak, or broken, valve spring.
Valve not seating properly.
Contact points dirty.
Incorrect contact point gap.

Engine misses fire may be due to :

Defective, or oiled, sparking plugs.
Incorrect contact point gap.
Contact breaker rocker arm sticking.
Contact breaker points loose.
Rocker adjustment incorrect.
Oil on contact breaker points.
Weak valve springs.
Defective sparking plug wire.
Partially obstructed petrol supply.

Loss of power may be due to :

Faulty sparking plugs.
Lack of oil in tank.
No rocker clearance, or too much clearance.
Weak, or broken, valve spring.
Sticky valve stem.
Valve not seating properly.
Brakes adjusted too closely.
Badly fitting, or broken, piston rings.
Punctured carburetter float.
Engine carbonised.
Choked silencer.
Bad air leak between carburetter and manifold

Engine overheats may be due to :
Lack of proper lubrication.   (Quality or quantity of oil).
Faulty sparking plugs.
Air control to carburetter out of order.
Punctured carburetter float.
Engine carbonised.
Weak valve springs.
Pitted valve seats.
Worn piston rings.
Ignition setting incorrect.
Choked silencer.

Engine stops suddenly may be due to :
Stuck up valve.
No petrol in tank, or choked petrol supply.
Choked main jet.
Oiled up, or fouled, sparking plugs.
Water on high-tension pick-up, or sparking plugs.
Water in float chamber.
Vent hole in petrol tank filler cap choked.

EXCESSIVE OIL CONSUMPTION
Excessive oil consumption may be due to :
Stoppage, or partial stoppage, in the pipe returning oil from the engine to the oil tank.
Badly worn, or stuck up, piston rings.   (Causing high pressure in the crankcase.)
Air leak in dry sump oiling system.
Worn inlet valve stems.
Improper non-return valve action.

EXCESSIVE PETROL CONSUMPTION
Excessive petrol consumption may be due to :
Leaks in the petrol feed system.   (Damaged fibre washers, loose union nuts on piping, defective float needle action).
Incorrect ignition setting.   (Ignition not advanced sufficiently).
Defective engine valve action.
Incorrect use of air control lever.
Moving parts of carburetter badly worn.   (Only possible after very considerable mileage).
Bad air leak at carburetter junction, or inlet manifold joint.

STEERING UNSATISFACTORY
Incorrect steering head adjustment (too tight or excessively slack.)
Pitted steering head ball races resulting from loose adjustment.
Wheels out of alignment.
Front and/or rear tyre tread not correctly manipulated to run true with wheel (causes handlebar oscillation at low road speed.)
Damaged front fork main tubes resulting from impact.

ABNORMAL TYRE WEAR
Abnormal tyre wear may be due to :
Incorrect tyre pressure.
Wheels not in alignment.
Harsh driving methods.   (Misuse of acceleration and braking)

CLEANING THE MACHINE

Do not attempt to rub, or brush, mud off the enamelled surfaces because this will soon destroy the sheen of the enamel. Mud, and other road dirt, should be soaked off with water.

The best method is to use a small hose, taking care not to direct water on to the engine, carburetter, magneto and other such parts. As a poorer substitute, a pail of water and a sponge may be used.

After washing down with water, the surplus moisture should be removed with a chamois leather, and, when the enamelled surfaces are thoroughly dry, they may be polished with a good wax polish and soft dusters.

Such parts as the engine crankcase and the gear box can be cleaned by applying paraffin with a stiff brush, and, with a final application of petrol, will come up like new.

CHROMIUM PLATING

Under some climatic conditions, a rusty looking deposit may be observed on ferrous parts that are chromium plated. This is not ordinary rust (ferric oxide) but is a salt deposit that, in most cases and in its early stages, can be quickly and easily removed with a damp chamois leather. In stubborn cases it may be necessary to use a special chromium cleaning compound.

The safest precaution during Winter is to wipe over all chromium plated parts with a soft rag soaked in "**TEKALL,**" which is a lanoline base rust preventative marketed in small tins and available at most garages. This material, so applied, leaves an almost invisible film that is impervious to moisture and its use cannot be too highly recommended to owners who value the appearance of their mounts.

In Summer, when those conditions do not prevail, chromium parts should be frequently cleaned with a damp chamois leather and afterwards polished with a soft duster, or, better still, with a polishing cloth of the "**Selvyt**" type.

If a polish is used it must be one of the special compounds for chromium plating only. Ordinary metal polishing liquids, in particular, must not, on any account, be used because these, almost without exception, contain acids, which attack chromium.

NOTE—"**Tekall**" is a product of **20th Century Finishes Ltd., 175-177, Kirkgate, Wakefield,** and is retailed in $\frac{1}{2}$ pint and I pint tins. It can be obtained from our Spare Parts Department, as follows :

$\frac{1}{2}$ pint tin " Tekall," Part number 011957.

I pint tin " Tekall," Part number 011958.

REPAIRS AND SERVICE

REPAIRS

The instructions regarding repairs should be clear and definite, otherwise the cost may be greater than that expected. We shall be pleased to give estimates for repairs if parts are sent to us for that purpose. If the estimate is accepted, no charge is made for the preliminary examination, but, should it be decided not to have the work carried out, it **MAY** be necessary to make a charge to cover the cost of whatever dismantling and re-assembly may have been done to prepare the estimate.

Customers desiring that old parts which are replaced with new during the course of overhaul or repair be retained must make the fact known prior to the work being put in hand because, normally, such parts, having no further useful life, are scrapped upon removal.

Parts sent to us as patterns, or for repair, should have attached to them a label bearing the sender's full name and address. The instructions regarding such parts should be sent under separate cover.

If it is necessary to bring a machine, or parts, to the Works for an urgent repair, **IT IS ESSENTIAL** you **MAKE AN APPOINTMENT** beforehand to **AVOID DISAPPOINTMENT**. This can be done by letter or telephone.

CORRESPONDENCE AND ORDERS

Our routine is organised into different departments, therefore delay cannot be avoided if matters relating to more than one department are contained in one letter.

Consequently, it is desirable, when communicating with more than one department, to do so on **SEPARATE SHEETS**, each of which should bear your name and address. When writing on a technical matter, or when ordering spares, it is essential to quote the **COMPLETE ENGINE NUMBER**. Some numbers have one, or more, letters incorporated in them and these letters **MUST BE QUOTED**, otherwise model identification is not possible.

Orders should always be sent in list form and not as part of a letter.

Owners are strongly advised to purchase a Spare Parts List so that correct part numbers can be quoted. Most parts are clearly illustrated in this list which makes it very easy to recognize the part or parts required.

PROPRIETARY FITTINGS

No expense is spared to secure and fit the most suitable, and highest quality, instruments and accessories for the standard equipment of our machines.

Nevertheless, our Guarantee does not cover such parts and, in the event of trouble being experienced, the parts in question should be returned to, and claims made, direct on the actual manufacturers who will deal with them on the terms of their respective guarantees.

Those manufacturers are :

Carburetters	Messrs. Amalgamated Carburetters Ltd., Holford Road, Witton, Birmingham, 6
Chains	The Renold and Coventry Chain Co. Ltd., Didsbury, Manchester
Electrical Equipment	Messrs. Joseph Lucas Ltd., Great King Street, Birmingham, 19
Gear Boxes	Messrs. Burman & Sons Ltd., Wychall Lane, King's Norton, Birmingham, 30
Sparking Plugs	K.L.G. Sparking Plugs Ltd., Putney Vale, London, S.W.15
Speedometers	Messrs. S. Smith & Sons (M.A.) Ltd., Cricklewood, London
Tyres	Messrs. Dunlop Rubber Co. Ltd., Fort Dunlop, Birmingham
Air Filter	Messrs. Vokes Ltd., Henley Park, Nr. Guildford, Surrey

All the above manufacturers except S. Smith & Sons (M.A.) Ltd., issue instructive literature regarding their products which is obtainable by writing to them.

SERVICE

The **Service and Repair Department** is situated in **Burrage Grove, Plumstead, London, S.E.18**, and is open on Mondays to Fridays from 8.30 a.m. to 12.55 p.m.—2.0 p.m. to 5.30 p.m. It is closed on Saturdays, Sundays and National Holidays.

It exists for the purposes of :

(a) Giving technical assistance verbally or through the post.

(b) Supplying spare parts over the counter or through the post.

(c) Repairing and re-conditioning machines, or parts of machines, of our make.

Burrage Grove is the first turning on the left from Burrage Road when entering Burrage Road from the Plumstead Road. (See final paragraph below.)

The nearest Railway Station is WOOLWICH ARSENAL, SOUTHERN REGION RAILWAY. This Station is five minutes walk from our Service Depot in Burrage Grove. There is an excellent service of electric trains from Charing Cross, Waterloo, Cannon Street and London Bridge Stations, Southern Region Railway.

Bus routes 53, 53a, 54, 99 and 122. Trolleybus routes, 696 and 698 pass the end of Burrage Road (one minute from the Service Depot).

Bus routes 21a, 75 and 161 serve **Beresford Square** which is three minutes walk from the **Service and Repair Department.**

Visitors from the North can pass into Woolwich via the Free Ferry between North Woolwich and Woolwich. North Woolwich is a British Railways terminus and is also served by Bus and Trolleybus routes 101, 569, 669 and 685. There is also a tunnel under the River Thames at this point for foot passengers. The Free Ferry accommodates all types of motor vehicles and there is a very frequent service. The Southern landing stage is less than a mile from the Service Depot.

Visitors arriving by road, if they are strangers to the locality, should enquire for **Beresford Square, Woolwich.** Upon arrival there, the road skirting the Royal Arsenal should be followed in an Easterly direction for about four hundred yards, and Burrage Road is the second turning on the right after leaving the Square. Burrage Grove is then the first turning on the left.

THE DRIVER AND THE LAW

The driver of a motor cycle **MUST** be **INSURED** against Third Party Claims and **MUST** be able to produce an **INSURANCE CERTIFICATE** showing that such an insurance is in force.

If your Insurance Certificate specifies you can only drive one particular machine you **MUST NOT DRIVE** any other machine unless its owner has a current Certificate covering **" ANY DRIVER "** and it is advisable to remember that, in the absence of such a provision the penalties for doing so are very heavy.

The driver of a motor cycle **MUST** hold a current **DRIVING LICENCE.** If you are a learner and hold a Provisional Driving Licence, your machine must show, front and back, the standard " L " plates in red and white and you must not take a **PILLION PASSENGER** unless that passenger is the holder of a current **UNRESTRICTED** driving licence.

As soon as you receive your driving licence, sign it in the appropriate place and do so each time it is renewed. It is an offence not to.

Make sure you are well acquainted with the recommendations set down in the " Highway Code," a copy of which can be obtained from any main Post Office.

THE MACHINE AND THE LAW

Every motor cycle used on the public roads must be registered and carry the registration numbers and licence disc allotted to it. The dealer, from whom the machine is bought, will, generally, attend to all matters legally essential before it is used on the public roads.

To register a new machine

Send to the Local Registration Authority the following :

(a) Form " RFI/2," duly completed.
(b) The certificate of insurance.
(c) The invoice you received from your dealer when you purchased the machine.
(d) The appropriate registration fee.

In due course you will receive :

(1) A Registration Book. (Commonly called the " log " book).
(2) A Licence Disc.
(3) Your Insurance Certificate.
(4) Your Invoice.

The Registration Book and the Licence Disc will bear the registration numbers that have been allotted to your machine and will also show the date the Road Licence expires.

Your number plates must then be painted, in white upon a black background, with the registration numbers in characters of even thickness as follows :

The numbers on the front plate must be $1\frac{3}{4}''$ high, $1\frac{1}{4}''$ wide and $\frac{5}{16}''$ thick with spaces of $\frac{1}{2}''$ between each two characters.

The numbers on the rear plate must be $2\frac{1}{2}''$ high, $1\frac{3}{4}''$ wide and $\frac{3}{8}''$ thick with spaces $\frac{1}{2}''$ between each two characters.

The Licence Disc must be enclosed in a water-tight container, having a transparent front, and this must be fixed to the machine in a conspicuous position, near the front and on the left-hand side.

It is not legally necessary to carry your Driving Licence, Insurance Certificate and Registration Book while driving your machine.

Ignition Suppressors

As required by law all 1956 models for the Home Market are issued with an approved type of radio interference suppressor already installed.

Speedometer

A speedometer MUST be fitted and it MUST BE so ILLUMINATED that it is possible to read the dial after lighting up time.

Lamps

During the official " **LIGHTING UP** " hours the machine must exhibit a white light facing forwards and a red light facing rearwards. The rear number plate must be adequately illuminated by a white light.

Each front electric light bulb **MUST** be marked with its "Wattage." (Beware of cheap, imported, bulbs that do not have this marking).

All motor cycles made by us have electric equipment that complies with the law regarding position, size of bulbs, marking on bulbs and the correct illumination of the rear number plate.

FREE SERVICE SCHEME

FREE SERVICE SCHEME

All owners of **NEW MODELS** are entitled to one **FREE SERVICE AND INSPECTION** at 500 miles, or, at latest, three months after taking delivery.

This service is arranged by the supplying dealer to whom the **Free Service Voucher** must be handed. This voucher, together with the Instruction Manual, are supplied by us upon receipt of the signed application card to be found in the tool box upon taking delivery of a new motor cycle.

The **INSPECTION AND SERVICE** consists of :

(a) Check, and, if necessary, adjust :

- (1) Rocker clearances.
- (2) Contact breaker points.
- (3) Sparking plugs.
- (4) Clutch.
- (5) Chains.
- (6) Wheel bearings.
- (7) Brakes.
- (8) Forks, legs, and steering head.
- (9) Alignment of wheels.
- (10) Tyre pressures.

(b) Tighten all external nuts and bolts, including **cylinder head nuts and fork crown pinch screws**.

(c) Top-up battery and check all lighting equipment.

(d) Clean out carburetter and check for correct idling.

(e) Adjust and lubricate all cables.

(f) Grease all nipples.

(g) Drain oil system. Clean filter and replenish.

(h) Check oil level in front chaincase.

(i) Top-up gear box.

(j) Test machine on the road.

NOTE—Oils, greases and materials used are chargeable to the customer.

FOR THE CONVENIENCE OF OWNERS,

SPARES STOCKISTS

ARE APPOINTED FOR MOST DISTRICTS. TO SAVE DELAY, AND THE DELIVERY SURCHARGE CUSTOMERS ARE RECOMMENDED TO ALWAYS APPLY TO THEIR NEAREST SPARES STOCKIST.

SPARE PARTS

GENUINE SPARE PARTS purchased from an Authorised Dealer, or from the Factory, are identical with the parts originally built into your motorcycle. By using them you are assured that they will fit accurately and give satisfactory service.

SPARES STOCKISTS

For the convenience of owners Spares Stockists are appointed for most districts. To prevent delay and save the delivery surcharge, customers are recommended always to apply to their nearest Spares Stockist.

CORRESPONDENCE AND SPARES ORDERS

Always quote the complete engine number, including all the letters in it. This will enable us to identify the machine.

Each series of frames is numbered from zero upwards, therefore, the quotation of a frame number only does not facilitate identification.

SPARES LIST

An illustrated spares list covering the models described in this Instruction Book is available on application. Price 2s. 6d. each.

PART NUMBERS

If there is any doubt about the names of parts required, or their part numbers, please send the old parts as patterns.

REMINDER

Do not forget to include your name and full postal address. We do receive orders without this very necessary information.

PAYMENT

(1) Cash with order.*
(2) Cash against pro-forma invoice.
(3) Approved ledger account.

We do not send C.O.D. (Cash on delivery).

*Add 5% of total value for carriage and packing. Minimum 6d.

GUARANTEE

Full details of the guarantee relating to the models described in this book are given on page 84.

INSTRUCTION BOOKS

A copy of this book is issued free of charge to all purchasers of a new machine. Additional copies may be obtained, price 2s. 6d. each.

TOOLS AND SPECIAL EQUIPMENT

TOOLS

The standard tool kit, issued with each new machine, contains:

1	017253	Tool bag.
1	017114	Tyre inflator.
2	017007	Tyre lever.
1	017248	Pliers.
1	011188	Gudgeon pin circlip pliers.
1	017256	Screwdriver.
1	017246	Grease gun.
1	017249	Adjustable wrench.
1	017252	Sparking plug box spanner and tommy bar.
1	018178	Spanner 1·010 in. and 1·200 in.
1	017052	Double end spanner. $\frac{3}{16}'' \times \frac{1}{4}''$ in.
1	017053	Double end spanner. $\frac{5}{16}'' \times \frac{3}{8}''$ in.
1	015023	Contact point spanner and gauge.
1	018153	Spanner, for petrol tap (Special Overseas Models only).
1	018055	Key, for handlebar clip screw and rocker cover bolts.
1	017257	Double end spanner. $\frac{3}{16}'' \times .375''$ in.
1	015264	S.E. spanner. (Rocker clamping bolt nut).
1	015213	Box spanner.
1	017254	Clutch spring stud nut adjuster.
1	018667	Key for fork crown pinch screw.

OPTIONAL EQUIPMENT

The following items of optional equipment are available. They are described and priced in the Spares List.

Stop rear light fittings (see page 72.)

Air cleaner.

Gear extractor 015374. A bridge type extractor, consisting of bridge, central screw and two side bolts, for removing the gears on the camshafts.

Detachable luggage carrier.

Timing disc 022011. A circular timing disc, graduated in degrees and made of ivorine. A very useful device.

Pinion extractor 015273. A two piece extractor for removing the timing gear small pinion and the gear on the magneto shaft.

Pannier frames and bags.

Holder for valve grinding. Part number 011381.

Pillion footrests, specially designed fold up type.

GASKET SETS

For convenience in ordering, standard sets of engine washers and gaskets are stocked. Full details of contents and prices are included in the Spares List.

BADGES

Neat monogram badges are now available at a cost of 1/6, plus 6d. postage. They can be supplied as a tie pin, as a brooch or for fitting in a button hole. When ordering state type required.

TOOL KIT

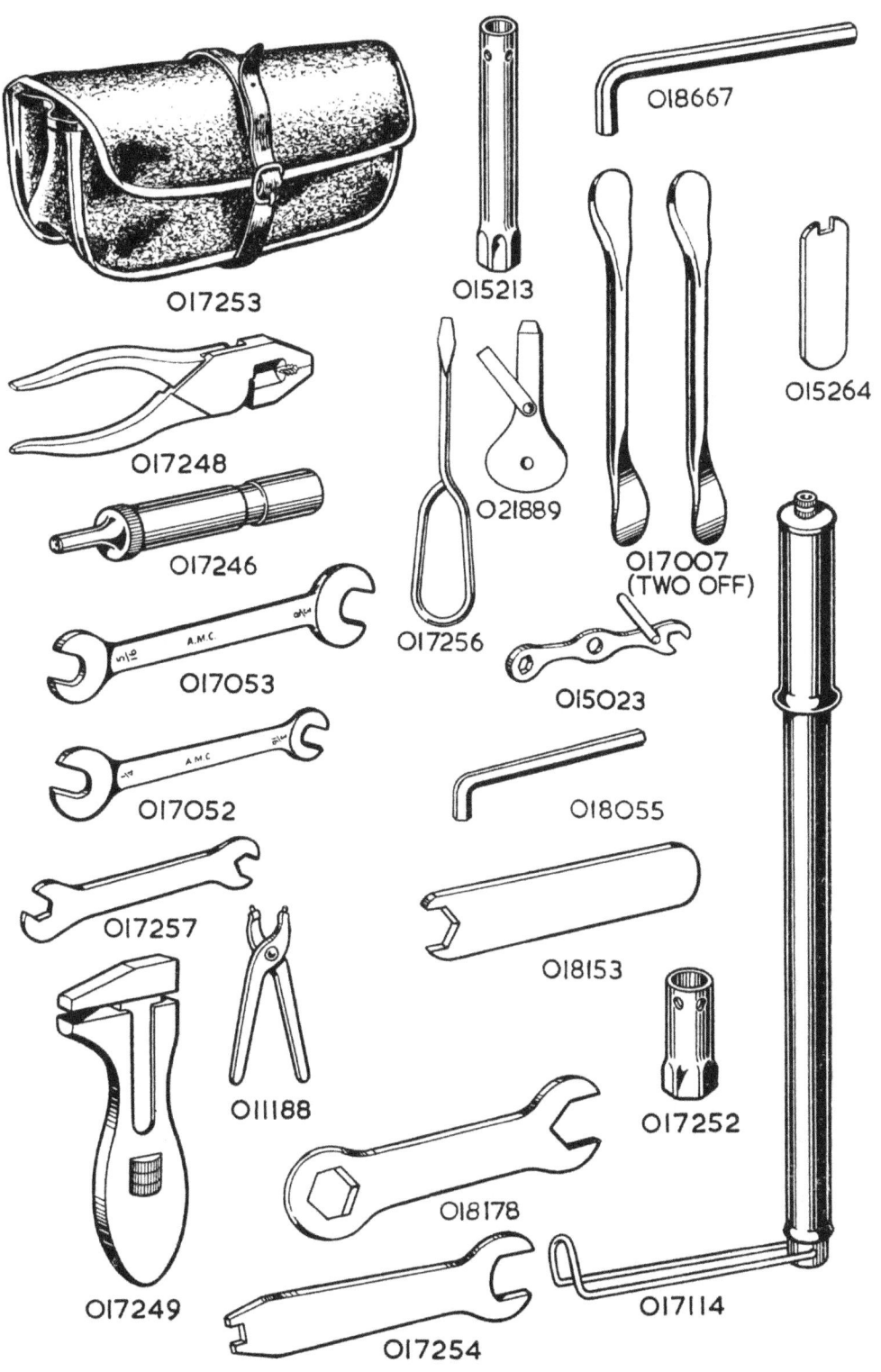

Illustration 36

GUARANTEE

We give the following guarantee with our motorcycles, motorcycle combinations and sidecars, which is given in place of any implied conditions, warranties or liabilities whatsoever, statutory or otherwise, all such implied conditions, warranties and liabilities being in all cases excluded. Any statement, description, condition or representation contained in any catalogue, advertisement, leaflet or other publication shall not be construed as enlarging, varying or overriding this guarantee. In the case of machines (a) which have been used for " hiring-out " purposes or (b) any motorcycle and/or sidecar used for any dirt track, cinder track or grass track racing or competitions (or any competition of any kind within an enclosure for which a charge is made for admission to take part in or view the competition) or (c) machines from which the trade mark, name or manufacturing number has been removed, no guarantee, condition or warranty of any kind is given or is to be implied.

We guarantee, subject to the conditions mentioned below, that all precautions which are usual and reasonable have been taken by us to secure excellence of materials and workmanship, but this guarantee is to extend and be in force for six months only from date of purchase, and damages for which we make ourselves responsible under this guarantee are limited to the free supply of a new part in exchange for the part of the motorcycle, motorcycle combination or sidecar which may have proved defective. We do not undertake to replace or refix, or bear the cost of replacing or refixing, such new part in the motorcycle, motorcycle combination or sidecar. We undertake, subject to the conditions mentioned below, to make good at any time within six months any defects in these respects. As motorcycles, motorcycle combinations and sidecars are easily liable to derangement by neglect, or misuse, this guarantee does not apply to defects caused by wear and tear, misuse or neglect.

The term " misuse " shall include amongst others the following acts :—

1. The attaching of a sidecar to a motorcycle in such a manner as to cause damage or calculated to render the latter unsafe when ridden.
2. The use of a motorcycle or of a motorcycle and sidecar combined, when carrying more persons or a greater weight than that for which the machine was designed by the manufacturers.
3. The attaching of a sidecar to a motorcycle by any form of attachment not provided, supplied or approved by us or to a motorcycle which is not designed for such use.

Any motorcycle, motorcycle combination or sidecar sent to us to be plated, enamelled or repaired will be repaired upon the following conditions, i.e., we guarantee that all precautions which are usual and reasonable have been taken by us to secure excellence of materials and workmanship, such guarantee to extend and be in force for three months only from the time such work shall have been executed or until the expiration of the six months above referred to, and this guarantee is in lieu and in exclusion of any common law or statute warranty or condition, and the damages recoverable are limited to the cost of any further work which may be necessary to amend and make good the work found to be defective.

CONDITIONS OF GUARANTEE

If a defective part should be found in our motorcycles, motorcycle combinations or sidecars, or in any part supplied by way of exchange before referred to, it must be sent to us CARRIAGE PAID, and accompanied by an intimation from the owner that he desires to have it repaired or exchanged free of charge under our guarantee, and he must also furnish us at the same time with the number of the machine, the date of the purchase or the date when the alleged defective part was exchanged as the case may be.

Failing compliance with the above, such articles will lie here AT THE RISK OF THE OWNER, and this guarantee and any implied guarantee, warranty or condition shall not be enforceable.

We do not guarantee specialities such as tyres, saddles, chains, electrical equipment, lamps, etc., or any component parts supplied to the order of the Purchaser differing from standard specifications supplied with our motorcycles, motorcycle combinations, sidecars or otherwise.

NOTICE

We do not appoint agents for the sale on our behalf of our motor cycles or other goods, but we assign to motor cycle dealers areas in which we supply to such dealers exclusively for re-sale in such areas. No such Dealer is authorised to transact any business, give any warranty, make any representation or incur any liability on our behalf.

INDEX

	Page
Air filter	35
A.V.C.	68
Badge	82
Battery	69
Brake controls, lubrication	19
Brake cover plate, front	56
Brake drums	57
Brake, front	59
Brake, pedal	61
Brake, rear	60
Brake shoes	57
Brake shoe adjustment	58
Carbon deposit, removal	26
Carburetter adjustment	33
Carburetter, function	33
Carburetter, tuning	35
Centre stand	52
Chain adjustment	42
Chain lubrication	18
Chain rear, fitting	43
Chaincase, front	38
Chainguard, removal	52
Chrome plating	76
Cleaning	76
Clutch	37, 38
Clutch actuating mechanism	37
Clutch adjustment	41
Controls	8, 9
Correspondence	77
Crankcase release valve	32
Cylinder barrel, removal	28
Cylinder barrel, replacement	28
Cylinder head, removal	25
Cylinder head, replacement	29

	Page
Data	6, 7
Decarbonisation	25
Driving notes	12
Dynamo, removal	68
Dynamo, test	68
Electrical equipment	64
Engine lubrication	14
Engine oil pumps	14
Engine shock absorber	38
Forks, front	44/49
Forks, rear lubrication	19
Free service	80
Fuel	10
Fuel tank fixing details	24
Gasket sets	82
Gearbox	36
Gearbox end-plate removal	38
Gearbox lubrication	18
Gear change	37
Headlamp	72
Horn	72
Hub lubrication	19
Ignition	64, 65
Ignition timing	31
Kickstarter	37

	Page
Law, the	78, 79
Lighting	71
Lubricants	13
Lubrication chart	20
Magneto adjustment	65
Magneto cleaning	65
Magneto removal	67
Oil consumption excessive	75
Oil circulation	15, 16
Oil filter	16
Oil filter, cleaning	17
Oil tank	16
Oil tank removal	52
Optional equipment	82
Overhead rocker adjustment	23
Periodic maintenance	21
Petrol consumption excessive	75
Petrol tank removal	25
Piston removal and re-fitting	28
Primary chain	38
Prop stand	52
Proprietary fittings	77
Rear lamp	72
Rear suspension	50/52
Repairs	77
Running in	11

	Page
Service	78
Sparking plug	66
Sparking plug removal	32
Speedometer, lubrication	19
Starting	10
Steering, causes of unsatisfactory	75
Steering head adjustment	44
Steering head lubrication	19
Stopping	11
Terminals, electrical equipment	72
Timing gear removal	29
Tools and toolkit	82, 83
Tracing troubles	74
Twist grip, adjustment	33
Tyres	62, 63
Tyre wear	75
Valve grinding	26
Valve guide removal	26
Valve removal	26
Valve timing	29
Wheel bearing adjustment	54
Wheel bearing, front	54
Wheel bearing, rear	56
Wheel removal, front	53
Wheel removal, rear	53
Wire connector	72

SPARES LIST
for
1956

A·J·S "SPRINGTWIN"
VERTICAL TWINS

| Bore 66 m.m. | Stroke 72.8 | Capacity 498 c.c. |
| Bore 72 m.m. | Stroke 72.8 | Capacity 592 c.c. |

Compiled and Issued by the Manufacturers

A·J·S MOTOR CYCLES

(Proprietors : ASSOCIATED MOTOR CYCLES LIMITED)

Registered Offices :

PLUMSTEAD ROAD, PLUMSTEAD
LONDON, S.E.18 . ENGLAND

Nearest Station :
WOOLWICH ARSENAL
(Southern Region Railway)

Factories :
BURRAGE GROVE and MAXEY ROAD
PLUMSTEAD, S.E.18

Telegrams and Cables : "ICANHOPIT, TELEX-LONDON"
Telephone : WOOLWICH 1223 (7 Lines)
Codes : A.B.C. 5th and 6th Edition ; Bentley's ; and Private Codes

All correspondence to :—
A·J·S MOTOR CYCLES, PLUMSTEAD ROAD, LONDON, S.E.18

Price : TWO SHILLINGS and SIXPENCE

DETAILED INDEX

	Page
BRAKES	40-41
CARBURETTER	12-14
CABLES (Control)	35-37
CARRIER	31
ELECTRICAL	
Battery	41
Battery carrier	32
Cable clips	43
Dynamo	14
Horn	42
Lamp, Head	41
Lamp, Rear	42
Magneto	14
Sundries	43
Voltage Regulator	41
ENGINE	5 to 10
ENGINE PLATES	15
FOOTRESTS	32
FORKS (Front)	26-27
FORKS (Rear)	24
FRAME	24
GASKETS	17
GRIPS	33
GUARDS	
Chaincase, front	31
Chainguard rear	32
Mudguard, front	29
Mudguard, rear	31
Number plate, front	31
Number plate, rear	31

	Page
HANDLEBAR	29
LEVERS (Control)	33-35
OFFICE INFORMATION	
Guarantee	3
How to order parts	2
Instruction Book	3
Repairs	3
Service	2
Terms of Business	2
PIPES	
Exhaust	17
Oil	39
Petrol	39
SEATS	33
SERVICE	
How to reach Factory	44
SILENCERS	17
SPEEDOMETER	43
STANDS	29
TANKS	37
TELEDRAULIC LEG	26
TOOLS	44
TOOL BOXES	32
TRANSFERS	33
TRANSMISSION	17 to 22
VARIOUS	43
WHEELS	39-40

ILLUSTRATIONS

	Page
CARBURETTER	13
CLUTCH AND KICK-STARTER	23
CONTROL LEVERS	34
CRANKCASE, CRANKSHAFT, AND CONNECTING RODS	4
CYLINDERS, HEADS, PISTONS, VALVES, AND TIMING GEAR ...	8
EXHAUST PIPES, SHOCK ABSORBER AND CHAINS	16
FRAME AND TELEDRAULIC REAR LEG	25
FRONT TELEDRAULIC FORKS AND STEERING DAMPER	28
GEARS AND SHAFTS	21
GEAR BOX SHELLS	18
OIL PUMPS, DYNAMO AND MAGNETO	11
STANDS, GUARDS, CHAINCASES AND TOOL BOXES	30
TANKS AND PIPES	36
WHEELS AND BRAKES	38

ALWAYS QUOTE

THE COMPLETE ENGINE NUMBER

(Including all the Letters in it)

THIS ENABLES THE MACHINE TO BE IDENTIFIED

EACH SERIES OF FRAMES IS NUMBERED FROM ZERO UPWARDS. THEREFORE THE QUOTATION OF A FRAME NUMBER ONLY DOES NOT FACILITATE IDENTIFICATION.

(1) **TERMS OF BUSINESS.**

Our terms are :— CASH WITH ORDER,
CASH AGAINST PRO-FORMA INVOICE, OR
APPROVED LEDGER ACCOUNT.

Customers who wish to avoid delay can open deposit accounts and the usual deposit is £5.

Orders from abroad should be accompanied by a remittance to cover the costs of goods and postal charges.

We do not send goods by "CASH ON DELIVERY" (C.O.D.).

(2) **PRICES AND SPECIFICATIONS.**

All prices, specifications and conditions are subject to alteration without notice. The prices of spares do not include the costs of packing and carriage.

(3) **CARRIAGE AND PACKING.**

All invoices for spare parts will be SURCHARGED by 5 PER CENT. to cover the cost of packing and postage, or carriage, and the minimum surcharge is sixpence. (Home orders only.)

A special packing case, or crate, is required for some spares to ensure freedom from damage in transit. In such circumstances a special charge for the value of the case, or crate, will be made in addition to the 5 per cent. surcharge but the special charge will be credited in full if the container is promptly returned to our factory carriage paid and in good condition.

(4) **HOW TO ORDER SPARES.**

STATE :— (a) The Model of the machine.
         (b) The complete engine number. (See paragraph 5.)
         (c) The frame number. (See paragraph 5.)
         (d) The part numbers of the spares required.
         (e) A description of each spare.
         (f) The quantity required of each item.
         (g) How the spares are to be sent. (Post, Parcels Post, Passenger train or Goods train.)
         (h) Your full name and address. These particulars are best written in BLOCK LETTERS.
         (i) Mention if, or not, you have an account with us.

ALSO :— Unless you have a deposit or ordinary account, enclose a remittance to cover the cost of the spares plus the 5 per cent. surcharge. (See paragraph 3.)

When cash is sent any excess will be refunded without prior application.

NOTE :— When sending orders by telegram or cable do not omit your name and address from the message.

(5) **IDENTITY.**

To ensure the supply of correct spares it is essential we can identify the machine for which they are required. The ONLY WAY to do that is for us to know the COMPLETE ENGINE and frame numbers.

The engine number is stamped on the left crankcase, in front of the left cylinder, and may have one or more letters incorporated in it. THE COMPLETE NUMBER MUST BE QUOTED.

The frame number is stamped on the right-hand side of the frame lug that is below the saddle.

(6) **SERVICE.**

The **SERVICE AND REPAIR DEPARTMENT** is situated in **BURRAGE GROVE, PLUMSTEAD, LONDON, S.E.18,** and is open on Mondays to Fridays from 8.30 a.m. to 12.55 p.m.—2 p.m. to 5.30 p.m. It is closed on Saturdays, Sundays and National Holidays.

It exists for the purpose of :—
         (a) Giving technical assistance verbally or through the Post.
         (b) Supplying spare parts over the counter or through the Post.
         (c) Repairing and re-conditioning machines, or parts of machines, of our make.

If it is considered necessary to bring a machine, or parts, to the factory for an urgent repair IT IS ESSENTIAL you make an appointment beforehand to avoid disappointment. This can be done by letter or telephone.

(7) REPAIRS.

The instructions regarding repairs should be clear and definite, otherwise the cost may be greater than that expected. We shall be pleased to give estimates for repairs if parts are sent to us for that purpose. If the estimate is accepted, no charge is made for the preliminary examination, but, should it be decided not to have the work carried out, it may be necessary to make a charge to cover the cost of whatever dismantling and re-assembly may have been done to prepare the estimate.

(8) REPAIRS TO PROPRIETARY FITTINGS.

We do not repair carburetters, chains, electrical equipment, saddles, sparking plugs, speedometers and tyres. On page 77 of the "**MAINTENANCE MANUAL AND INSTRUCTION BOOK**" will be found the names and addresses of the manufacturers of the proprietary equipment we fit, all of whom service and repair equipment they make.

(9) PATTERNS.

Parts sent to us as patterns, or for repair, should have attached to them a label bearing the sender's full name and address. The instructions regarding such parts should be sent under separate cover.

(10) GUARANTEE.

All parts made by us, and sold as spares, are subject to the same Limited Guarantee as that issued with each new motor cycle and that guarantee is printed in full on Page 84 of the "**MAINTENANCE MANUAL AND INSTRUCTION BOOK.**"

(11) INSTRUCTION BOOK.

A "**MAINTENANCE MANUAL AND INSTRUCTION BOOK**" has been compiled and published by us.

One copy is supplied free, upon application, with each new motor cycle. Replacement copies are two shillings and sixpence each.

(12) CORRESPONDENCE.

Our routine is organised into different departments. Therefore delay cannot be avoided if matters relating to more than one department are contained in one letter.

Consequently when communicating with more than one department it is desirable to do so on SEPARATE SHEETS. Each sheet should bear the sender's name and address. **IN PARTICULAR, requests** for TECHNICAL ADVICE should not be on the same sheets as ORDERS FOR SPARE PARTS.

A·J·S MOTOR CYCLES,
PLUMSTEAD, LONDON, S.E.18.

ALL PRICES, EXCEPT THOSE MARKED *, ARE SUBJECT TO 10% INCREASE.

NOTE

The numbers, in brackets, that appear in the "Description" columns relate to the numbered foot notes regarding items so specially indicated.

The quantities per machine of each item are entered in the "Qty." columns. "R" indicates as may be required.

The illustrations are not to scale and are not necessarily accurate in detail.

Some items are not illustrated.

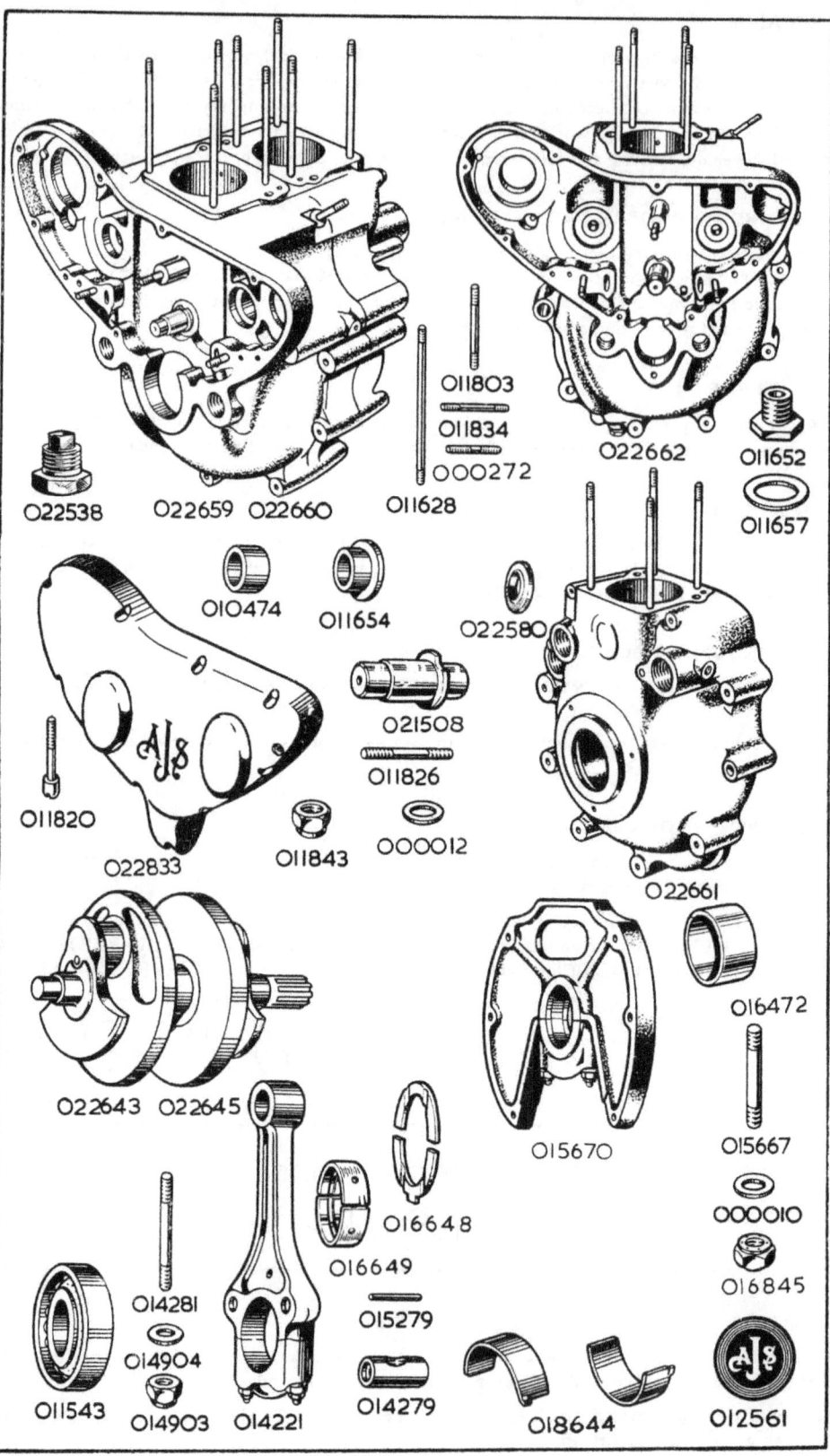

PART NUMBER	DESCRIPTION	QTY. OFF	USED ON	PRICE EACH £ s. d.

CRANKCASE

Part Number		Description	Qty. Off	Price
022660	...	Crankcase, complete (1)	1	20-30
022661	...	Crankcase, driving side only (2)	1	,,
022662	...	Crankcase, timing side only (3)	1	,,
015670	...	Web, centre, with cap, studs, washers and nuts (no bearing and thrust washers)	1	,,
022833	...	Cover, for timing gear	1	,,
012561	...	Badge, monogram, for driving side crankcase	1	,,
011826	...	Stud, fixing centre web, $1\frac{15}{32}$ in. by $\frac{1}{4}$ in. by 26 and 20	6	,,
000012	...	Washer, plain, for centre web top fixing studs	2	,,
000012	...	Washer, plain, for centre web centre fixing studs	2	,,
000012	...	Washer, plain, for centre web bottom fixing studs	2	,,
011843	...	Nut, for centre web fixing studs	6	,,
015667	...	Stud, for centre web bearing cap, $2\frac{11}{16}$ in. by $\frac{3}{8}$ in. by 20 and 20	2	,,
000010	...	Washer, plain, for centre web bearing cap stud	2	,,
016845	...	Nut, for centre web bearing cap stud	2	,,
011628	...	Stud, in driving side crankcase, for cylinder and head, $5\frac{7}{16}$ in. by $\frac{5}{16}$ in. by 26 and 22	4	,,
011628	...	Stud, in timing side crankcase, for cylinder and head, $5\frac{7}{16}$ in. by $\frac{5}{16}$ in. by 26 and 22	4	,,
011834	...	Stud, in timing side crankcase, for pump carrying plate, $1\frac{5}{8}$ in. by $\frac{5}{16}$ in. by 26 and 22	3	,,
000272	...	Stud, in timing side crankcase, for fixing magneto, $1\frac{1}{4}$ in. by $\frac{5}{16}$ in. by 26 and 22	2	,,
011803	...	Stud, in timing side crankcase, for dynamo strap, $1\frac{3}{16}$ in. by $\frac{1}{4}$ in. by 26 and 20	1	,,
021508	...	Shaft, in timing side crankcase, for intermediate gear	1	,,
011820	...	Screw, retaining timing gear cover	10	,,
011652	...	Adaptor, to accommodate oil feed and return pipe retaining banjo pins. (Screws into timing side crankcase)	2	,,
011657	...	Washer, fibre, for banjo pin adaptors	2	,,
010474	...	Bush, plain, for camshafts. (In driving side crankcase)	2	,,
011654	...	Bush, flanged, for camshafts. (In timing side crankcase)	4	,,
016472	...	Tunnel, for camshaft chamber (fits between crankcase halves)	2	,,
011648	...	Cap, in crankcase housing for inlet camshaft	1	,,
011642	...	Washer, fibre, for crankcase housing cap	1	,,

1.—Includes :—*Driving crankcase. Timing crankcase, centre web with studs (no bearing and washers). Bushes for camshafts. Cylinder studs. Shaft for intermediate gear. Cam follower spindles. Studs for pump plate. Two magneto studs. Dynamo strap stud. Timing gear cover and screws. Monogram badge. Three bolts. One stud. Two nuts. Five washers.*

2.—Includes :—*Two camshaft bushes. Four cylinder studs. Cam follower spindles. Six studs for centre web. (No badge.)*

3.—Includes :—*Four camshaft bushes. Four cylinder studs. Shaft for intermediate gear. Three studs for pump plate. Two studs for magneto. One stud for dynamo strap. (No timing gear cover and screws.)*

WHEN IN DOUBT REGARDING THE NAMES AND PART NUMBERS OF THE PARTS YOU REQUIRE, PLEASE SEND THE OLD PARTS TO SERVE AS PATTERNS

PART NUMBER	DESCRIPTION	QTY. OFF	USED ON	PRICE EACH £ s. d.

CRANKSHAFT, CONNECTING RODS AND BEARINGS

Part Number	Description	Qty. Off	Used On
022643	Crankshaft, plugged, but bare	1	20
022645	Crankshaft, plugged, but bare	1	30
016649	Bearing, plain, for centre bearing (in halves)............per pair	1	20-30
016648	Washer, thrust, for centre bearing	2	,,
011543	Bearing, roller, for crankshaft. (Parts of this bearing are not sold separately), $1\frac{3}{8}$ in. internal, 3 in. external, $\frac{11}{16}$ in. wide. Manufacturers part number RLS-$12\frac{1}{2}$	2	,,
014221	Connecting rod assembly. (No big end bearing)	2	,,
014281	Stud, for connecting rod, $2\frac{23}{32}$ in. by $\frac{5}{16}$ in. by 26	4	,,
014279	Trunnion, for connecting rod	4	,,
015279	Rivet, locating connecting rod stud	4	,,
014904	Washer, plain, for connecting rod stud	4	,,
014903	Nut, for connecting rod stud	4	,,
018644	Bearing, plain, for connecting rod, top or bottom half...each half	4	,,
	The following undersize bearings can be supplied. It is necessary to have the journals ground to suit.		
016670	Bearing, plain, for centre bearing, ·010 in. undersize (2 halves)	1	20-30
016671	Bearing, plain, for centre bearing, ·020 in. undersize (2 halves)	1	,,
016672	Bearing, plain, for centre bearing, ·030 in. undersize (2 halves)	1	,,
018564	Bearing, plain, for connecting rod, ·010 in. undersize, top or bottom, each half	4	,,
018565	Bearing, plain, for connecting rod, ·020 in. undersize, top or bottom, each half	4	,,
018566	Bearing, plain, for connecting rod, ·030 in. undersize, top or bottom, each half	4	,,

CYLINDERS, PISTONS, HEADS AND VALVES

Part Number	Description	Qty. Off	Used On
022230	Cylinder, barrel only	2	20
022231	Cylinder, barrel only	2	30
022233	Washer, paper, for cylinder base	2	20-30
022598	Piston, bare, normal size	2	20
022226	Piston, bare, normal size	2	30
022669	Piston, bare, ·020 in. oversize	2	20
022670	Piston, bare, ·020 in. oversize	2	30
022671	Piston, bare, ·040 in. oversize	2	20
022672	Piston, bare, ·040 in. oversize	2	30
022663	Piston, complete, normal size	2	20
022664	Piston, complete, normal size	2	30
022665	Piston, complete, ·020 in. oversize	2	20
022666	Piston, complete, ·020 in. oversize	2	30
022667	Piston, complete, ·040 in. oversize	2	20
022668	Piston, complete, ·040 in. oversize	2	30
	The above complete pistons include :—		
	Piston, two compression rings (1 chrome plated), one scraper ring. Gudgeon pin, two circlips for gudgeon pin.		
018297	Ring, compression, chrome plated, normal size	2	20
022228	Ring, compression, chrome plated, normal size	2	30
018298	Ring, compression, chrome plated, ·020 in. oversize	2	20
022315	Ring, compression, chrome plated, ·020 in. oversize	2	30
018299	Ring, compression, chrome plated, ·040 in. oversize	2	20
022316	Ring, compression, chrome plated, ·040 in. oversize	2	30
010631	Ring, compression, normal size	2	20
022227	Ring, compression, normal size	2	30
015522	Ring, compression, ·020 in. oversize	2	20
022317	Ring, compression, ·020 in. oversize	2	30
016441	Ring, compression, ·040 in. oversize	2	20
022318	Ring, compression, ·040 in. oversize	2	30
018366	Ring, scraper, normal size	2	20
022229	Ring, scraper, normal size	2	30
022677	Ring, scraper, ·020 in. oversize	2	20
022319	Ring, scraper, ·020 in. oversize	2	30
022679	Ring, scraper, ·040 in. oversize	2	20
022320	Ring, scraper, ·040 in. oversize	2	30
011731	Pin, gudgeon	2	20
022277	Pin, gudgeon	2	30

PART NUMBER	DESCRIPTION	QTY. OFF	USED ON	PRICE EACH £ s. d.

CYLINDERS, PISTONS, HEADS AND VALVES—continued.

014283	Circlip, gudgeon pin	4	20-30	
022234	Head, for cylinder, bare, left	1	,,	
022235	Head, for cylinder, bare, right	1	,,	
022681	Head, for cylinder, with valve guides, valve guide circlips and manifold studs, left	1	,,	
022682	Head, for cylinder, with valve guides, valve guide circlips and manifold studs, right	1	,,	
022236	Gasket, for cylinder head	2	,,	
014163	Valve, inlet	2	,,	
014165	Valve, exhaust	2	,,	
011770	Spring, inner, for valve	4	,,	
011769	Spring, outer, for valve	4	,,	
014169	Seat, for valve spring	4	,,	
014168	Collar, for valve spring	4	,,	
014167	Collet, for valve stems (in pairs)	4	,,	
014170	Guide, for inlet valves	2	,,	
014171	Guide, for exhaust valves	2	,,	
011111	Circlip, locating valve guides	4	,,	
011634	Spacer, $\frac{25}{32}$ in. long, for head retaining nuts	8	,,	
000004	Nut, retaining cylinders and heads	8	,,	
000011	Washer, plain, for head retaining nuts	8	,,	
010625	Stud, retaining inlet manifold, $1\frac{11}{16}$ in. by $\frac{1}{4}$ in. by 26 and 20	4	,,	
014352	Bush, for rocker spindle	4	,,	

RE-BORING

Cylinders may be re-bored to ·020 in. or ·040 in. oversize and pistons (with rings) supplied to suit. The charge is £5 9s. 4d. for the pair, with an additional 11s. 4d. if new gudgeon pins and circlips are also supplied. Cylinders sent for re-boring should be packed in stout cases which will be used by us for their return. Carriage is additional.
If a complete machine, or engine, is sent to us for cylinder re-boring, there will be an additional charge, according to the time taken, for dismantling and assembly.

TIMING GEAR

018961	Camshaft, inlet	1	20-30	
018962	Camshaft, exhaust	1	,,	
011620	Gear, on camshaft, 60 teeth	2	,,	
000573	Key, locating camshaft gears	2	,,	
011653	Nut, retaining camshaft gears	2	,,	
016209	Pinion, on crankshaft, 30 teeth	1	,,	
016210	Spacer, $\frac{7}{32}$ in. long, for crankshaft pinion	1	,,	
000573	Key, locating crankshaft pinion	1	,,	
011776	Bolt, retaining crankshaft pinion, threaded $\frac{1}{2}$ in. by 20	1	,,	
010589	Washer, plain, for crankshaft pinion bolt	1	,,	
021506	Gear, intermediate, with bush, 60 teeth	1	,,	
022016	Bush, for intermediate gear	1	,,	
018576	Follower, for camshaft	4	,,	
011626	Spindle, for camshaft followers	2	,,	
022102	Spacer, $1\frac{19}{64}$ in. long between camshaft followers	2	,,	

ROCKERS AND PUSH RODS

022017	Rocker, with bushes (left inlet and right exhaust)	2	20-30	
022018	Rocker, with bushes (right inlet and left exhaust)	2	,,	
014222	Spindle, for rockers	4	,,	
014226	Washer, spring, double coil, for rocker spindle	4	,,	
014275	Washer, plain, for either side of rocker spindle spring washer	8	,,	
014275	Washer, plain, for clamping end of rocker spindle	4	,,	
011760	Bolt, clamping rocker spindle. (Thread No. 2 B.A.)	4	,,	
015021	Washer, plain, for rocker spindle clamping bolt	4	,,	
011846	Nut, for rocker spindle clamping bolt	4	,,	
014245	Bush, for rockers. (One in each rocker)	4	,,	
019987	Bush for rockers. (One in each rocker)	4	,,	
018623	Cover, for rockers	4	,,	
018493	Gasket, for rocker covers	4	,,	
018492	Screw, retaining rocker covers	8	,,	
018517	Rod, push, assembled with ends	4	,,	
018508	Rod, push, bare	4	,,	
018518	End, upper, for push rod	4	,,	
018519	End, lower, for push rod	4	,,	

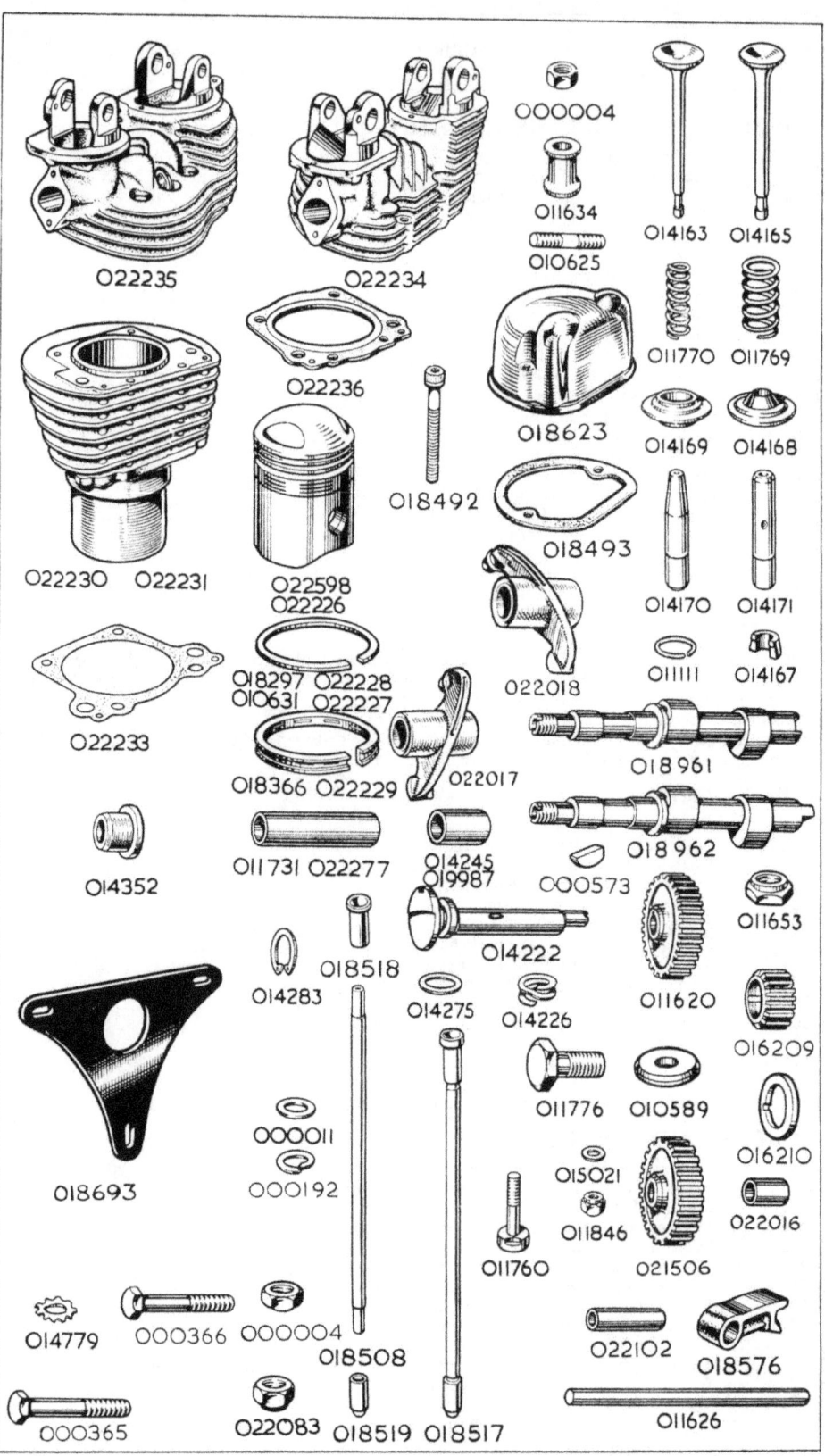

PART NUMBER	DESCRIPTION	QTY. OFF	USED ON	PRICE EACH £ s. d.

ENGINE STEADY STAY

018693	... Plate, engine steady..	1	20-30	
000365	... Bolt, securing rear of steady stay, $1\frac{1}{16}$ in. by $\frac{5}{16}$ in. by 26	2	,,	
014779	... Washer, lock, for steady stay frame front bolt	1	,,	
022083	... Nut, for steady stay rear bolt	2	,,	
000366	... Bolt, securing steady stay to frame, $1\frac{1}{4}$ in. by $\frac{5}{16}$ in. by 26	1	,,	
000004	... Nut, for steady stay to frame securing bolt	1	,,	
000011	... Washer, plain, under heads of rear bolts	2	,,	
000192	... Washer, spring, for rear bolts	2	,,	

OIL PUMPS

018037	... Oil pumps, complete, assembled on carrying plate (4)	1	20-30	
015017	... Plate, carrying, oil pumps, bare (5).......................................	1	,,	
014903	... Nut, securing pump carrying plate to timing side crankcase ...	3	,,	
000011	... Washer, plain, for pump carrying plate fixing nuts	3	,,	
000021	... Ball, $\frac{1}{4}$ in. steel, for return pump bleed valve	1	,,	
000701	... Spring, for return pump bleed valve ball	1	,,	
015001	... Screw, securing return pump bleed valve spring. (Grub screw $\frac{1}{4}$ in. long by $\frac{5}{16}$ in. by 22)	1	,,	
016137	... Gasket, oval, behind pump carrying plate	2	,,	
016138	... Gasket, round, behind pump carrying plate	1	,,	
015568	... Body, oil feed pump, for $\frac{1}{4}$ in. gears with $\frac{7}{16}$ in. shaft	1	,,	
015599	... Pin, dowel, for oil feed pump	2	,,	
015576	... Plate, front end, for oil pump feed body	1	,,	
015573	... Plate, back end, for oil pump feed body...............................	1	,,	
011617	... Washer, paper, between oil feed pump and carrying plate......	1	,,	
000453	... Screw, retaining oil feed pump to carrying plate. 1 in. by 2 B.A.	3	,,	
015579	... Gear, driving, for oil feed pump, $\frac{1}{4}$ in. wide. $\frac{7}{16}$ in. shaft	1	,,	
015580	... Gear, driven, for oil feed pump, $\frac{1}{4}$ in. wide. $\frac{7}{16}$ in. shaft	1	,,	
015567	... Body, oil return pump, for $\frac{3}{8}$ in. gears with $\frac{7}{16}$ in. shaft	1	,,	
015599	... Pin, dowel, for oil return pump	2	,,	
015576	... Plate, front end, for oil pump return body	1	,,	
015573	... Plate, back end, for oil pump return body............................	1	,,	
011617	... Washer, paper, between oil return pump and carrying plate...	1	,,	
000453	... Screw, retaining oil return pump to carrying plate. 1 in. by 2 B.A.	3	,,	
015577	... Gear, driving, for oil return pump, $\frac{3}{8}$ in. wide. $\frac{7}{16}$ in. shaft ...	1	,,	
015578	... Gear, driven, for oil return pump, $\frac{3}{8}$ in. wide. $\frac{7}{16}$ in. shaft ...	1	,,	

NOTE 4.—Includes all the items listed above except the three 014903 and 000011 fixing nuts and washers.

NOTE 5.—Includes the 000021, 000701 and 015001 bleed valve ball, spring and retaining grub screw.

BEFORE ORDERING SPARES
PLEASE NOTE THE INFORMATION GIVEN ON PAGES
TWO AND THREE

PART NUMBER	DESCRIPTION	QTY. OFF	USED ON	PRICE EACH £ s. d.

OIL FELT FILTER (IN ENGINE)

014235	Filter, felt, for engine crankcase	1	20-30	
018120	Seat, for oil felt filter	1	,,	
014240	Valve, relief, for oil felt filter	1	,,	
014241	Spring, for oil felt filter relief valve	1	,,	
016179	Cap, for felt filter housing (also accommodates oil non-return valve)	1	,,	
011642	Washer, fibre, for filter housing cap	1	,,	
011645	Ball, ⅜ in. steel, for non-return valve	1	,,	
013564	Spring, for non-return valve ball	1	,,	
013332	Plug, screwed, retaining non-return valve spring	1	,,	
012118	Washer, fibre, for non-return valve spring plug	1	,,	
015034	Gasket, paper, for oil filter chamber (fits between the two crankcase halves)	1	,,	
022538	Filter, magnetic	1	,,	
000182	Washer, for magnetic filter	1	,,	

OIL DISTRIBUTOR

022385	Distributor, oil	1	20-30	
014247	Cap, housing, for oil distributor	1	,,	
011642	Washer, fibre, for oil distributor housing cap	1	,,	
022580	Washer, sealing crankcase bolt	1	,,	

GENUINE A·J·S SPARES

PURCHASED FROM

AN AUTHORISED "A·J·S" DEALER

OR FROM THE FACTORY, ARE IDENTICAL

WITH THE PARTS ORIGINALLY BUILT

INTO YOUR MOTOR CYCLE

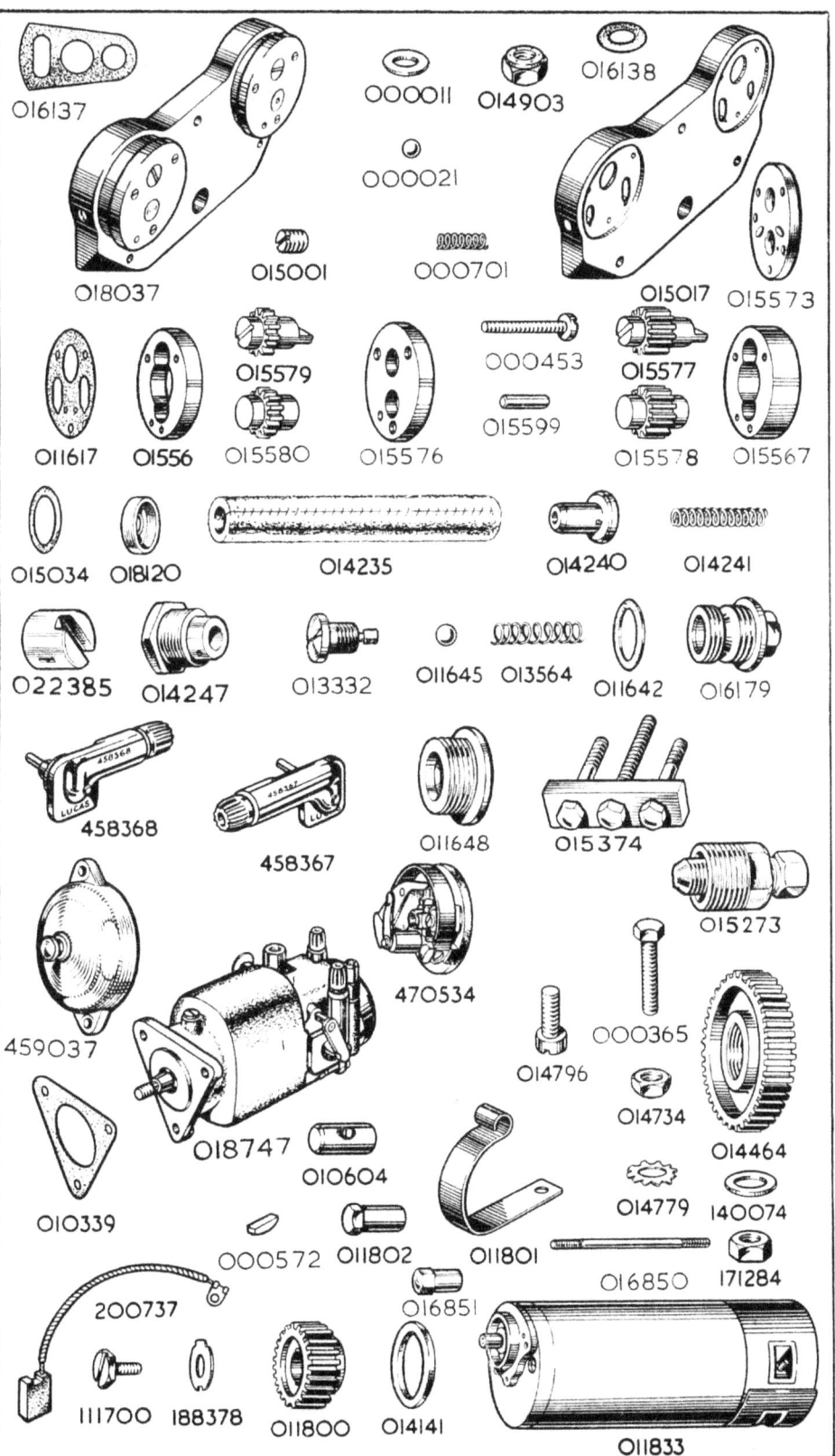

PART NUMBER	DESCRIPTION	QTY. OFF	USED ON	PRICE EACH £ s. d.

CARBURETTER

Part Number	Description	Qty.	Price
021875	Carburetter complete (less controls) Monobloc type 376/6	1	20
022768	Carburetter complete (less controls) Monobloc type 376/6	1	30
011633	Inlet manifold (bare) see cylinder head for fixing studs	1	20-30
000012	Washer for manifold retaining studs	4	,,
000005	Nut for manifold retaining studs	4	,,
011771	Gasket between manifold and cylinder head	2	,,
018503	Ring, rubber between carburetter and manifold	1	,,
016724	Bolt retaining carburetter to manifold	2	,,
000011	Washer for carburetter retaining bolts	2	,,
376-002	Carburetter body	1	,,
376-077	Side cover	1	,,
376-078	Side cover jointing washer	1	,,
376-079	Side cover screw	3	,,
376-083	Float	1	,,
376-094	Float spindle bush	1	,,
376-089	Float needle	1	,,
376-088	Float needle seating	1	,,
376-065	Mixing chamber cap securing ring	1	,,
4-235	Mixing chamber cap securing ring spring	1	,,
4-241	Screw securing cap securing ring spring	1	,,
376-064	Mixing chamber cap	1	,,
4-035	Control cable adjuster	2	,,
376-062	Air valve	1	,,
6-047	Air valve guide	1	,,
376-060	Throttle valve	1	,,
4-046	Air valve spring	1	,,
376-061	Throttle valve spring	1	,,
376-068	Throttle stop screw	1	,,
376-069	Throttle stop screw spring	1	,,
332-017	Pilot air adjusting screw	1	,,
4-148	Pilot air adjusting screw spring	1	,,
376-063	Taper jet needle	1	,,
4-230	Taper jet needle clip	1	,,
376-072	Needle jet	1	,,
376-100	Main jet (specify size when ordering)	1	,,
376-073	Main jet holder	1	,,
376-074	Jet holder washer	1	,,
376-075	Main jet cover	1	,,
376-076	Pilot jet	1	,,
376-095	Pilot jet cover nut	1	,,
116-162	Pilot jet cover nut washer	1	,,
376-056	Jet block complete	1	,,
376-070	Locating peg for jet block	1	,,
376-067	Jet block washer	1	,,
376-097	Petrol pipe banjo	1	,,
376-091	Petrol pipe banjo bolt	1	,,
376-092	Petrol pipe banjo bolt washer	1	,,
14-175	Banjo seating washer	1	,,
376-093	Filter gauze	1	,,
343-011	Tickler body	1	,,
376-086	Tickler plunger	1	,,
376-087	Tickler Spring	1	,,
376-066	Air intake venturi	1	,,

BY USING GENUINE SPARES YOU ARE ASSURED THEY WILL FIT ACCURATELY AND GIVE SATISFACTORY SERVICE

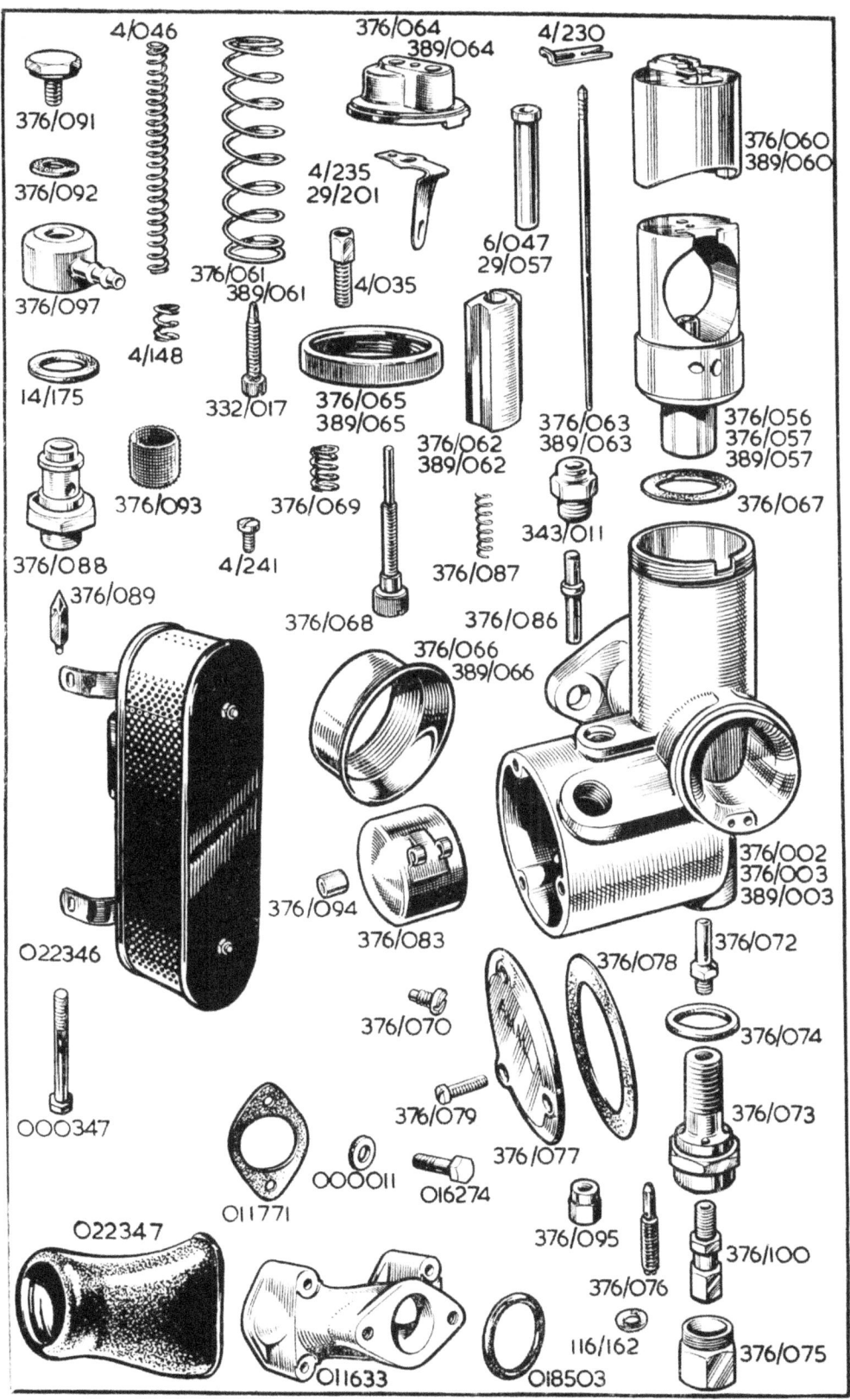

PART NUMBER	DESCRIPTION	QTY. OFF	USED ON	PRICE EACH £ s. d.

AIR CLEANER. (This is optional extra equipment)

022346	... Cleaner, air	1	20-30	
022347	... Sleeve, rubber, connecting air cleaner to carburetter............	1	,,	
016983	... Set of air cleaner elements comprising filter element and two fabric end gaskets	1	,,	
000347	... Bolt, for frame..	1	,,	
000005	... Nut, for fixing bolt...	1	,,	
000012	... Washer, for fixing bolt	1	,,	

When an air cleaner is fitted it is essential to :—

	Fit a smaller jet, viz., use jet 376-100 (size 230)	1	20	
	(size 250)	1	30	

MAGNETO

018747	... Magneto, complete, Type K2F (Lucas number 42230-A)	1	20-30	
458367	... Pick-up, with brush and spring, right	1	,,	
458368	... Pick-up, with brush and spring, left.......................................	1	,,	
470534	... Contact breaker, complete	1	,,	
470609	... Contact set	1	,,	
459037	... Cover, for contact breaker with switch	1	,,	
010339	... Gasket, for magneto flange	1	,,	
000365	... Bolt, retaining magneto, $1\frac{1}{16}$ in. by $\frac{5}{16}$ in. by 26 .... *For the two magneto retaining studs, see " Crankcase Group."*	1	,,	
014779	... Washer, lock, for magneto retaining bolt and studs...............	3	,,	
000004	... Nut, for magneto retaining bolt and studs............................	3	,,	
014464	... Gear, on magneto shaft	1	,,	
140074	... Washer, plain, on magneto shaft	1	,,	
171284	... Nut, on magneto shaft, retaining magneto driving gear	1	,,	

★ *Price on application.*

DYNAMO

011833	... Dynamo, Type E3L-L-1-0 (Lucas Number 20009-B)	1	20-30	
200826	... Cover assembly	1	,,	
200737	... Brush, for dynamo, set of two, per set	1	,,	
014141	... Gasket, between dynamo and crankcase.............................	1	,,	
011801	... Strap, retaining dynamo to crankcase..................................	1	,,	
014796	... Screw, retaining lower end of dynamo strap to crankcase, $\frac{7}{16}$ in. by $\frac{1}{4}$ in. by 20	1	,,	
000012	... Washer, plain, for dynamo strap retaining screw	1	,,	
010604	... Crosshead, in eye of dynamo retaining strap.........................	1	,,	
011802	... Nut, tensioning dynamo strap. (The stud on which this nut screws, is listed with the crankcase parts).........................	1	,,	
000012	... Washer, plain, for dynamo strap tensioning nut	1	,,	
011800	... Gear on dynamo shaft	1	,,	
000572	... Key, locating dynamo shaft gear	1	,,	
111700	... Bolt, retaining gear on dynamo shaft	1	,,	
188378	... Washer, lock, for dynamo gear retaining bolt	1	,,	
016850	... Stud, drawing dynamo to crankcase, and passing through timing cover, $2\frac{1}{2}$ in. long by 2 B.A.	1	,,	
016851	... Nut, for dynamo draw stud	1	,,	

★ *Price on application.*

PART NUMBER	DESCRIPTION	QTY. OFF	USED ON	PRICE EACH £ s. d.

CRANKCASE BOLTS, with engine plates and all bolts passing through same.

014292	... Bolt, clamping crankcase throat, $3\frac{11}{16}$ in. by $\frac{5}{16}$ in. by 22. (These bolts pass through the driving side crankcase and thread into the timing side crankcase)	3		20-30
000011	... Washer, plain, for 014292 crankcase bolts	3		,,
013944	... Plate, engine front, right side	1		,,
013943	... Plate, engine front, left side	1		,,
000303	... Stud, passing through crankcase and upper holes in engine, front plates. (This stud also supports the stays for the exhaust pipes)	1		,,
000003	... Nut, for engine plate stud	2		,,
000278	... Stud, passing through crankcase and lower holes in engine front plates, $4\frac{9}{16}$ in. by $\frac{5}{16}$ in. by 26	1		,,
000011	... Washer, plain, for 000278 engine plate stud	2		,,
000004	... Nut, for 000278 engine plate stud	2		,,
000277	... Stud, passing through crankcase at bottom, $4\frac{3}{8}$ in. by $\frac{5}{16}$ in. by 26	1		,,
000011	... Washer, plain, for 000277 crankcase stud	2		,,
000004	... Nut for 000277 crankcase stud	2		,,
000303	... Stud, passing through front of main frame and top of engine front plate	1		,,
000003	... Nut, for 000303 frame stud	2		,,
021086	... Stud, passing through main frame front tube bottom lug, the crankcase, and the front ends of the rear frame rails, 6 in. by $\frac{3}{8}$ in. by 26	1		,,
000010	... Washer, plain, for 021086 frame stud	2		,,
000003	... Nut, for 021086 frame stud	2		,,
022291	... Plate, engine, rear left	1		,,
022292	... Plate, engine, rear right	1		,,
000278	... Stud, passing through top of engine rear plates and the crankcase, $4\frac{9}{16}$ in. by $\frac{5}{16}$ in. by 26	1		,,
000278	... Stud, passing through bottom of engine rear plates and the crankcase, $4\frac{9}{16}$ in. by $\frac{5}{16}$ in. by 26	1		,,
000011	... Washer, plain, for 000278 studs	3		,,
000004	... Nut, for 000278 studs	3		,,
000316	... Stud, passing through engine rear plates, rear of crankcase, and centre of front chaincase, $7\frac{7}{16}$ in. by $\frac{7}{16}$ in. by 26. (Stud should be fitted so that the longer thread is on left-hand side of machine)	1		,,
014084	... Spacer, $1\frac{17}{32}$ in. long, on 000316 stud, between back of front chaincase and crankcase	1		,,
021230	... Wide nut spacer, on 000316 stud, inside front chaincase	1		,,
000009	... Washer, plain, for 000316 stud	2		,,
000002	... Nut, for 000316 stud	1		,,
000220	... Nut, chaincase stud (outer)	1		,,
000306	... Stud, passing through top of engine, rear plates, and lower end of main frame seat tube	1		,,
000003	... Nut, for 000306 stud	2		,,
000278	... Stud, passing through back ends of engine rear plates, $4\frac{9}{16}$ in. by $\frac{5}{16}$ in. by 26	1		,,
	(The front chain adjusting eye bolt block screws on the right-hand end of this stud.)			
000011	... Washer, plain, for 000278 stud	1		,,
000004	... Nut, for 000278 stud	1		,,

For the bolt stud passing through the top and bottom of the gear box and the engine rear plates, see " Gear Box Fixing Bolts."

For the footrest rod, which passes through the bottoms of the engine rear plates and the frame rails, see " Footrests."

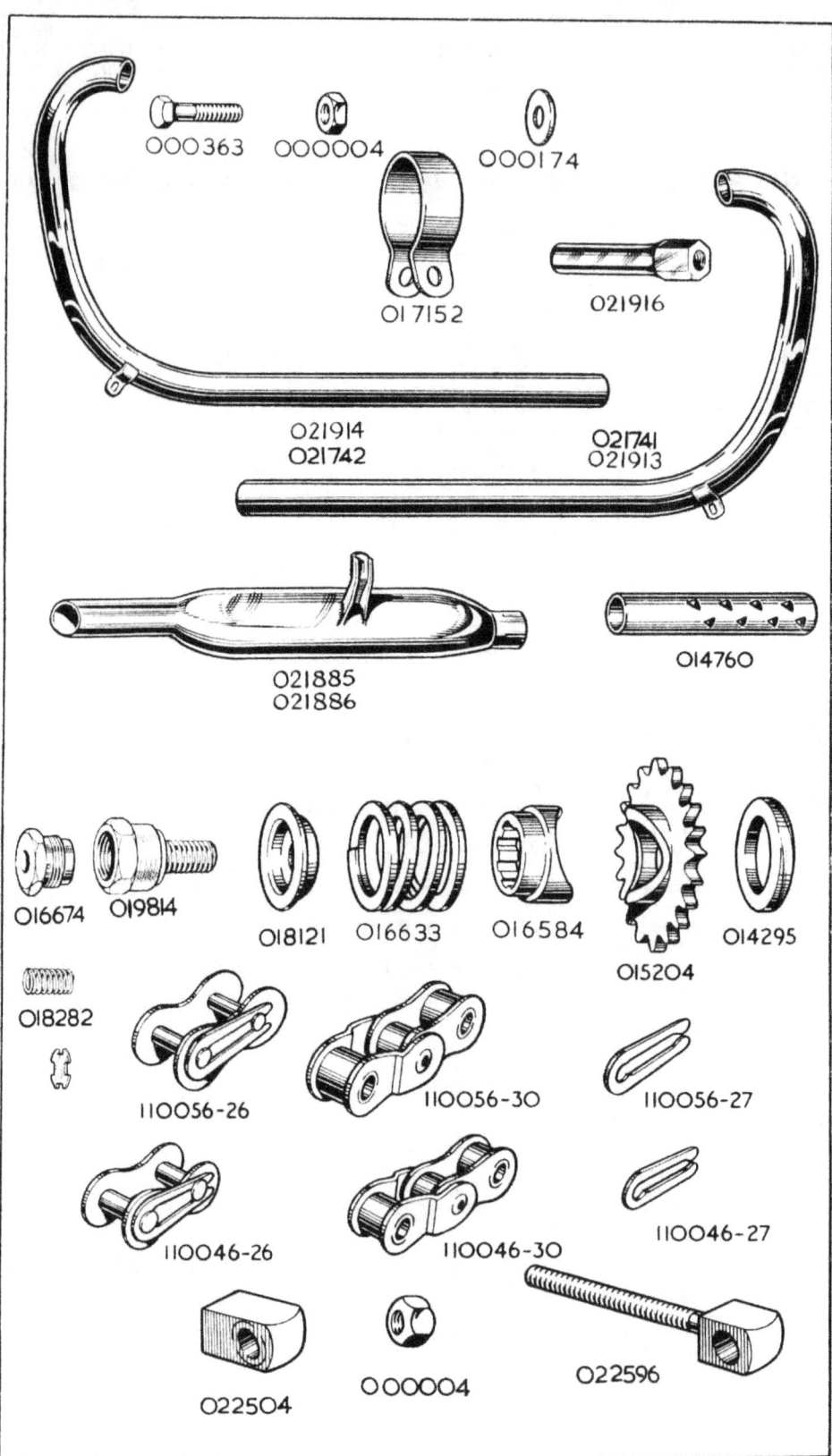

PART NUMBER	DESCRIPTION	QTY. OFF	USED ON	PRICE EACH £ s. d.

GASKETS

We supply engine gaskets, either as separate spares, or in complete sets.

Single gaskets, are listed in the groups to which they belong.

Gaskets in complete sets are listed below.

022696	... Complete gasket set for vertical twin engine	1	20-30	
022697	... Decarbonising gasket set for vertical twin engine	1	,,	

Each complete gasket set contains :—
1—011642 Washer, fibre, for engine filter housing cap.
1—011642 Washer, fibre, for oil distributor housing cap.
4—000183 Washer, fibre, for banjo end of oil pipes.
2—011617 Washer, paper, for oil pump bodies.
2—022233 Washer, paper, for cylinder bases.
1—015034 Washer, paper, for oil filter chamber.
1—010339 Gasket, between magneto and crankcase.
2—022236 Gasket, for cylinder head.
2—011771 Gasket, between inlet manifold and cylinder head.
1—014141 Gasket, between dynamo and crankcase.
4—018493 Gasket, for rocker covers.
2—016137 Gasket, oval, behind pump carrying plate.
1—016138 Gasket, round, behind pump carrying plate.

Each decarbonising gasket set includes :—
2—022236 Gasket, for cylinder heads.
4—018493 Gasket, for rocker covers.
2—011771 Gasket, between inlet manifold and cylinder heads.
2—022233 Washer, paper, for cylinder bases.

EXHAUST PIPES AND SILENCERS

021913	... Pipe, exhaust, bare, left side	1	20	
022741	... Pipe, exhaust, with baffle, left side	1	30	
021914	... Pipe, exhaust, bare, right side	1	20	
022742	... Pipe, exhaust, with baffle, right side	1	30	
014760	... Baffle, for exhaust pipe	2	20	
021916	... Support, for exhaust pipe, left side or right side	2	20-30	
000362	... Bolt, fixing exhaust pipe to support	2	,,	
000174	... Washer, plain, for exhaust pipe fixing bolt	2	,,	
000192	... Washer, spring, for exhaust pipe fixing bolt	2	,,	
021885	... Silencer, bare, left side	1	,,	
021886	... Silencer, bare, right side	1	,,	
017152	... Clip, clamping silencer to pipe	2	,,	
000363	... Bolt, for silencer clip, $\frac{3}{4}$ in. by $\frac{5}{16}$ in. by 26	2	,,	
000174	... Washer, plain for silencer clip bolt	2	,,	
000004	... Nut, for silencer clip bolt	2	,,	
000363	... Bolt, fixing silencer to frame	2	,,	
000174	... Washer, plain, for silencer to frame fixing bolt	2	,,	
000192	... Washer, spring, for silencer to frame fixing bolt	2	,,	

ENGINE SPROCKETS (and Crankcase Release Valve)

016665	... Sprocket, engine, bare, 18 teeth (for sidecar use only on 20)	1	20	
015203	... Sprocket, engine, bare, 19 teeth (for sidecar use only on 30)	1	30	
015204	... Sprocket, engine, bare, 20 teeth. (This is the standard sprocket)	1	20-30	
014294	... Sprocket, engine, bare, 21 teeth	1	,,	
014295	... Spacer (collar), $\frac{9}{32}$ in. wide, for engine sprocket	1	,,	
016584	... Cam, engine shock absorber	1	,,	
016633	... Spring, engine shock absorber	1	,,	
018121	... Cap, for engine shock absorber spring	1	,,	
019814	... Bolt, locking shock absorber assembly, threaded $\frac{1}{2}$ in. by 20. (Also houses crankcase release valve)	1	,,	
016676	... Diaphragm, for crankcase release valve	1	,,	
018282	... Spring, for crankcase release valve diaphragm	1	,,	
016674	... Plug, retaining crankcase release valve. (Screws into bolt 019814)	1	,,	

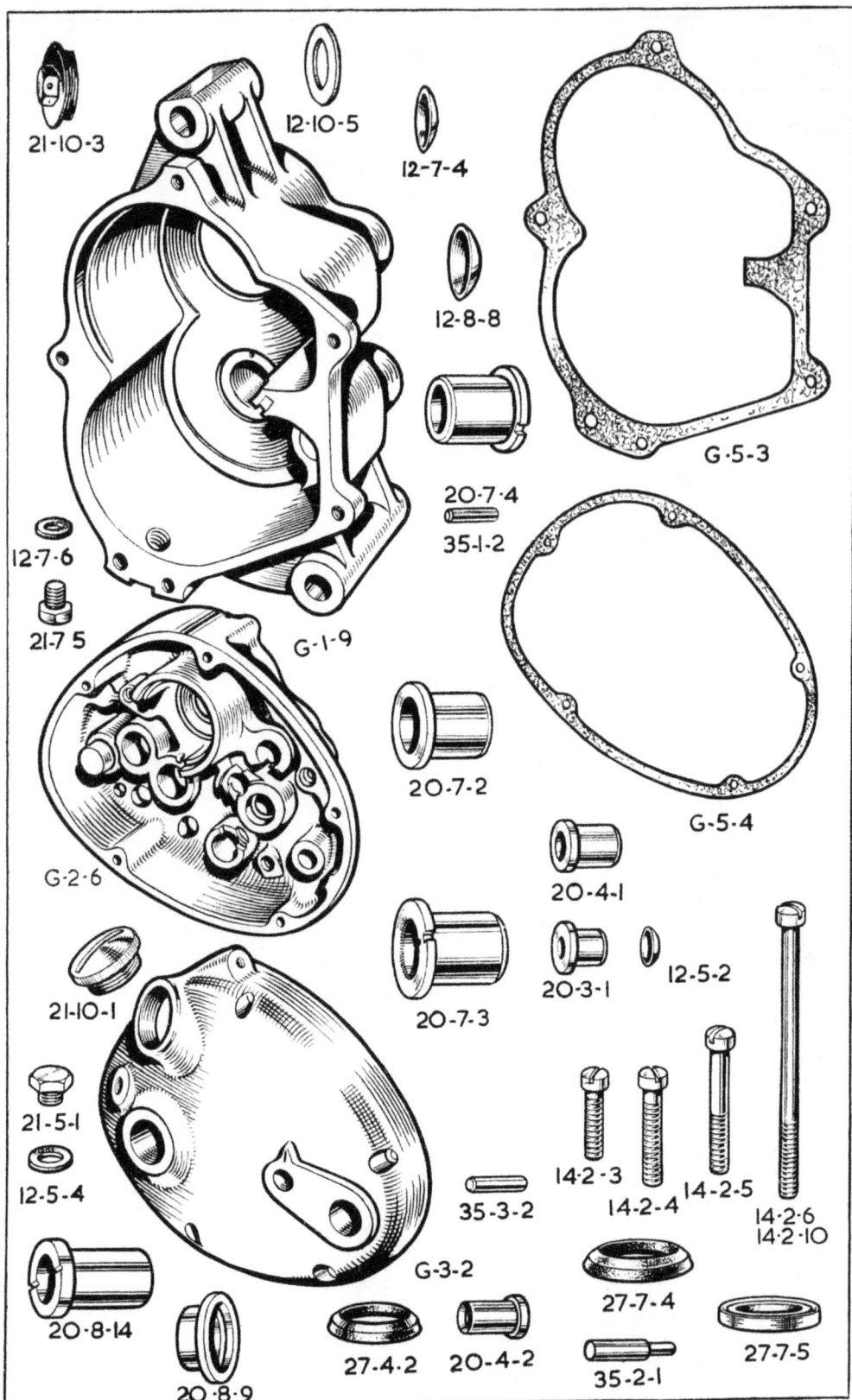

PART NUMBER	DESCRIPTION	QTY. OFF	USED ON	PRICE EACH £ s. d.

CHAINS

017298	Chain, front, 66 links, $\frac{1}{2}$ in. by ·305 in.	1	20-30	
017375	Chain, rear, 96 links, $\frac{5}{8}$ in. by ·380 in.	1	,,	
110046-26	Link, connecting, for $\frac{1}{2}$ in. chains	R	,,	
110056-26	Link, connecting, for $\frac{5}{8}$ in. chains	R	,,	
110046-30	Link, cranked, double, for $\frac{1}{2}$ in. chains	R	,,	
110056-30	Link, cranked, double, for $\frac{5}{8}$ in. chains	R	,,	
110046-27	Clip, spring, for 110046-26 connecting links ($\frac{1}{2}$ in.)	R	,,	
110056-27	Clip, spring, for 110056-26 connecting links ($\frac{5}{8}$ in.)	R	,,	

The prices of front and rear chains include spring connecting links and these are also included in the number of links per chain.

We do not sell odd lengths of chains.

GEAR BOX

016709	Gear box, complete, with clutch and with kick-starter and gear control levers	1	20-30	

★ *Price on application.*

GEAR BOX FIXING PARTS

022509	Bolt, gearbox top fixing	1	20-30	
000318	Stud, gearbox bottom fixing, $4\frac{9}{16}$ in. by $\frac{7}{16}$ in. by 26	1	,,	
000002	Nut, for gearbox top fixing bolt	1	,,	
000002	Nut, for gearbox bottom fixing stud	2	,,	
000009	Washer, plain, for top fixing bolt, left side	1	,,	
022596	Gearbox adjuster	1	,,	
000215	Nut, for front chain adjustment eye-bolt	1	,,	
022504	Block, crosshead, for front chain adjustment eye-bolt. (This threads on the right-hand end of 000278 stud that passes through the rear of the engine rear plates and the bottom frame lug)	1	,,	
000402	Bolt, gear box adjuster crosshead	1	,,	
000010	Washer, gearbox adjuster crosshead bolt	1	,,	

GEAR BOX SHELL

G-1-9	Shell, gearbox, bare	1	20-30	
21-10-3	Inspection plug	1	,,	
12-10-5	Inspection plug washer	1	,,	
21-7-5	Plug, drain, for gearbox shell	1	,,	
12-7-6	Washer, fibre, for gearbox shell drain plug	1	,,	
12-7-4	Cap, in shell, covering bore for selector spindles	2	,,	
35-3-2	Pin, dowel, locating, kick-starter case on gearbox shell	1	,,	
G-2-6	Case, kick-starter	1	,,	
G-5-3	Washer, paper, between shell and kick-starter case	1	,,	
G-3-2	Cover, for kick-starter case	1	,,	
G-5-4	Washer, paper, between kick-starter case and cover	1	,,	
28-12-45	Piece, locating, between kick-starter case and cover	1	,,	
35-1-1	Pin, dowel, locating fixed cam-plate in kick-starter case	2	,,	
21-10-1	Cap, filler, for kick-starter case cover	1	,,	
21-5-1	Plug, oil level, in kick-starter case cover	1	,,	
12-5-4	Washer, fibre, for oil level plug	1	,,	
35-2-1	Pin, anchor, in cover, for kick-starter spring	1	,,	
14-2-3	Screw, $\frac{7}{8}$ in. under head	1	,,	
14-2-4	Screw, $1\frac{1}{4}$ in. under head	4	,,	
14-2-5	Screw, $1\frac{3}{8}$ in. under head	1	,,	
14-2-6	Screw, $2\frac{7}{8}$ in. under head	1	,,	
14-2-10	Screw, $3\frac{1}{8}$ in. under head	1	,,	
12-2-5	Washer, fibre, end plate fixing screw	8	,,	

Above screws have cheese heads and are threaded $\frac{1}{4}$ in. Whit.

PART NUMBER	DESCRIPTION	QTY. OFF	USED ON	PRICE EACH £ s. d.

SHAFTS AND GEARS

G-18-2	... Mainshaft, for gearbox	1	20-30	
G-19-6	... Layshaft for gearbox overall length 5½ in.	1	,,	
G-6-2	... Gear, driving, mainshaft, with bushes, 28 teeth	1	,,	
G-12-2	... Gear, first, mainshaft, 17 teeth	1	,,	
G-10-2	... Gear, second, mainshaft, 22 teeth	1	,,	
G-8-1	... Gear, third, mainshaft, 25 teeth	1	,,	
G-7-2	... Pinion, on layshaft, 18 teeth	1	,,	
G-13-2	... Gear, first, layshaft, with bush, 29 teeth	1	,,	
G-11-2	... Gear, second, layshaft, with bush, 24 teeth	1	,,	
G-9-1	... Gear, third, layshaft, 21 teeth	1	,,	
19-8-13	... Bush, for mainshaft driving gear	2	,,	
19-8-15	... Bush, for mainshaft third gear	1	,,	
19-8-15	... Bush, for layshaft second gear	1	,,	
19-8-14	... Bush, for layshaft first gear	1	,,	

GEARBOX BEARINGS, CAPS AND OIL-SEALS

38-11-1	... Bearing, ball, 1$\frac{9}{32}$ in. by 62 mm. by 16 mm. for driving gear on mainshaft	1	20-30	
27-12-2	... Oil-seal, for driving gear bearing	1	,,	
39-12-1	... Housing, for driving gear bearing oil-seal	1	,,	
31-12-2	... Ring, split, retaining driving gear bearing	1	,,	
38-7-1	... Bearing, ball, 17 mm. by 40 mm. by 12 mm. for mainshaft (kick-starter end)	1	,,	
31-11-1	... Ring, split, retaining mainshaft ball bearing	1	,,	
20-7-4	... Bush, for layshaft (clutch end) (·968 in. long)	1	,,	
35-1-2	... Pin, dowel, locating layshaft bush	1	,,	
12-8-8	... Cap, in shell, covering bore, for layshaft	1	,,	
20-7-3	... Bush, for layshaft (kick-starter end) (·779 in. long)	1	,,	
35-1-2	... Pin, dowel, locating layshaft bush	1	,,	
20-7-2	... Bush, in kick-starter case, for kick-starter spindle	1	,,	
20-8-14	... Bush, in cover, for kick-starter spindle	1	,,	
27-7-5	... Oil-seal, in cover bush, for kick-starter spindle	1	,,	
20-4-1	... Bush, in kick-starter case, for cam spindle	1	,,	
20-4-2	... Bush, kick-starter case cover	1	,,	
27-4-2	... Oil-seal, in cover bush, for cam spindle	1	,,	
20-3-1	... Bush, in kick-starter case, for control quadrant spindle	1	,,	
12-5-2	... Cap, in kick-starter case, covering bore for control quadrant spindle	1	,,	
20-8-9	... Bush, in cover, for control quadrant spindle	1	,,	
27-7-4	... Oil-seal, in cover bush, for control quadrant spindle	1	,,	

GEARBOX SMALL SPROCKET

G-31-1	... Sprocket, gearbox, 16 teeth by $\frac{5}{8}$ in. by ·380 in.	1	20-30	
28-12-16	... Collar, spacing, gearbox sprocket, ·435 in. wide	1	,,	
12-11-3	... Spacer, $\frac{1}{16}$ in. wide, for Sprocket	2	,,	
12-11-1	... Washer, lock, for gearbox sprocket nut	1	,,	
11-11-1	... Nut, fixing gearbox sprocket to driving gear	1	,,	

GEAR OPERATING PARTS

G-29-4	... Spindle and fork, gear selection, left	1	20-30	
G-29-6	... Spindle and fork, gear selection, right	1	,,	
35-3-1	... Peg, for selector spindles	2	,,	
16-1-4	... Pin, cotter, for selector spindle pegs	2	,,	
018337	... Cam, assembly	1	,,	

The cam assembly comprises :—
 1—G-27-2 Spindle.
 1—G-28-1 Cam.
 3—35-2-4 Pegs.
 1—35-2-2 Locating pegs.
 2—35-1-4 Cam stop pegs.
 (Above parts not sold as separate spares)

G-42-3	... Plunger, locating cam assembly	1	20-30	
36-2-1	... Spring, for cam assembly locating plunger	1	,,	

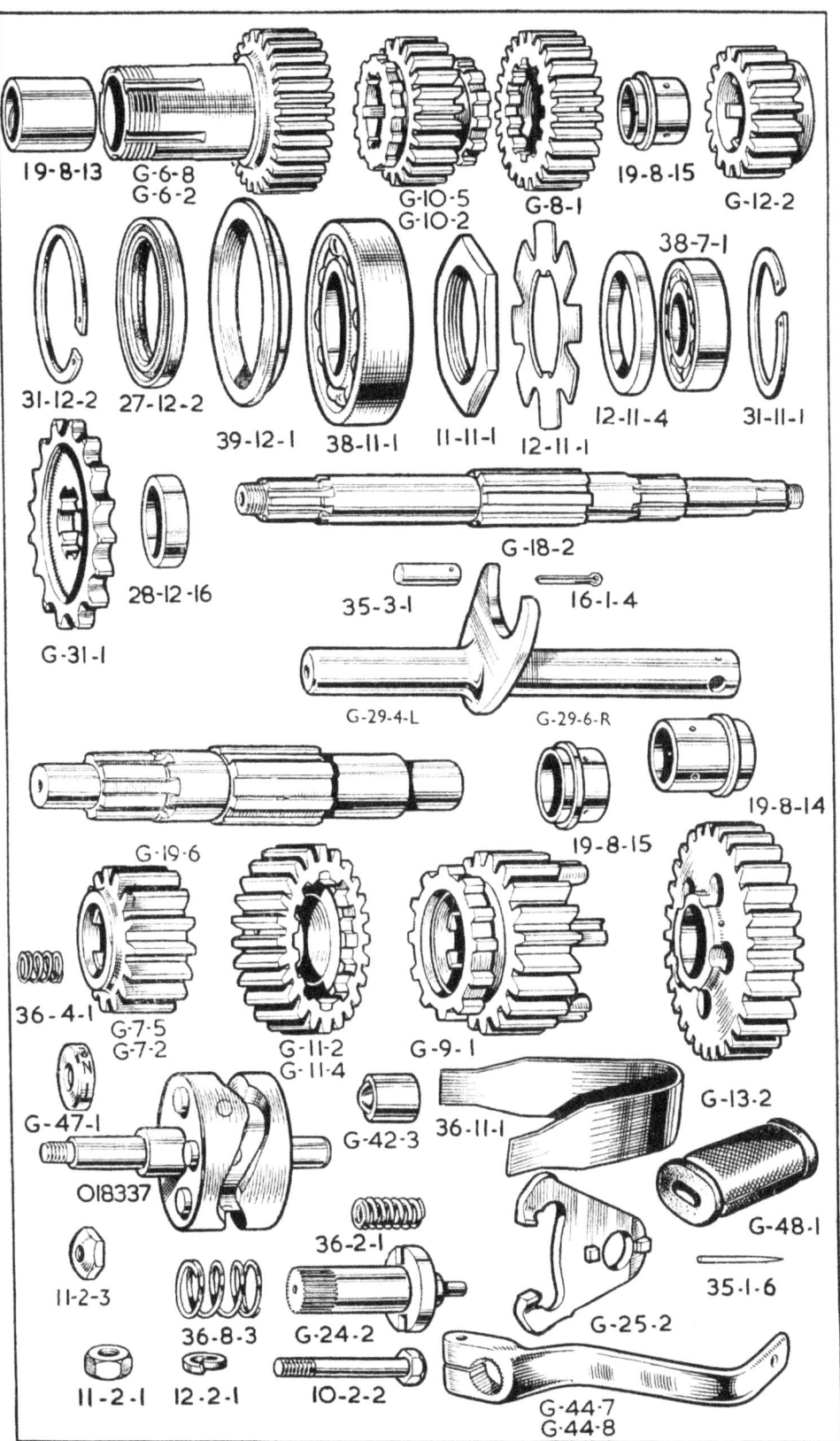

PART NUMBER	DESCRIPTION	QTY. USED OFF ON	PRICE EACH £ s. d.

GEAR OPERATING PARTS—continued.

Part No.	Description	Qty.	Price
G-25-2	Quadrant, for control spindle	1	20-30
35-2-6	Peg, quadrant drive	1	,,
G-24-2	Spindle, for gear control quadrant	1	,,
36-11-1	Spring, primary, for control quadrant	1	,,
36-8-3	Spring, secondary, for control quadrant	1	,,
G-47-1	Indicator	1	,,
36-4-1	Spring under indicator	1	,,
11-2-3	Nut, retaining indicator	1	,,
G-44-7	Lever, foot, for gear control	1	,,
G-48-1	Pad, rubber, for gear foot lever	1	,,
35-1-6	Pin, fixing gear foot lever rubber pad	1	,,
10-2-2	Bolt, clamping gear foot lever	1	,,
12-2-1	Washer, spring, for gear foot lever bolt	1	,,
11-2-1	Nut, for gear foot lever bolt	1	,,

CLUTCH

Part No.	Description	Qty.	Price
G-36-3	Case, for five plate clutch	1	20-30
29-2-4	Rivet, for clutch case and chainwheel	8	,,
G-34-2	Chainwheel, 40 teeth by $\frac{1}{2}$ in. by ·305 in.	1	,,
018339	Case and chainwheel, assembled (five plate)	1	,,
G-35-2	Sleeve, for mainshaft	1	,,
12-10-2	Race, roller, for clutch bearing chainwheel	1	,,
18-2-1	Rollers, for chainwheel bearing........price per set of	24	,,
12-10-3	Washer, thin, chainwheel bearing	1	,,
12-10-4	Washer, thick, chainwheel bearing	1	,,
G-37-3	Centre, for five plate clutch	1	,,
12-7-7	Washer, plain, for centre retaining nut	1	,,
12-7-5	Washer, lock, for centre retaining nut	1	,,
11-7-11	Nut, retaining clutch centre	1	,,
G-39-4	Plate, clutch, plain, steel	6	,,
G-40-12	Plate, clutch, friction, with inserts	5	,,
G-41-5	Inserts, fabric, for friction plate ...price per dozen	120	,,
G-38-2	Plate, clutch, spring pressure	1	,,
25-7-3	Cup, thrust, for spring pressure plate	1	,,
11-7-8	Nut, lock, for pressure plate thrust cup	1	,,
14-2-8	Stud, for clutch spring, 2 in. long (five plate clutch)	5	,,
36-6-1	Spring, for clutch	5	,,
G-42-2	Cup, for clutch spring	5	,,
11-2-2	Nut, adjusting, for clutch spring	5	,,

CLUTCH OPERATING PARTS

Part No.	Description	Qty.	Price
37-3-1	Rod, thrust, $10\frac{3}{16}$ in. long (five plate clutch)	1	20-30
17-3-2	Ball, $\frac{5}{16}$ in., steel, for clutch thrust rod	1	,,
G-32-2	Cam-plate, fixed, actuating clutch	1	,,
G-33-3	Cam-plate, moving, actuating clutch	1	,,
35-3-4	Dowel, thrust (passes through both cam-plates)	1	,,
12-2-4	Washer, plain, for cam-plate dowel	1	,,
36-2-3	Spring, for cam-plate dowel	1	,,
16-1-5	Pin, split, for cam-plate dowel	1	,,
17-3-2	Ball, $\frac{5}{16}$ in., steel, for cam-plates	3	,,

KICK-STARTER

Part No.	Description	Qty.	Price
G-21-2	Ratchet, driving, kick-starter	1	20-30
G-20-1	Pinion, ratchet, kick-starter	1	,,
19-7-3	Bush, kick-starter ratchet pinion	1	,,
36-8-2	Spring, kick-starter ratchet pinion	1	,,
11-7-10	Nut, retaining ratchet driver to mainshaft	1	,,
G-23-1	Spindle, for kick-starter quadrant	1	,,
G-22-1	Quadrant, for kick-starter	1	,,
018340	Kick-starter quadrant and spindle assembled	1	,,
36-8-1	Spring, return, for kick-starter foot lever	1	,,
G-43-2	Lever, foot, kick-starter, bare	1	,,
G-45-1	Pin, pedal, rigid, for kick-starter lever	1	,,
10-4-1	Bolt, clamping, kick-starter foot lever to spindle	1	,,
12-4-1	Washer, spring, for foot lever clamping bolt	1	,,
11-4-1	Nut, for foot lever clamping bolt	1	,,
12-7-22	Lock washer, for nut retaining ratchet driver	1	,,

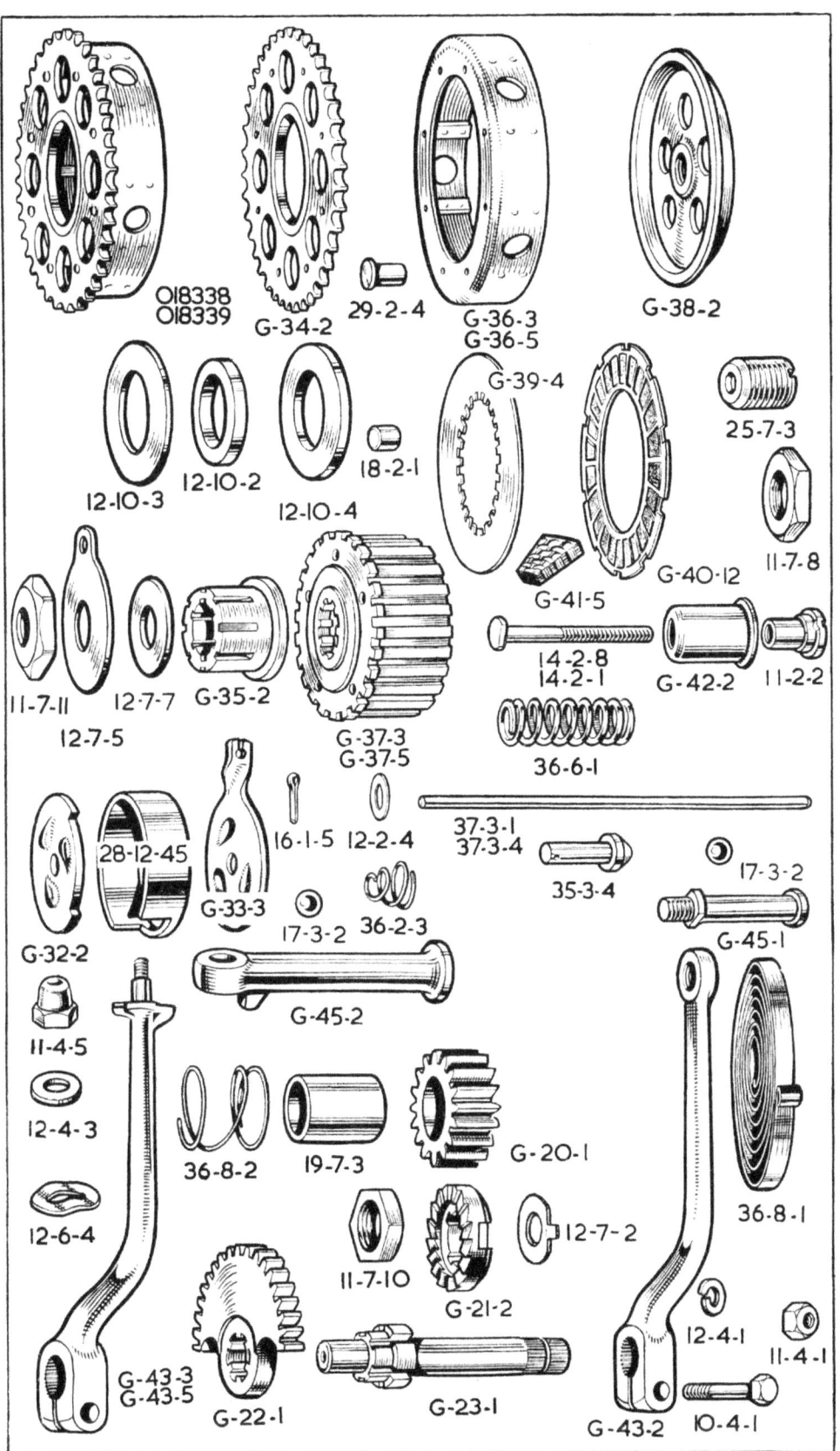

PART NUMBER	DESCRIPTION	QTY. OFF	USED ON	PRICE EACH £ s. d.

FRONT FRAME

022239	... Frame, front portion only, bare	1		20-30
000806	... Race, ball, for frame head lug	2		,,
000072	... Balls, $\frac{3}{16}$ in. diameter, for steering head, per set of	56		,,
000051	... Nipple, grease, for frame head lug	1		,,
021768	... Stud, for seat lug (below saddle), $4\frac{7}{16}$ in. by $\frac{1}{2}$ in. by 26	1		,,
000008	... Washer, plain, for seat lug stud	2		,,
000001	... Nut, for seat lug stud	2		,,
022390	... Cover, for frame	1		,,
022541	... Bead, for frame cover	2		,,
014357	... Screw, for frame cover	2		,,
000191	... Washer, spring, for cover screw	2		,,

REAR FRAME

022247	... Rail, frame, right side	1		20-30
022246	... Rail, frame, left side	1		,,
022249	... Loop, rear frame	1		,,
022248	... Stud, for rear loop at bottom, $10\frac{5}{8}$ in. by $\frac{7}{16}$ in. by 26. (Also passes through frame lug and both frame rails)	1		,,
000002	... Nut, for rear loop bottom stud	1		,,
000009	... Washer, plain, for rear loop bottom stud	2		,,
018617	... Tube, supporting rear mudguard, right side	1		,,
018616	... Tube, supporting rear of rear mudguard, left side	1		,,
000351	... Bolt, fixing mudguard support tube to mudguard, $1\frac{3}{16}$ in. by $\frac{1}{4}$ in. by 26 (chrome head)	2		,,
018648	... Bolt, fixing mudguard support tube to frame loop (also fixes top end of rear leg)	2		,,

If a carrier is fitted the above 018648 bolts are discarded and bolt 014521 used. See Carrier page 31.

022549	... Washer, chrome, for mudguard support tube bolt	2		20-30
000191	... Washer, spring, for mudguard support tube bolt	2		,,
000005	... Nut, for mudguard support tube bolt	2		,,

REAR FORK

021543	... Fork, rear	1		20-30
021595	... Adjuster, rear chain	1		,,
011373	... Nut, lock, for chain adjuster	1		,,
014746	... Sleeve, assembly (bushed)	2		,,
010116	... Tube	1		,,
010095	... Cap, for rear fork bearing, right side	1		,,
010096	... Cap, for rear fork bearing, left side	1		,,
010093	... Washer, felt, for rear fork bearing	2		,,
010098	... Gasket, for rear fork bearing caps	2		,,
010094	... Spoke, for rear fork bearing (central tie bolt)	1		,,
012472	... Nipple, for rear fork bearing spoke	1		,,
000485	... Screw, plug, for oil, in end cap, $\frac{1}{4}$ in. by $\frac{1}{4}$ in. by 26	1		,,
000203	... Washer, fibre, for oil plug screw	1		,,
022510	... Pin, cotter, for bearing tube	2		,,
022083	... Nut, for bearing cotter pin	2		,,
000011	... Washer, for bearing cotter pin	2		,,

BEFORE ORDERING SPARES
PLEASE NOTE THE INFORMATION GIVEN ON PAGES
TWO AND THREE

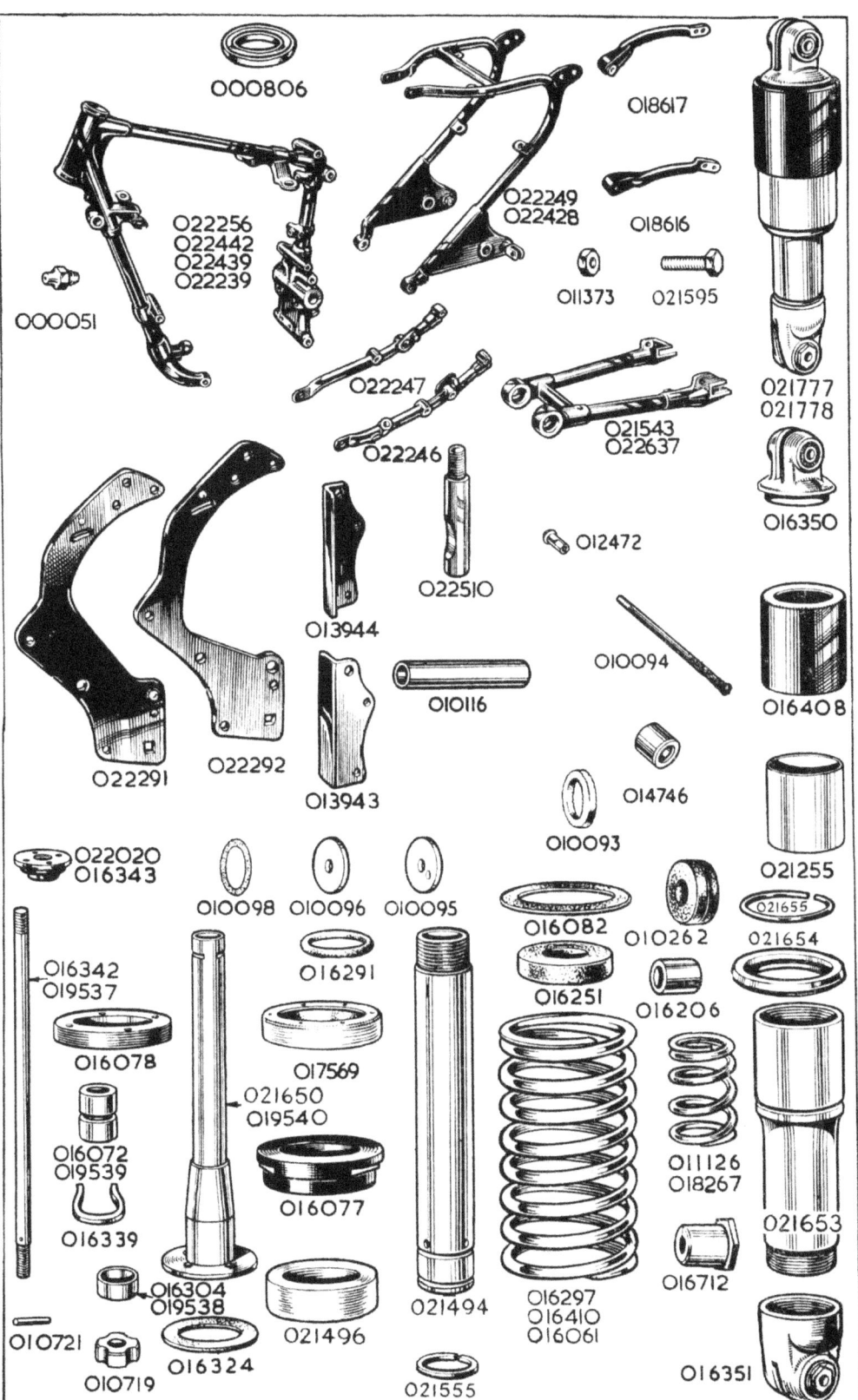

PART NUMBER	DESCRIPTION	QTY. OFF	USED ON	PRICE EACH £ s. d.

TELEDRAULIC REAR LEG

Part Number	Description	Qty. Off	Used On
021777	Leg, TELEDRAULIC, rear complete assembly (no fixing bolts, washers and nuts)	2	20-30
016350	Pivot, top, assembled (this assembly includes the next three items)	2	,,
016059	Pivot, top, bare	2	,,
010262	Bush, rubber, for top pivot	4	,,
016206	Spacer, for top pivot rubber bush	4	,,
016351	Pivot, bottom, assembled (this assembly includes the next five items)	2	,,
016060	Pivot, bottom, bare	2	,,
010262	Bush, rubber, for bottom pivot	4	,,
016206	Spacer, for bottom pivot rubber bush	2	,,
016712	Nut, with sleeve, for bottom pivot bolt	2	,,
016873	Washer, plain, for 016712 sleeve nut	2	,,
021494	Tube, inner (fits in top pivot recess)	2	,,
016291	Ring, sealing inner tube at top	2	,,
021496	Bush, lower end of inner tube	2	,,
021555	Circlip, retaining inner tube bush	2	,,
021653	Tube, outer (screws into bottom pivot)	2	,,
016324	Washer, sealing lower end of outer tube	4	,,
016077	Bush, for outer tube	2	,,
017569	Oil-seal, between inner and outer tubes	2	,,
016078	Collar, retaining oil-seal	2	,,
021650	Tube, for damper	2	,,
016072	Sleeve, plunger, for damper rod	2	,,
016339	Clip, locating plunger sleeve	2	,,
016342	Rod, for damper	2	,,
016343	Collar, for top end of damper rod	2	,,
000074	Nut, locking collar top-end of damper rod	2	,,
016304	Valve, for damper	2	,,
010721	Pin, stop, for damper valve	2	,,
010719	Seat, for damper valve	2	,,
000005	Nut, retaining damper seat to damper rod	2	,,
011126	Spring, buffer	2	,,
016297	Spring, main (solo)	2	,,
016061	Spring, main (sidecar)	2	,,
016082	Washer, leather, at both ends of main spring	4	,,
016408	Tube, outer, covering top end of main spring	2	,,
021255	Tube, outer, covering bottom end of main spring	2	,,
021654	Collar, retaining bottom outer cover tube	2	,,
021655	Circlip, retaining collar	2	,,
016251	Buffer, for TELEDRAULIC Leg	2	,,
018648	Bolt, fixing top pivot, $3\frac{1}{8}$ in. by $\frac{3}{8}$ in. by 26	2	,,
014521	Bolt, fixing top pivot (replaces 018648 when carrier is fitted)	2	,,
000010	Washer, plain, for top pivot bolt	4	,,
016712	Nut for top pivot bolt	2	,,
016359	Bolt, fixing bottom pivot, $2\frac{1}{32}$ in. by $\frac{3}{8}$ in. by 26	2	,,
000010	Washer, plain, for bottom pivot bolt	2	,,

FORK ASSEMBLIES

The following fork assemblies are complete and include ball races for the fork crown and top head lug (but not the two frame ball races).

Part Number	Description	Qty. Off	Used On
022689	Fork, assembly (TELEDRAULIC Front Fork, Solo)	1	20-30
022690	Fork, assembly (TELEDRAULIC Front Fork, Sidecar)	1	,,

For ease of servicing, the inner tube unit and damper unit are listed and supplied as separate assemblies. This enables a complete assembly to be exchanged in minimum time.

The units are listed below.

Part Number	Description	Qty. Off	Used On
022693	Front fork inner tube assembly, Solo	2	20-30
022694	Front fork inner tube assembly, Sidecar	2	,,

The above assemblies comprise :—

Inner tubes with rubber buffers, bushes and circlips, top bolts with washers and sealing rings, slider extensions with oil seals, fork springs and washers.

021974	Front fork damper assembly	2	20-30

The above assembly comprises :—

Rod and two nuts, damper tube with valve, seat and pin, sleeve and clip and bottom fixing bolt with washer.

PART NUMBER	DESCRIPTION	QTY. OFF	USED ON	PRICE EACH £ s. d.

FRONT FORK

Part Number	Description	Qty. Off	Used On
021927	... Crown, assembly, comprising crown, stem and circlip (these parts not sold separately)	1	20-30
000805	... Race, ball, for fork crown	1	,,
021740	... Screw, pinch, for fork crown	2	,,
021749	... Lug, for handlebar and steering head	1	,,
012620	... Race, ball, for handlebar lug	1	,,
000051	... Nipple, grease, for handlebar lug	1	,,
021741	... Nut, adjusting, for fork crown stem	1	,,
021642	... Nut, lock (domed), for fork crown stem	1	,,
021652	... Tube, fork, inner	2	,,
021911	... Buffer, rubber, for fork inner tube	6	,,
021495	... Bush, bottom, for fork inner tube	2	,,
021651	... Circlip, for fork inner tube bush	2	,,
022215	... Bolt, top, for fork inner tube	2	,,
022216	... Grommet for top bolt	2	,,
022213	... Adaptor for damper rod	2	,,
014355	... Ring, sealing, for fork inner tube top bolt	2	,,
022792	... Slider, fork, with cap, studs and nuts, left	2	,,
022793	... Slider, fork, with cap, studs, and nuts, right	1	,,
022799	... Cap, for fork slider	2	,,
010713	... Stud, securing fork slider cap, $1\frac{3}{16}$ in. by $\frac{5}{16}$ in. by 26 and 22...	4	,,
000011	... Washer, plain, for fork slider cap stud	4	,,
000004	... Nut, for fork slider cap stud	4	,,
021907	... Extension, for fork slider	2	,,
022700	... Bush, plastic, for fork inner tube	2	,,
022699	... Oil-seal, for fork inner tube (rubber)	2	,,
022369	... Spring, main, for front fork, solo	2	,,
021789	... Spring, main, for front fork, sidecar	2	,,
022079	... Spring, buffer, for front fork	2	,,
022021	... Collar, for buffer spring	2	,,
021785	... Washer, leather, fork spring seating, top	2	,,
021786	... Washer, leather, fork spring seating, bottom	2	,,
021732	... Tube, fork cover, top, right, with lamp lug	1	,,
021731	... Tube, fork cover, top, left, with lamp lug	1	,,
021742	... Spigot, for top of fork top cover tubes	2	,,
021910	... Seat (rubber), for cover tube	2	,,
021912	... Housing, for fork top cover tube	2	,,
021735	... Tube fork cover, bottom	2	,,
000485	... Screw, plug, oil drain, for fork slider, $\frac{1}{4}$ in. by $\frac{1}{4}$ in. by 26	2	,,
000203	... Washer, fibre, for fork slider screw oil plug	2	,,
021662	... Tube, fork damper	2	,,
010697	... Bolt, fixing fork damper to slider $\frac{7}{16}$ in. by $\frac{5}{16}$ in. by 26	2	,,
010706	... Washer, fibre, for damper tube bolt	2	,,
017357	... Rod, for fork damper	2	,,
000004	... Nut, lock, top end of damper rod	2	,,
016072	... Sleeve, plunger, for fork damper rod	2	,,
016339	... Clip, retaining damper rod sleeve	2	,,
016304	... Valve, for fork damper	2	,,
010721	... Pin, stop, for fork damper valve	2	,,
010719	... Seat, for fork damper valve	2	,,
000005	... Nut, lock, for fork damper valve seat	2	,,
018691	... Steering locking bar (own padlock to be used)	1	,,

---

ALWAYS INCLUDE ALL THE LETTERS WHEN QUOTING THE ENGINE NUMBER

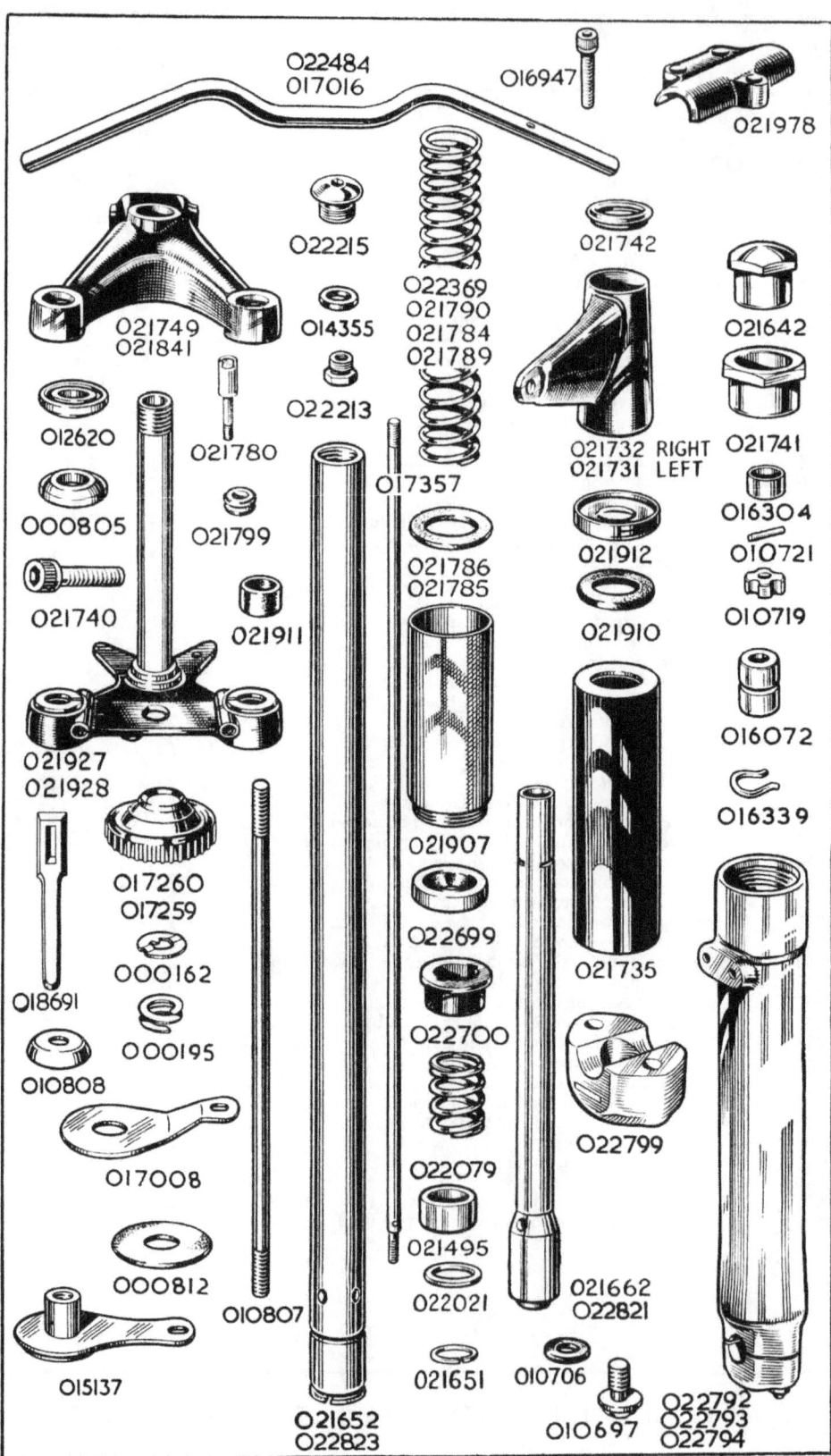

PART NUMBER	DESCRIPTION	QTY. OFF	USED ON	PRICE EACH £ s. d.

STEERING DAMPER. (This is an optional extra)

022059	... Damper, steering, complete set of parts....................	1		20-30
017260	... Knob, control, for steering damper..........................	1		,,
000162	... Washer, ratchet, for steering damper knob	1		,,
000195	... Washer, spring, for steering damper knob.................	1		,,
010808	... Cap, for top of steering stem..................................	1		,,
010807	... Drawbolt, for steering damper.................................	1		,,
015137	... Sleeve, assembly, lower end of drawbolt	1		,,
000073	... Nut, locking sleeve to drawbolt	1		,,
014577	... Bolt, fixing sleeve assembly, $\frac{7}{16}$ in. by $\frac{1}{4}$ in. by 26.............	1		,,
000191	... Washer, spring, for bolt 014577	1		,,
000012	... Washer, plain, for bolt 014577	1		,,
017008	... Plate, anchor, top position	1		,,
014577	... Bolt, fixing top anchor plate, $\frac{7}{16}$ in. by $\frac{1}{4}$ in. by 26	1		,,
000191	... Washer, spring, for bolt 014577	1		,,
000812	... Washer, friction, for steering damper........................	2		,,
021811	... Nut, lock, for fork crown stem (this replaces the domed lock-nut 021642 when a steering damper is fitted)	1		,,

HANDLEBAR

022484	... Handlebar, bare	1		20-30
021978	... Clip (half only), for handlebar lug	1		,,
016947	... Screw, for handlebar clip, $\frac{7}{8}$ in. by $\frac{1}{4}$ in. by 26 (socket head) ...	3		,,

PROP STAND

014719	... Stand, prop, bare...	1		20-30
014713	... Bolt, hinge, for prop stand, $2\frac{1}{16}$ in. by $\frac{7}{16}$ in. by 26	1		,,
014139	... Nut, for prop stand hinge bolt.................................	1		,,
000049	... Pin, split, for prop stand hinge bolt..........................	1		,,
021261	... Spring, return, for prop stand	1		,,

CENTRE STAND

016438	... Stand, centre, bare	1		20-30
014626	... Bush, for centre stand, ·7 in. long	2		,,
014629	... Stud, hinge, for centre stand, $8\frac{15}{16}$ in. by $\frac{7}{16}$ in. by 26	1		,,
014630	... Spacer, central, for centre stand hinge stud, 4·2 in. long	1		,,
010912	... Washer, spigot, for centre stand hinge stud	2		,,
000002	... Nut, for centre stand hinge stud	2		,,
014627	... Spring, return, for centre stand	1		,,
016399	... Spring, clip, for centre stand...................................	1		,,
000250	... Stud, for centre stand clip......................................	2		,,
000080	... Nut, for centre stand stop spring stud	2		,,
000039	... Washer, plain, for centre stand stop spring fixing nuts	2		,,

FRONT MUDGUARD

022372	... Mudguard, front, bare	1		20-30
010795	... Bolt, fixing mudguard bridge to right fork slider, $\frac{1}{2}$ in. by $\frac{5}{16}$ in. by 22	2		,,
000192	... Washer, spring, for bridge right fixing bolt	2		,,
010624	... Stud, fixing mudguard bridge to left fork slider, also retains brake anchor stay and bracket for brake cable adjuster, $1\frac{1}{32}$ in. by $\frac{5}{16}$ in. by 26 and 22	2		,,
014117	... Washer, lock, for bridge left fixing stud...................	2		,,
000004	... Nut, for bridge left fixing stud.................................	2		,,
022373	... Stay, front mudguard	1		,,
000070	... Bolt, fixing stay to mudguard	2		,,
000191	... Washer, spring stay to mudguard bolt	2		,,
000005	... Nut, stay to mudguard bolt	2		,,

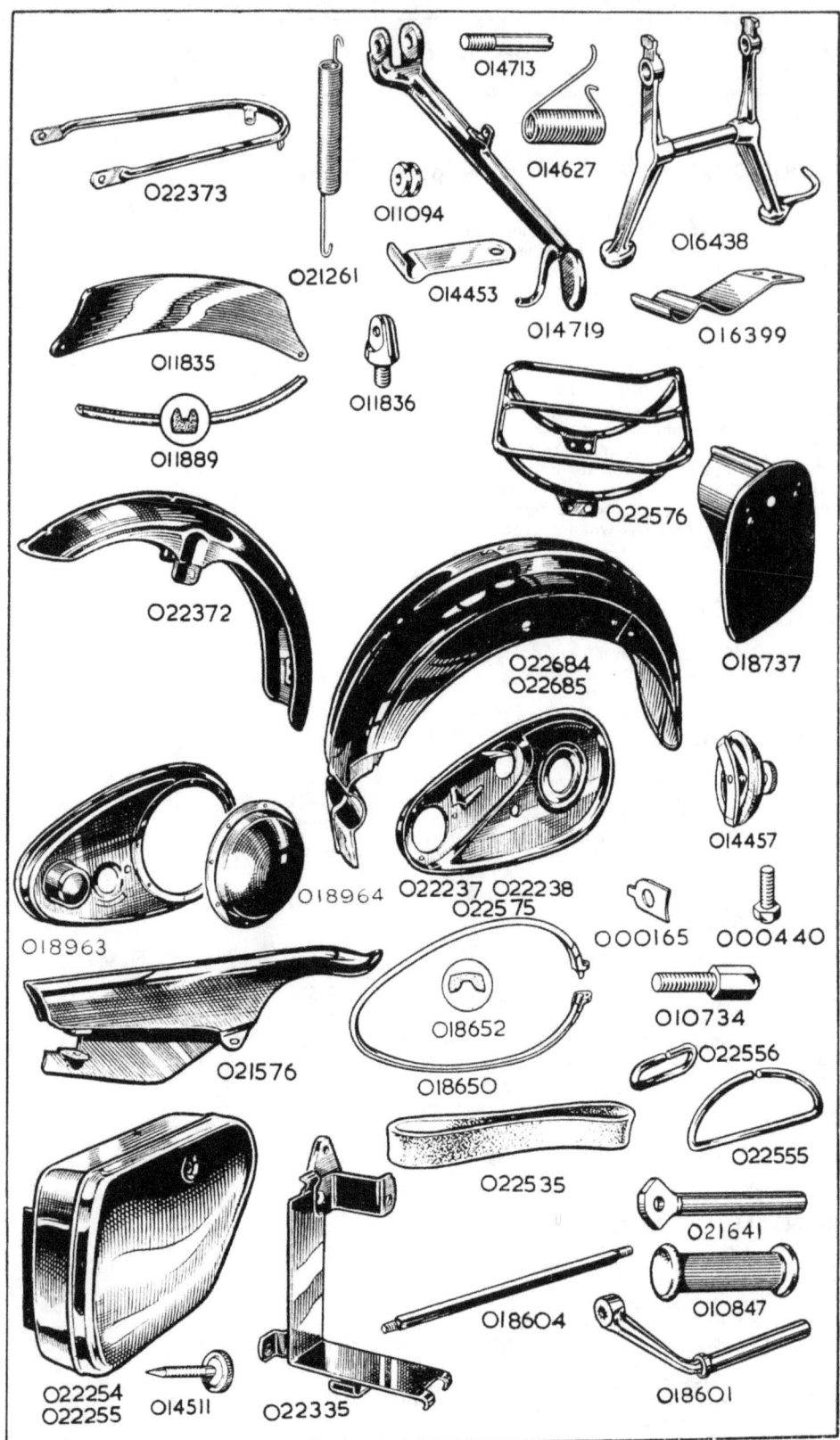

PART NUMBER	DESCRIPTION	QTY. OFF	USED ON	PRICE EACH £ s. d.

REAR MUDGUARD

022685	Rear mudguard (both portions with joint bolts)	1	20-30	
022389	Rear mudguard, forward portion only	1	,,	
021710	Rear mudguard, rear portion only	1	,,	
021098	Bolt, for mudguard joint	3	,,	
021099	Washer, for mudguard joint bolt	3	,,	
022250	Bracket, for bottom of rear mudguard	2	,,	
000342	Bolt, fixing bracket to rear mudguard, $1\frac{1}{16}$ in. by $\frac{1}{4}$ in. by 26	2	,,	
000012	Washer, plain, for bracket fixing bolt	4	,,	
000005	Nut, for bracket fixing bolt	2	,,	
000275	Stud, fixing rear mudguard brackets to frame, $3\frac{9}{16}$ in. by $\frac{5}{16}$ in. by 26	1	,,	
000011	Washer, plain, for bracket fixing stud	2	,,	
000004	Nut, for bracket fixing stud	2	,,	
000346	Bolt, fixing rear mudguard to frame loop bridge, $1\frac{7}{16}$ in. by $\frac{1}{4}$ in. by 26	1	,,	
000191	Washer, spring, for bridge fixing bolt	1	,,	
000005	Nut, for bridge fixing bolt	1	,,	
000012	Washer, plain, for bridge fixing bolt	1	,,	

REAR CARRIER

022576	Carrier, rear, bare	1	20-30	
014521	Front fixing bolt (replaces 018648 when carrier is fitted)	2	,,	
022738	Bolt, fixing carrier	2	,,	
022737	Washer, for carrier fixing bolt	2	,,	

FRONT NUMBER PLATE

011835	Plate, number, front	1	20-30	
011836	Stud, fixing front number plate	2	,,	
000012	Washer, plain, front number plate stud	2	,,	
000005	Nut, front number plate stud	2	,,	
000861	Screw, fixing front number plate to stud, $\frac{5}{16}$ in. by 2 B.A.	2	,,	
011889	Fillet, rubber, front number plate	1	,,	

REAR NUMBER PLATE

018737	Plate, number, rear, 8 in. wide	1	20-30	
000363	Bolt, fixing rear number plate, $\frac{3}{4}$ in. by $\frac{5}{16}$ in. by 26	2	,,	
000192	Washer, spring, rear number plate bolt	2	,,	

FRONT CHAINCASE

022683	Chaincase, complete (comprises both halves, metal and rubber bands, clamping screw and inspection caps—NO FIXING BOLTS, SPACERS, WASHERS AND NUTS ARE INCLUDED)	1	20-30	
022238	Chaincase, back half, bare	1	,,	
018963	Chaincase, front half, bare	1	,,	
018650	Band, metal, for chaincase	1	,,	
022750	Screw, clamping, chaincase metal band, 1 in. by 2 B.A.	1	,,	
018652	Band, rubber, for chaincase	1	,,	
014457	Cap, assembly, chaincase inspection (components not sold as separate spares)	1	,,	
000580	Washer, cork, chaincase inspection cap	1	,,	
018964	Domed clutch cover	1	,,	
018966	Washer, cork, for clutch dome	1	,,	
000450	Screw, $\frac{3}{8}$ in. by 2 B.A., round head, for clutch dome	8	,,	
000440	Bolt, fixing chaincase to engine, $\frac{1}{2}$ in. by 0 B.A.	3	,,	
000165	Washer, lock, chaincase engine bolt	3	,,	

PART NUMBER	DESCRIPTION	QTY. OFF	USED ON	PRICE EACH £ s. d.

REAR CHAINGUARD

021576	... Chainguard, rear, bare	1	20-30	
000350	... Bolt, fixing chainguard in front, $2\frac{1}{16}$ in. by $\frac{1}{4}$ in. by 26	1	,,	
000012	... Washer, plain, chainguard, front fixing bolt	2	,,	
000005	... Nut, for chainguard front fixing bolt	1	,,	
000349	... Bolt, fixing rear of chainguard, $1\frac{7}{8}$ in. by $\frac{1}{4}$ in. by 26	1	,,	
021579	... Washer, spring, for chainguard rear fixing bolt	1	,,	
021578	... Spacer, $1\frac{5}{16}$ in. long (located inside chainguard), on bolt 000349	1	,,	

BATTERY CARRIER

022335	... Carrier, battery assembled (less strap and loops)	1	20-30	
022535	... Carrier, battery strap	1	,,	
022555	... Loop, battery carrier strap, large	1	,,	
022556	... Loop, battery carrier strap, small	1	,,	
000371	... Bolt, fixing battery carrier to frame	2	,,	
000004	... Nut, for battery carrier fixing bolt	2	,,	
000011	... Washer, for battery carrier fixing bolt	4	,,	
000070	... Bolt, earthing cable	1	,,	
000012	... Washer, earthing cable bolt	1	,,	
022721	... Rubber, for battery carrier	1	,,	

TOOL BOXES

022255	... Box, tool, bare (with lid but no other fittings)	1	20-30	
014511	... Screw, knurled, for tool box lid	2	,,	
000189	... Washer, spring, for tool box lid screw	2	,,	
000005	... Nut, for tool box lid screw	4	,,	
000070	... Bolt, fixing tool box, $\frac{9}{16}$ in. by $\frac{1}{4}$ in. by 26	2	,,	
000012	... Washer, plain, for tool box fixing bolt	4	,,	
000005	... Nut, for tool box fixing bolts	4	,,	
000070	... Bolt, tool box, battery carrier, $\frac{9}{16}$ in. by $\frac{1}{4}$ in. by 26	2	,,	
000005	... Nut, tool box, battery carrier bolt	2	,,	
000012	... Washer, tool box, battery carrier bolt	2	,,	

FOOTRESTS

018601	... Arm, for footrest	2	20-30	
010847	... Pad, rubber, for footrest arm	2	,,	
018604	... Rod, for footrests, overall length $10\frac{1}{2}$ in.	1	,,	
010924	... Spacer, $3\frac{1}{2}$ in. long, for footrest rod, between engine rear plates	1	,,	
013837	... Spacer, 1 in. long, for footrest rod, outside right plate	1	,,	
010911	... Spacer, $\frac{13}{16}$ in. long, for footrest rod, outside left plate	1	,,	
000009	... Washer, for footrest rod	2	,,	
000002	... Nut, for footrest rod	2	,,	

PILLION FOOTRESTS

021984	... Pair of pillion footrests, complete (includes all the following items)	1	20-30	
021641	... Spindle, bare for pillion footrest	2	,,	
011599	... Bolt, hinge, for pillion footrest spindle, $1\frac{3}{16}$ in. by $\frac{3}{8}$ in. by 26	2	,,	
000073	... Nut, for pillion footrest hinge bolt	2	,,	
010847	... Pad, rubber, for pillion footrest spindle	2	,,	

PART NUMBER	DESCRIPTION	QTY. OFF	USED ON	PRICE EACH £ s. d.

TWIN SEAT

022375	Seat, Twin	1		20-30
021208	Screw, fixing seat at rear to loop, $\frac{5}{16}$ in. by $\frac{1}{4}$ in.	2		,,
000012	Washer, plain, for seat fixing screw	2		,,
018160	Nut, for seat fixing screw	2		,,
021219	Rubber Grommet, for base	2		,,

TRANSFERS

009203	Transfer, for side of oil tank (oil level indicator)	1		20-30
009186	Transfer, for front chaincase (oil level indicator)	1		,,
009187	Transfer, for front chaincase (patent)	1		,,
009202	Transfer, for tool box and oil tank cover	2		,,
009194	Transfer, for rear mudguard (" A·J·S ")	1		,,
009199	Transfer, for front forks (patent)	1		,,
009195	Transfer, for petrol tank (reserve)	1		,,
009204	Transfer, for side of oil tank (" Fill to Here ")	1		,,
009200	Transfer, for forks (" Made in England ")	1		,,
009197	Transfer, for rear fork hinge (patent)	1		,,
009206	Transfer for top of petrol tank	1		30
022808	Complete set of transfers	1		20
022809	Complete set of transfers	1		30

DUMMY GRIP

16-069	Grip, rubber, dummy	1		20-30

TWIST GRIP

16-117	Twist grip, complete assembly	1		20-30
16-070	Grip, rubber, for twist grip	1		,,
16-091	Rotor, and sleeve, for twist grip (does not include rubber grip)	1		,,
16-060	Body, twist grip, top (plain clip)	1		,,
16-061	Body, twist grip, bottom (for friction spring)	1		,,
11-013	Screw, long, clamping twist grip body	1		,,
11-014	Screw, short, clamping twist grip body	1		,,
16-008	Spring, friction, for twist grip	1		,,
16-009	Screw, for twist grip friction spring	1		,,
16-010	Nut, for twist grip friction spring screw	1		,,
16-011	Stop, for twist grip (throttle) cable	1		,,

CLUTCH AND IGNITION CONTROL LEVERS

18-694	Lever, assembly, clutch and ignition	1		20-30
18-528	Lever only, clutch	1		,,
12-557	Lever only, ignition	1		,,
18-241	Bracket, for clutch lever	1		,,
12-008	Bracket, for ignition lever	1		,,
11-013	Screw, long, clamping clutch and ignition brackets	1		,,
11-014	Screw, short, clamping clutch and ignition brackets	1		,,
18-087	Pin, fulcrum, for clutch lever	1		,,
18-053	Nut, clutch, lever fulcrum pin	1		,,
12-029	Bolt, central, for ignition lever	1		,,
12-031	Cap, for ignition lever	1		,,
12-033	Washer, spring, for ignition lever	1		,,

WHEN ORDERING SPARES, IF IN DOUBT REGARDING THE NAMES AND PART NUMBERS OF THE PARTS YOU REQUIRE, PLEASE SEND THE OLD PARTS TO SERVE AS PATTERNS.

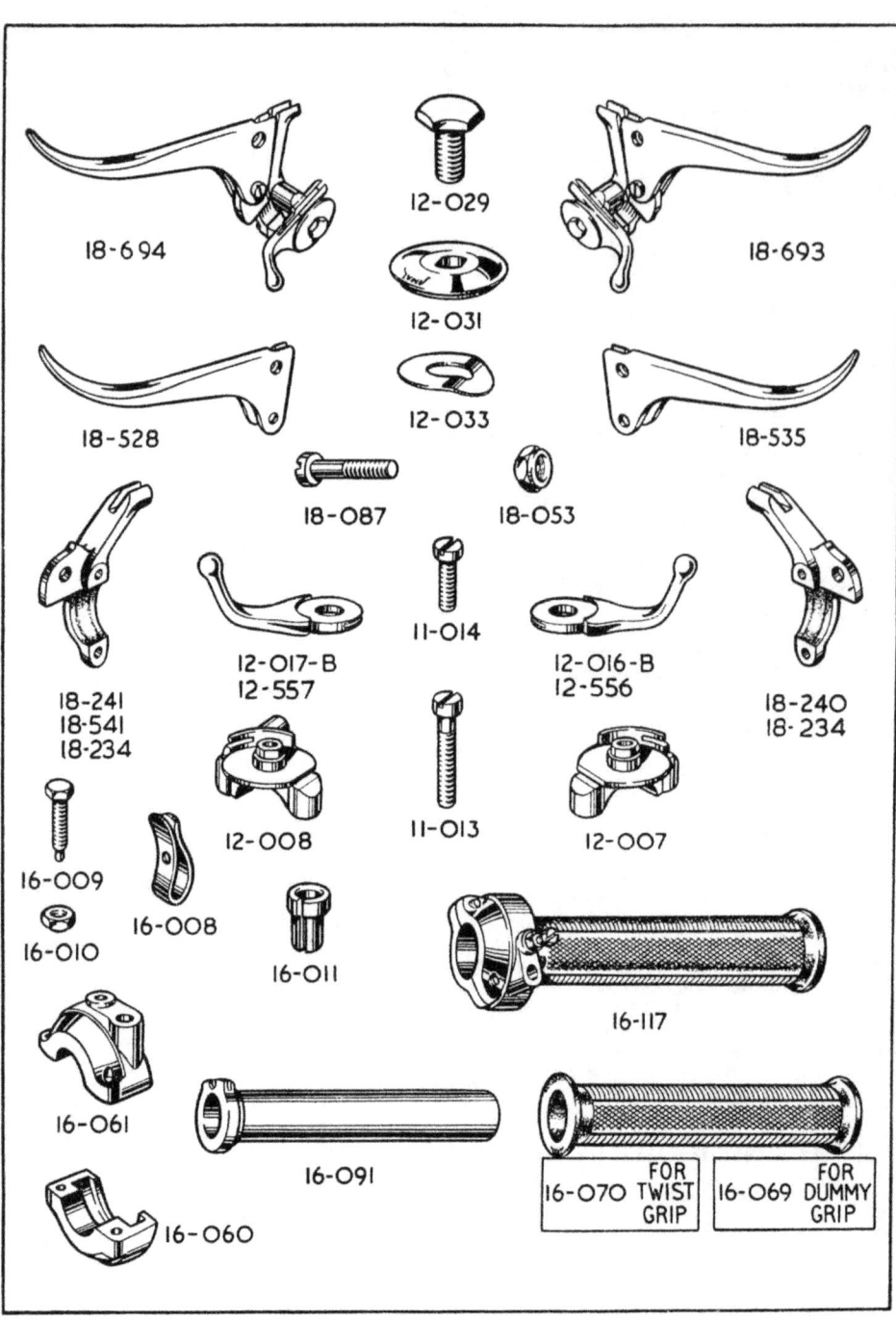

PART NUMBER	DESCRIPTION	QTY. OFF	USED ON	PRICE EACH £ s. d.

BRAKE AND AIR CONTROL LEVERS

18-693	Lever, assembly, brake and air	1	20-30	
18-535	Lever, only, brake	1	,,	
12-556	Lever, only, air	1	,,	
18-240	Bracket, for brake lever	1	,,	
12-007	Bracket, for air lever	1	,,	
11-013	Screw, long, clamping brake and air brackets	1	,,	
11-014	Screw, short, clamping brake and air brackets	1	,,	
18-087	Pin, fulcrum, for brake lever	1	,,	
18-053	Nut, brake lever fulcrum pin	1	,,	
12-029	Bolt, central, for air lever	1	,,	
12-031	Cap, for air lever	1	,,	
12-033	Washer, spring, for air lever	1	,,	

FRONT BRAKE CABLE

022874	Cable, complete, assembled, front brake	1	20-30	
000530-36$\frac{1}{2}$	Wire, inner, front brake, 36$\frac{1}{2}$ in. finished length	1	,,	
18-689	Nipple, brake end, for brake inner wire	1	,,	
18-689	Nipple, handlebar end, for brake inner wire	1	,,	
18-690	Nipple, roller adaptor, handlebar end for inner wire	1	,,	
000529-26	Casing, outer, front brake, 26 in. long	1	,,	
000531	Ferrule, front brake outer casing	2	,,	
011348	Adjuster, front brake cable	1	,,	
017217	Nut, lock, front brake cable adjuster	1	,,	
017049	End, yoke, front brake cable	1	,,	
000736	Pin, for yoke end, front brake cable	1	,,	
000014	Pin, split, for front brake cable yoke and pin	1	,,	
012478	Sleeve, rubber, for front brake cable inner wire	1	,,	

CLUTCH CABLE

021405	Cable, complete, assembled, clutch, with oil nipple	1	20-30	
000530-43$\frac{1}{2}$	Wire, inner, clutch, 43$\frac{1}{2}$ in. finished length	1	,,	
017241	Nipple, gearbox end, clutch inner wire	1	,,	
18-689	Nipple, handlebar end, clutch inner wire	1	,,	
18-690	Nipple, roller adaptor, handlebar end for inner wire	1	,,	
021406	Casing, outer, clutch, with adaptor for oil nipple	1	,,	
000531	Ferrule, clutch outer casing	2	,,	
014225	Adjuster, clutch cable	1	,,	
011373	Nut, lock, clutch cable adjuster	1	,,	
000051	Oil nipple only	1	,,	
018986	Adaptor for oil nipple	1	,,	

THROTTLE CONTROL CABLE

022019	Cable, complete, assembled, throttle with oil nipple	1	20-30	
000535-40$\frac{1}{16}$	Wire, inner, throttle, 40$\frac{1}{16}$ in. finished length	1	,,	
017242	Nipple, carburetter end, throttle inner wire	1	,,	
017266	Nipple, handlebar end, throttle inner wire	1	,,	
021408	Casing, outer, throttle, with adaptor for oil nipple	1	,,	
000528	Ferrule, throttle outer casing	2	,,	
000051	Oil nipple only	1	,,	
018987	Adaptor for oil nipple	1	,,	

AIR CONTROL CABLE

022022	Cable, complete, assembled, air	1	20-30	
000527-37$\frac{7}{8}$	Wire, inner, air, 37$\frac{7}{8}$ in. finished length	1	,,	
017242	Nipple, carburetter end, air inner wire	1	,,	
017266	Nipple, handlebar end, air inner wire	1	,,	
000526-32$\frac{13}{16}$	Casing, outer, air, 32$\frac{13}{16}$ in. finished length	1	,,	
000528	Ferrule, air, outer casing	2	,,	

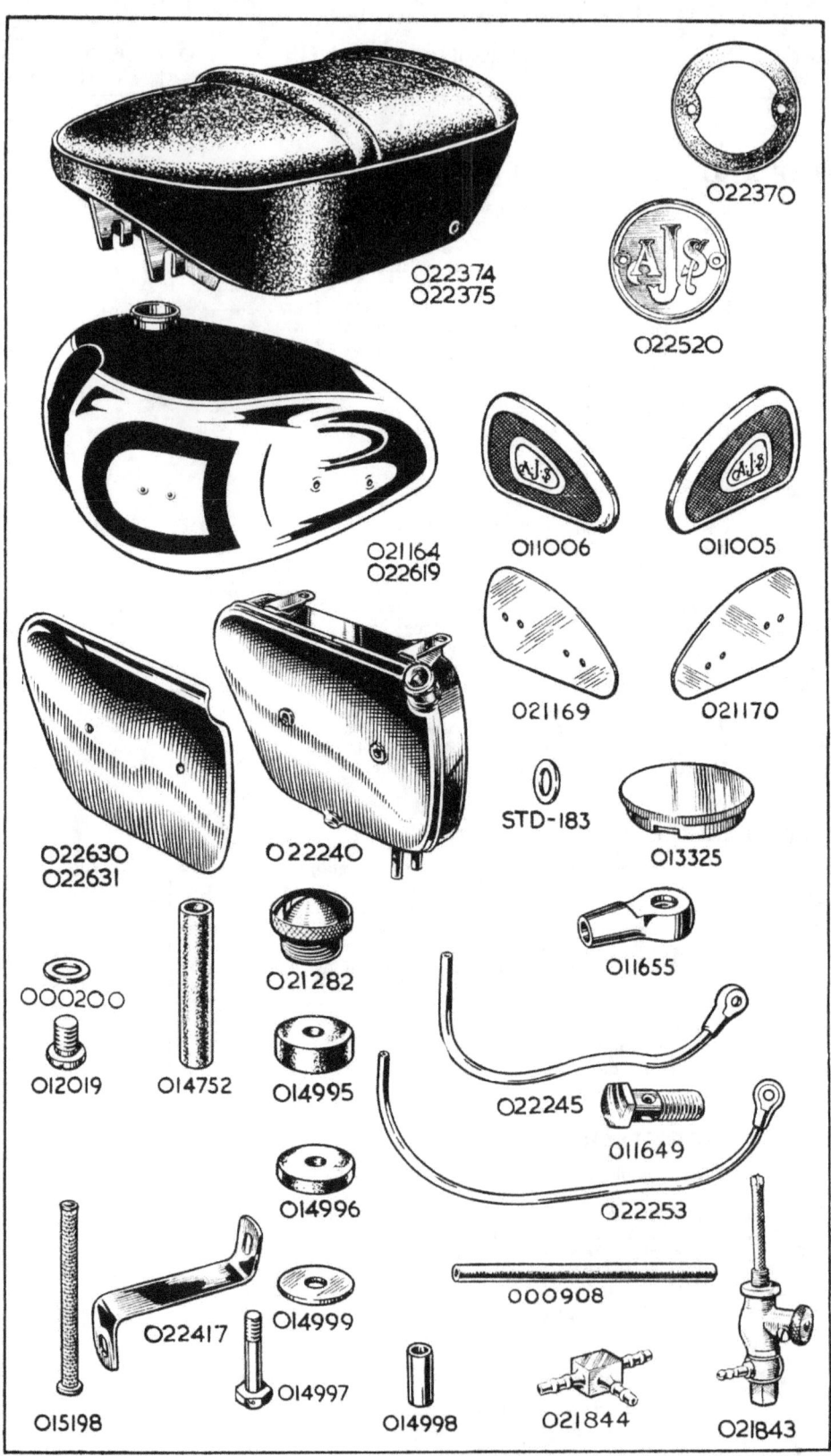

PART NUMBER	DESCRIPTION	QTY. OFF	USED ON	PRICE EACH £ s. d.

IGNITION CONTROL CABLE

Part Number	Description	Qty. Off	Used On
018749	Cable, complete, assembled ignition	1	20-30
000526-37½	Wire, inner, ignition, finished length 37½ in.	1	,,
017379	Nipple, magneto end, ignition inner wire	1	,,
017266	Nipple, handlebar end, ignition inner wire	1	,,
000526-34⅞	Casing, outer, ignition, 34⅞ in. long	1	,,
000528	Ferrule, ignition outer casing	2	,,
458731	Cap, rubber, cable entry to magneto	1	,,
458727	Cap, metal, cable entry to magneto	1	,,
163343	Washer, fibre, for cable entry metal cap	1	,,
454969	Plunger, for ignition cable	1	,,
458732	Spring, return, for ignition cable	1	,,

PETROL TANK

Part Number	Description	Qty. Off	Used On
021164	Tank, petrol, bare, plated, black panels	1	20
022619	Tank, petrol, bare, plated, black panels	1	30
022362	Motif, for tank	2	20-30
022370	Seating, rubber, for tank motif	2	,,
000153	Screw, fixing tank motif	4	,,

PETROL TANK FITTINGS

Part Number	Description	Qty. Off	Used On
013325	Cap, filler, for petrol tank	1	20-30
021843	Tap, for petrol feed, with filter and banjo	2	,,
000200	Washer, fibre, for petrol feed tap	2	,,
022110	Banjo, for petrol feed pipe	2	,,
022111	Nut, dome, retaining banjo	2	,,
022056	Washer, fibre for banjo	4	,,
022112	Cork, for petrol feed tap	2	,,
011006	Grip, knee, left hand side	1	,,
011005	Grip, knee, right hand side	1	,,
021169	Plate, for left hand knee grip	1	,,
021170	Plate, for right hand knee grip	1	,,
000348	Bolt, fixing knee grip plate	4	,,

PETROL TANK FIXING BOLTS

Part Number	Description	Qty. Off	Used On
014997	Bolt, fixing tank, all positions, 1¼ in. by $\frac{5}{16}$ in. by 26	4	20-30
014998	Sleeve, 1¾₁₆ in. long, for tank fixing bolts	4	,,
014995	Pad, rubber, thick (⅝ in.) for tank fixing bolts in front right and both rear positions	4	,,
014996	Pad, rubber, thin ($\frac{3}{16}$ in.), for all tank fixing bolts (three used on front left bolt)	4	,,
014999	Washer, metal, 1¼ in. diameter, plain, for tank fixing bolts	4	,,
017051	Wire, copper, 5 ft. by 20 S.W.G.	1	,,

OIL TANK

Part Number	Description	Qty. Off	Used On
022240	Tank, oil, bare	1	20-30
000070	Bolt, fixing oil tank	3	,,
000005	Nut, for tank fixing bolt	3	,,
000012	Washer, for tank fixing bolt	3	,,
021282	Cap, filler, oil tank	1	,,
021329	Washer, for filler cap	1	,,
012019	Plug, drain, for oil tank	1	,,
000200	Washer, fibre, oil tank drain plug	1	,,
022417	Bracket, fixing tank to seat tube	1	,,
000070	Bolt, seat, tube fixing bracket	1	,,
000012	Washer, bracket fixing bolt	1	,,
022631	Cover, for oil tank	1	,,
022632	Screw, for oil tank cover	2	,,
000203	Washer, fibre, for cover screw	2	,,
000012	Washer, plain, for cover screw	2	,,

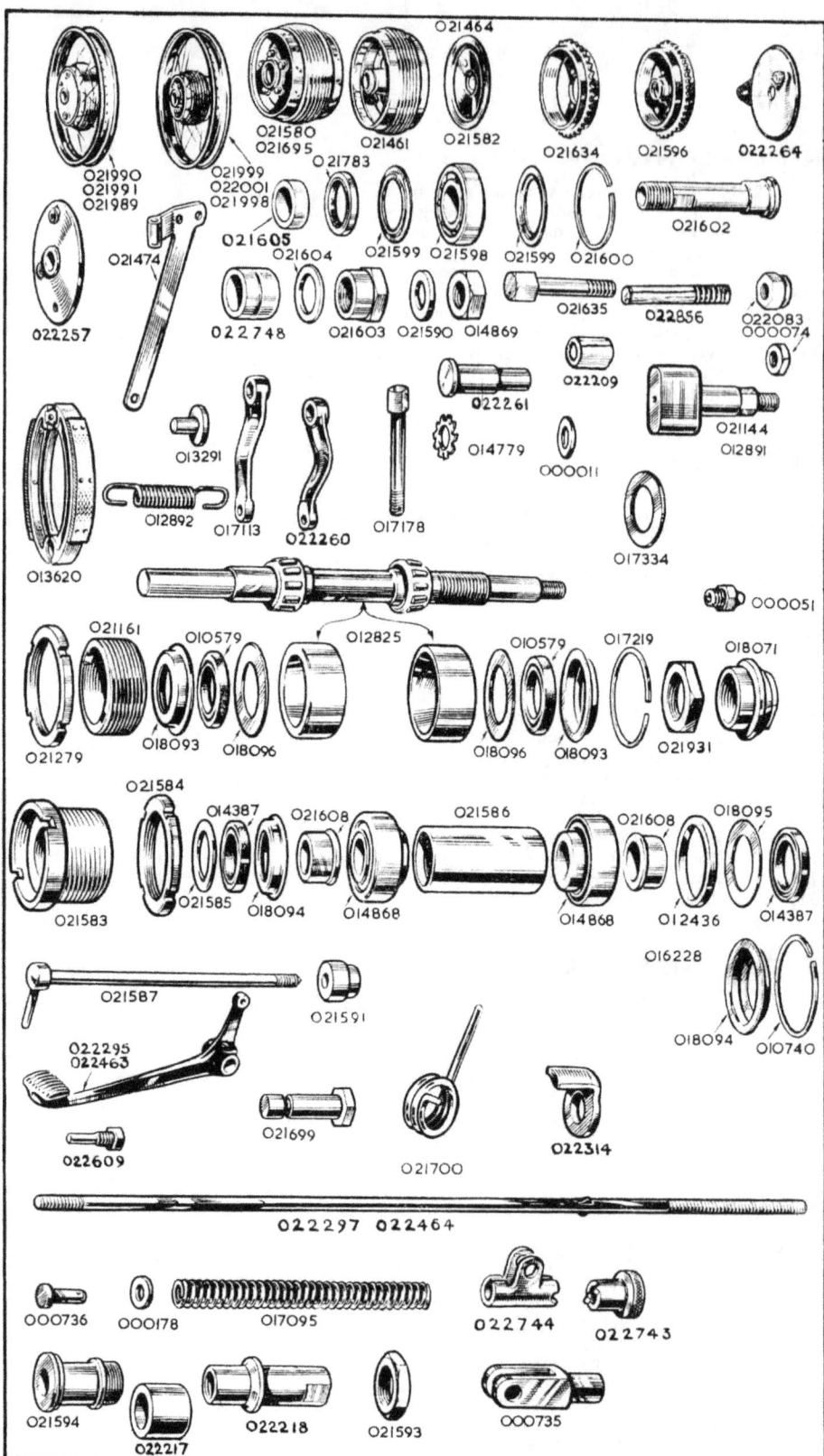

PART NUMBER	DESCRIPTION	QTY. OFF	USED ON	PRICE EACH £ s. d.

PETROL PIPE

000908-2½	Flexible tubing, short, 2½ in.	1	20-30	
000908-5	Flexible tubing, long, 5 in.	2	,,	
021844	Petrol pipe " T " piece	1	,,	

OIL PIPES

022253	Pipe, oil feed assembly	1	20-30	
022245	Pipe, oil return	1	,,	
011655	Union, banjo, feed and return oil pipes	2	,,	
011649	Pin, banjo, retaining feed and return oil pipes to engine	2	,,	
000183	Washer, fibre, for oil pipe banjo	4	,,	
014752	Connection, rubber, for feed and return oil pipes	2	,,	
015198	Filter, metal gauze, for oil feed pipe	1	,,	
022570	Pipe, vent, metal	1	,,	
000950-7¾	Hose, from oil tank to metal vent pipe	1	,,	

FRONT WHEEL

The complete wheel listed below comprises :—Rim, spokes, nipples, hub, grease nipple, all bearings, and all brake parts including cover plate and expander lever, but does not include the tyre.

022687	Wheel, front, with all fittings, chrome rim, black centre	1	20-30	

The bare wheel listed below comprises :—Rim, spokes, nipples and hub.

021990	Wheel, front bare, chrome rim, black centre	1	,,	
012220	Rim, front, chrome, black centre (A.M.C. 23)	1	,,	
021152	Spoke, front, 5⅞ in. by 11 G	40	,,	
021154	Nipple, front, ·250 in. by 11 G	40	,,	
021461	Hub, front wheel, shell only with brake drum	1	,,	
000051	Nipple, grease, for front wheel hub	1	,,	
011090	Tape, for 19 in. by 2½ in. rim	1	,,	
021464	Hub disc, covering right side	1	,,	

FRONT WHEEL BEARINGS

012825	Spindle, with roller bearings, for front wheel	1	20-30	
010579	Oil-seal, for front hub bearings	2	,,	
017219	Ring, spring, locating front hub bearings	1	,,	
018093	Cup, for front hub bearing oil-seal	2	,,	
018096	Ring, retaining front hub bearing oil-seals	2	,,	
021279	Nut, lock, for front hub bearing adjusting ring	1	,,	
021161	Ring, adjusting, for front hub bearing	1	,,	
021931	Nut, locating front brake cover plate	1	,,	
018071	Nut, outside, securing front brake cover plate	1	,,	
000001	Nut, front wheel spindle, left side	1	,,	
000008	Washer, plain, front wheel spindle, left side	1	,,	

REAR WHEEL

The complete wheel listed below comprises :—

Rim, spokes, nipples, hub, grease nipple and all bearings assembled, but does NOT include the centre solid spindle, washers, spacers, nuts, brake parts, sprocket and brake drum, speedometer drive and tyre.

021995	Wheel, rear, with all fittings, chrome rim, black centre	1	20-30	

The bare wheel listed below comprises :—
Rim, spokes, nipples and hub.

021999	Wheel, rear, bare, chrome, black centre	1	,,	
021814	Rim, rear, chrome, black centre (A.M.C. 24)	1	,,	
021691	Spoke, rear, left or right, 6 15/16 in. by 10 G	40	,,	
021693	Nipple, rear, left or right, ·250 in. by 10 G	40	,,	
021580	Hub, rear wheel, shell only	1	,,	
021582	Disc for right hand side of hub	1	,,	
000051	Nipple, grease, for rear wheel hub	1	,,	
011090	Tape, for 19 in. rear rim	1	,,	

PART NUMBER	DESCRIPTION	QTY. OFF	USED ON	PRICE EACH £ s. d.

REAR WHEEL BEARINGS

014868	... Bearings, roller, for rear hub (only sold as a complete bearing)	2	20-30	
014387	... Oil-seal, for rear hub bearings	2	,,	
010740	... Ring, spring, locating rear hub bearings	1	,,	
018094	... Cup, for rear hub bearing oil-seal	2	,,	
021585	... Ring, retaining, rear hub bearing oil-seals (small)	1	,,	
018095	... Ring, retaining, rear hub bearing oil-seals (large)	2	,,	
012436	... Collar, spacing, between bearing and rear hub bearing oil-seal	1	,,	
021586	... Spacer, $2\frac{9}{16}$ in. long between the two bearings of rear hub	1	,,	
021583	... Ring, adjusting, for rear hub bearing	1	,,	
021584	... Nut, lock, for rear hub bearing adjusting ring	1	,,	
021587	... Spindle, centre, solid, for rear wheel	1	,,	
021608	... Spacer, on rear wheel solid spindle, for oil seals	1	,,	
021594	... Spacer on rear wheel spindle for speedo gear box	1	,,	
021590	... Washer, for solid spindle	1	,,	
021593	... Nut, locking, speedometer gearbox	1	,,	
021591	... Spacer, on rear wheel solid spindle (abuts against fork end) speedo side	1	,,	
014869	... Nut, for rear wheel solid spindle	1	,,	

FRONT BRAKE

021744	... Drum, front brake (must be fitted at works)	1	20-30	
021766	... Screw, fixing front brake drum to hub shell	5	,,	
011846	... Lock nut for brake drum screw	5	,,	
022257	... Plate, cover, front brake	1	,,	
021474	... Stay, front brake cover plate anchor	1	,,	
014807	... Bolt, fixing anchor stay to front cover plate, $\frac{5}{8}$ in. by $\frac{3}{8}$ in. by 26	1	,,	
014119	... Washer, special, for anchor stay bolt	1	,,	
022261	... Pin, fulcrum, for brake shoes	1	,,	
000009	... Washer, plain (inner for pin)	1	,,	
021563	... Screw, front brake shoe pin	1	,,	
013620	... Shoes, pair of, for front brake, with brake linings and thrust pins (only supplied in pairs) ...... per pair	1	,,	
013291	... Pin, thrust, brake expander adjusting	2	,,	
000174	... Washer, plain, for thrust pin	R	,,	
022832	... Linings, brake, per pair of, less rivets ...... per pair	1	,,	
000113	... Rivets, for brake linings, per set of	14	,,	
012892	... Spring, for brake shoes	2	,,	
021144	... Expander, for brake shoes	1	,,	
017334	... Washer, packing, for expander bush	1	,,	
022260	... Lever, for front brake shoe expander	1	,,	
000051	... Nipple, grease, for brake shoe expander	1	,,	
000174	... Washer, plain, for brake shoe expander	1	,,	
000004	... Nut, for brake shoe expander	1	,,	

REAR BRAKE

021596	... Sprocket and brake drum, for rear wheel, 42 teeth	1	20-30	
021607	... Pin, driving in hub	5	,,	
022083	... Nut, for driving pin	5	,,	
022264	... Plate, cover, rear brake	1	,,	
022748	... Spacer, for brake cover plate (outer)	1	,,	
021605	... Spacer, for brake cover plate (inner)	1	,,	
021598	... Bearing, ball for brake drum	1	,,	
021599	... Washer, for brake drum bearing	2	,,	
021600	... Circlip, for brake drum bearing	1	,,	
021783	... Oil seal, for brake drum bearing	1	,,	
021602	... Dummy spindle, for bearing	1	,,	
021603	... Nut, for dummy spindle	1	,,	
021604	... Washer, for dummy spindle	1	,,	
013620	... Shoes, pair of, for rear brakes, with brake linings and thrust pins (only supplied in pairs) ...... per pair	1	,,	
013291	... Pin, thrust, brake, expander adjusting	2	,,	
000174	... Washer, plain, for thrust pin	R	,,	
022832	... Linings, brake, per pair of, less rivets ...... per pair	1	,,	

PART NUMBER	DESCRIPTION	QTY. OFF	USED ON	PRICE EACH £ s. d.

REAR BRAKE—*continued*

000113	... Rivets, for brake linings................................per set of	14	20-30	
012892	... Spring, for brake shoes	2	,,	
012891	... Expander, for brake shoes..	1	,,	
017113	... Lever, for rear brake shoe expander	1	,,	
000051	... Nipple, grease, for brake shoe expander	1	,,	
000174	... Washer, plain, for brake shoe expander................	1	,,	
000004	... Nut, for brake shoe expander	1	,,	

REAR BRAKE OPERATING PARTS

022295	... Pedal, foot, for rear brake..	1	20-30	
022314	... Stop, for brake pedal	1	,,	
021699	... Fulcrum, for rear brake foot pedal	1	,,	
000051	... Nipple, grease, for rear brake foot pedal	1	,,	
021700	... Spring, return, rear brake foot pedal	1	,,	
022609	... Bolt, adjusting, rear brake foot pedal	1	,,	
022297	... Rod, bare, rear brake..	1	,,	
000735	... End, yoke, for front end of brake rod....................	1	,,	
000736	... Pin, for brake rod yoke end	1	,,	
000014	... Pin, split, for brake rod yoke end pin....................	1	,,	
017095	... Spring, for brake rod	1	,,	
000178	... Collar, for brake rod, spring....................................	1	,,	
022744	... Clip, adjusting, for rear end of brake rod	1	,,	
000736	... Pin, for brake rod adjusting clip	1	,,	
000014	... Pin, split, for brake rod adjusting clip pin	1	,,	
022743	... Nut, adjusting, for rear brake rod	1	,,	

VOLTAGE REGULATOR

022544	... Regulator, complete unit, type MCR2 (Lucas No. 37097-B) ...	1	20-30	
022597	... Rubber, for regulator..	1	,,	
022220	... Pad, rubber, support for voltage control	1	,,	
011094	... Grommet for cable	1	,,	

BATTERY

022345	... Battery, with lid, dry and uncharged. This is a battery that has NOT been filled with electrolyte (acid) and is, of course, not charged. It requires no special packing, and can safely be packed with other goods. (Lucas No. PU7E/9). (We do not supply charged batteries—for such apply to nearest Lucas Service Station)	1	20-30 Plus	surcharge
4159062	... Lid, only, with rubber pads, for battery..............................	1	,,	

HEAD LAMP

021802	... Lamp, head, type 51655A with bulb, ammeter, switch, no cable harness (not Europe)	1	20-30	
021803	... Lamp, head, type 51655A with bulb, ammeter, switch, no cable harness (Europe except France)	1	,,	
021804	... Lamp, head, type 51655A with ammeter, switch, less bulb and cable harness (France only)	1	,,	
516951	... Shell only, top half, for head lamp, type 51655A	1	,,	
516952	... Shell only, bottom half, for hea dlamp, type 51655A	1	,,	
553248	... Rim, bare, for head lamp	1	,,	
553925	... Light unit, reflector and glass (all except Europe)	1	,,	
553940	... Light unit, reflector and glass (Europe except France)	1	,,	
553948	... Light unit, reflector and glass (France only)	1	,,	
555005	... Adaptor (bulb holder) all except France	1	,,	

See ELECTRICAL SUNDRIES for Ammeter, Switch, Cable Harness and Bulbs.

THE PRICES OF SPARES DO NOT INCLUDE THE COST OF CARRIAGE

PART NUMBER	DESCRIPTION	QTY. OFF	USED ON	PRICE EACH £ s. d.

SIDE LAMP

52224	... Side lamp, complete	2	20-30	
516719	... Rubber grommet, for side lamp	2	,,	
573615	... Lens for side lamp	2	,,	
573646	... Rim and bead for side lamp	2	,,	

REAR LAMP

022126	... Rear lamp, complete (Lucas L564)	1	20-30	
573839	... Window cover, red for rear lamp	1	,,	
575200	... Window cover, white for rear lamp	1	,,	
575208	... Rubber gasket, for window cover	1	,,	
552928	... Screw, retaining window cover	2	,,	
575207	... Grommet, rubber for bulb holder	1	,,	
575209	... Bulb holder	1	,,	
860428	... Rear lamp wires, with Paxolin washer	1	,,	
573825	... Rubber cap, covering cable entry	1	,,	
166014	... Nut, retaining body to rear number plate	2	,,	
188330	... Spring washer for fixing nut	2	,,	

STOP LIGHT PARTS (Optional Extra)

022031	... Stop light switch	1	20-30	
018727	... Pull off, spring for switch	1	,,	
022032	... Bracket, for switch	1	,,	
018764	... Clip, for pull off spring	1	,,	
000738	... Screw, securing switch and spring clip	3	,,	
000739	... Nut, for screw switch and spring clip	3	,,	
000039	... Washer, for spring clip screw	2	,,	
018220	... Extra rubber cable clip	1	,,	
011908	... Extra rubber cable clip	2	,,	
014453	... Metal cable clip	1	,,	
022836	... Cable (switch to lamp and battery) pair complete	1	,,	
000269	... Snap connector	1	,,	
022002	... Complete kit of parts for stop light conversion	1	,,	

HORN

022529	... Horn, type HF1441. Lucas replacement number is 70137A	1	20-30	
012565	... Horn, bolt	2	,,	
000039	... Horn, bolt washer	2	,,	

ELECTRICAL SUNDRIES

36084	... Ammeter, for head lamp panel	1	20-30	
351551	... Switch, main lighting, for head lamp panel	1	,,	
351567	... Handle, with screw, for main lighting switch	1	,,	
022548	... Switch, dipping, and horn button combined	1	,,	
380459	... Rubber packing, for dipping switch and horn switch	1	,,	
021229	... Screw, fixing switch, $\frac{3}{8}$ in. by 4 B.A.	2	,,	
	... Cable harness, main lighting (no dip switch wire, no horn wire, no regulator wires)	1	,,	
858795	... Cable harness, triple, for dipping switch	1	,,	
989981	... Cable, harness, for regulator	1	,,	
359218	... Cable, for horn	1	,,	
016681	... Sheath, for horn cable	1	,,	
016682	... Sheath, for dynamo cable	1	,,	
000543	... Cable, high tension, for sparking plug, price per foot	R	,,	
000541	... Terminal, for high tension cable	2	,,	

BY USING GENUINE SPARES YOU ARE ASSURED THEY WILL FIT ACCURATELY AND GIVE SATISFACTORY SERVICE

PART NUMBER	DESCRIPTION	QTY. OFF	USED ON	PRICE EACH £ s. d.

ELECTRICAL SUNDRIES—continued

000269	... Connector, snap, for rear lamp cable	1	20-30	
000269	... Connector, snap, for regulator to ammeter cable	1	,,	
011094	... Bush, rubber, fits in rear mudguard, for rear lamp cable	1	,,	
312	... Bulb, head lamp, main, 6 volt, 30 by 24 watts (not Europe)	1	,,	
	Plus Purchase Tax	—	,,	
988	... Bulb, head lamp, pilot, 6 volt, 3 watts	2	,,	
	Plus Purchase Tax	—	,,	
384	... Bulb, rear lamp, 6 volt, 18 and 6 watts double contact	1	,,	
	Plus Purchase Tax	—	,,	
015547	... Plug, sparking, KLG, type FE-80	2	,,	
021310	... Cover for dynamo terminals	1	,,	
018895	... Interference suppressor	2	,,	

CABLE CLIPS

011907	... Clip, rubber, $1\frac{1}{2}$ in.	4	20-30	
011908	... Clip, rubber, 3 in.	3	,,	
018220	... Clip, rubber, $4\frac{3}{4}$ in.	5	,,	
014453	... Clip, metal, holding rear lamp wire inside mudguard	1	,,	

SPEEDOMETER

022006	... Speedometer, complete, trip, 120 M.P.H.	1	20-30	
022010	... Speedometer, complete, trip, 180 K.P.H.	1	,,	
021793	... Head, only, speedometer, trip, 120 M.P.H.	1	,,	
021795	... Head, only, speedometer, trip, 180 K.P.H.	1	,,	
022057	... Bracket, retaining speedometer head	1	,,	
021798	... Grommet, rubber for speedometer head in lamp	1	,,	
021799	... Grommet, rubber for speedometer cable in fork crown	1	,,	
53279-1	... Set of bulb holding parts for head	1	,,	
53205	... Bulb, 6 volts, 1·8 watts, M.B.C. for head	1	,,	
	Plus Purchase Tax	—	,,	
N-1253	... Nut, fixing speedometer head to lamp	2	,,	
W-7216	... Washer, spring, speedometer bracket nut	2	,,	
53395-1-65	Cable, speedometer drive, complete	1	,,	
52108-1-65	Cable, speedometer drive, inner only	1	,,	
53398-1-65	Cable, speedometer drive, outer only	1	,,	
52283-5	... Gearbox, speedometer, complete	1	,,	
021454	... Washer, outside speedometer gearbox	1	,,	

VARIOUS EQUIPMENT

018691	... Bar, locking, for fork crown	1	20-30	
022829	... Set of panniers, complete, with frames, fixing bolts, nuts and washers ...set	1	,,	
	Plus Purchase Tax	—	,,	
022824	... Bag, pannier, left or right	2	,,	
	Plus Purchase Tax ...each bag	—	,,	
022825	... Frame only, for pannier bag, left	1	,,	
022826	... Frame only, for pannier bag, right	1	,,	
022827	... Bolt, fixing frames at bottom	2	,,	
000347	... Bolt, fixing frames at top	2	,,	
000073	... Nut, for bottom fixing bolt	2	,,	
018160	... Nut, for top fixing bolt	2	,,	
000012	... Washer, for top fixing bolt	2	,,	
011957	... " TEKALL " rust preventative, $\frac{1}{2}$ pint	R	,,	
011958	... " TEKALL " rust preventative, 1 pint	R	,,	
B-A-H	... Badge, monogram, " AJS," for button hole	R	,,	
B-A-T	... Badge, monogram, " AJS," for tie	R	,,	
B-A-B	... Badge, monogram, " AJS," for brooch	R	,,	
	Instruction manual	R	,,	

PART NUMBER	DESCRIPTION	QTY. OFF	USED ON	PRICE EACH £ s. d.

COMPLETE TOOL KITS

022107	... Tool kit, complete, with tyre inflator	1		20-30
022108	... Tool kit, complete, less tyre inflator	1		,,

The following comprise " TOOL KIT, COMPLETE, WITH TYRE INFLATOR," and is included as part of every motor cycle.

TOOLS

017253	... Bag for tools	1		20-30
021625	... Screwdriver	1		,,
017248	... Pliers, side cutting	1		,,
011188	... Pliers, for gudgeon pin circlips	1		,,
017246	... Gun, grease	1		,,
017114	... Inflator, tyre	1		,,
017007	... Lever, tyre	2		,,
017052	... Spanner, double end, $\frac{3}{16}$ in. by $\frac{1}{4}$ in.	1		,,
017053	... Spanner, double end, $\frac{5}{16}$ in. by $\frac{3}{8}$ in.	1		,,
018178	... Spanner, double end, 1·011 in. by 1·2 in.	1		,,
017257	... Spanner, double end, $\frac{3}{16}$ in. by ·375 in.	1		,,
017252	... Spanner, box, with tommy, for sparking plug	1		,,
017249	... Wrench, adjustable	1		,,
015023	... Spanner, double end, with gauge, for contacts (Lucas No. 415116)	1		,,
015264	... Spanner, single end, for rocker clamping bolts	1		,,
015213	... Spanner, box, for cylinder head nuts	1		,,
017254	... Spanner, clutch spring adjustment	1		,,
018055	... Key, for handlebar clip screws and rocker screws	1		,,
018667	... Key, for fork tube pinch screw	1		,,
000174	... Washer, for brake shoe thrust pin	8		,,

SPECIAL TOOLS

011381	... Holder, valve, for valve grinding	1		20-30
015273	... Extractor, for timing pinion and magneto gear	1		,,
015374	... Extractor, for camshaft gears	1		,,
022011	... Disc, timing (see Instructions Manual)	1		,,

The above tools are NOT INCLUDED in the equipment of a new motor cycle.

SERVICE

The **Service and Repair Department** is situated in **Burrage Grove, Plumstead, London, S.E.18. Burrage Grove** is the first turning on the left from Burrage Road when entering Burrage Road from the Plumstead Road. (See final paragraph below).

The nearest Railway Station is WOOLWICH ARSENAL, SOUTHERN REGION RAILWAY. This Station is five minutes' walk from our Service Depot in Burrage Grove. There is an excellent service of electric trains from Charing Cross, Waterloo, Cannon Street and London Bridge Stations, Southern Region Railway.

Bus Routes 53, 54, 163, 99, 122, 122a, 177 and Trolleybus routes 696 and 698, pass the end of Burrage Road (one minute from the Service Depot).

Bus routes 186, 75 and 161 serve **Beresford Square** which is three minutes' walk from the **Service and Repair Department.**

Visitors from the North can pass into Woolwich *via* the Free Ferry between North Woolwich and Woolwich. North Woolwich is a British Railways terminus and is also served by Bus and Trolleybus routes 101, 569, 669 and 685. There is also a tunnel under the River Thames at this point for foot passengers. The Free Ferry accommodates all types of motor vehicles and there is a very frequent service. The Southern landing stage is less than a mile from the Service Depot.

Visitors arriving by road, if they are strangers to the locality, should enquire for **Beresford Square, Woolwich.** Upon arrival there, the road skirting the Royal Arsenal should be followed in an Easterly direction for about four hundred yards, and Burrage Road is the second turning on the right after leaving the square. Burrage Grove is then the first turning on the left.

VELOCEPRESS MANUALS – MOTORCYCLE BY MAKE

- AJS 1932-1948 SINGLES & TWINS 250cc THRU 1000cc (BOOK OF)
- AJS 1945-1960 SINGLES MODELS 16 & 18 350cc & 500cc (BOOK OF)
- AJS 1948-1956 TWINS MODELS 20 & 30 FACTORY WSM & PARTS
- AJS 1955-1965 SINGLES MODELS 16 & 18 350cc & 500cc (BOOK OF)
- AJS 1957-1966 SINGLES & TWINS (ALL) FACTORY WSM
- AJS 1959-1969 G80CS G85CS & P11 OFF ROAD FACTORY WSM
- AJS 1968-1974 STORMER FACTORY WSM & PARTS LIST
- ARIEL UP TO 1932 (BOOK OF)
- ARIEL 1932-1939 PREWAR MODELS (BOOK OF)
- ARIEL 1933-1951 (WORKSHOP MANUAL)
- ARIEL 1939-1960 4 STROKE SINGLES (BOOK OF)
- ARIEL 1958-1964 LEADER & ARROW FACTORY WSM & PARTS LIST
- ARIEL 1958-1964 LEADER & ARROW (BOOK OF)
- BMW R26 R27 (1956-1967) FACTORY WORKSHOP MANUAL
- BMW R50 R50S R60 R69S (1955-1969) FACTORY WORKSHOP MANUAL
- BMW R50/5 R60/5 R75/5 (1969-1973) FACTORY WORKSHOP MANUAL
- BRIDGESTONE 90 SERIES FACTORY WSM & PARTS CATALOGUE
- BRIDGESTONE 175 SERIES FACTORY WSM & PARTS CATALOGUE
- BRIDGESTONE 350 SERIES FACTORY WSM & PARTS CATALOGUES
- BSA SERVICE SHEETS MASTER CATALOGUE ALL MODELS 1945-1967
- BSA BANTAM D1 TO D7 1948-1966 FACTORY SERVICE SHEETS MANUAL
- BSA BANTAM ALL MODELS FROM 1948 ONWARDS (BOOK OF)
- BSA BANTAM D14 FACTORY SERVICE MANUAL
- BSA DANDY FACTORY WORKSHOP MANUAL (COMPILATION)
- BSA SINGLES & V-TWINS UP TO 1926 inc. 1927 SUPPLEMENT (BOOK OF)
- BSA SINGLES & V-TWINS UP TO 1930 (BOOK OF)
- BSA SINGLES & V-TWINS UP TO 1935 (BOOK OF)
- BSA SINGLES & V-TWINS 1936-1939 (BOOK OF)
- BSA C10, C11 & C12 1945-1958 FACTORY SERVICE SHEETS MANUAL
- BSA OHV & SV SINGLES 250-600cc 1945-1959 (BOOK OF)
- BSA C15 & B40 1958-1967 FACTORY SERVICE SHEETS MANUAL
- BSA OHV & SV SINGLES 250cc (ONLY) 1954-1970 (BOOK OF)
- BSA B31, B32, B33 & B34 1945-60 FACTORY SERVICE SHEETS MANUAL
- BSA OHV SINGLES 350 & 500cc 1955-1967 (BOOK OF)
- BSA M20, M21 & M33 1945-1963 FACTORY SERVICE SHEETS MANUAL
- BSA TWINS A7 & A10 1948-1962 FACTORY SERVICE SHEETS MANUAL
- BSA TWINS A7 & A10 1948-1962 (BOOK OF)
- BSA TWINS A50 & A65 1962-1965 FACTORY WORKSHOP MANUAL
- BSA TWINS A50 & A65 1962-1969 (SECOND BOOK OF)
- BULTACO 125cc to 37cc SINGLES 1968-1979 WORKSHOP MANUAL
- CZ 125cc to 380cc SINGLES 1967-1974 WORKSHOP MANUAL
- DOUGLAS 1929-1939 PREWAR ALL MODELS (BOOK OF)
- DOUGLAS 1948-1957 POSTWAR ALL MODELS FACTORY SHOP MANUAL
- DUCATI 160cc, 250cc & 350cc OHC MODELS FACTORY SHOP MANUAL
- HODAKA 90cc,100cc & 125cc SINGLES 1964-1978 WORKSHOP MANUAL
- HONDA 50cc ALL MODELS UP TO 1970 INC MONKEY & TRAIL (BOOK OF)
- HONDA 90cc ALL MODELS UP TO 1966 (BOOK OF)
- HONDA TWINS & SINGLES 50cc THRU 305cc 1960-1966 (BOOK OF)
- HONDA TWINS ALL MODELS 125cc THRU 450cc UP TO 1968 (BOOK OF)
- HONDA C100 50cc SUPER CUB O.H.C. 1959-1962 FACTORY WSM
- HONDA C110 50cc SPORT CUB O.H.C. 1960-1962 FACTORY WSM
- HONDA 50-65-70-90cc O.H.C. SINGLES 1959-1983 WSM
- HONDA 100-125cc SINGLES CB/CD/CL/SL/TL 1970-1984 FACTORY WSM
- HONDA 125-150cc TWINS C/CS/CB/CA 1959-1966 FACTORY WSM
- HONDA 125-160-175-200cc TWINS 1965-1978 WORKSHOP MANUAL
- HONDA 250-305cc TWINS C/CS/CB 1961-1968 FACTORY WSM
- HONDA 250-350cc TWINS CB/CL/SL 1968-1973 FACTORY WSM
- HONDA 250-360cc TWINS CB/CL/CJ 1974-1977 FACTORY WSM
- HONDA 350F & 400F 4-CYLINDER 1972-1977 FACTORY WSM
- HONDA 450cc TWINS CB/CL 1965-1974 K0 TO K7 WORKSHOP MANUAL
- HONDA 500cc & 550cc 4-CYL 1971-1978 FACTORY WORKSHOP MANUAL
- HONDA 750 SHOC 4-CYL 1969-1978 K0~K8 WORKSHOP MANUAL
- HUSQVARNA 125cc to 450cc SINGLES 1965-1975 WORKSHOP MANUAL
- INDIAN PONYBIKE, BOY RACER & PAPOOSE ILL PARTS LIST & SALES LIT
- J.A.P. ENGINES 1927-1952 & MOTORCYCLES 1934-1952 (BOOK OF)
- MAICO 250cc to 501cc 1968-1978 WORKSHOP MANUAL
- MATCHLESS 1931-1939 ALL MODELS 250cc THRU 990cc (BOOK OF)
- MATCHLESS 1945-1956 SINGLES G3 & G80 350cc & 500cc (BOOK OF)
- MATCHLESS 1948-1956 TWINS G9 & G11 FACTORY WSM & PARTS
- MATCHLESS 1955-1966 SINGLES G3 & G80 350cc & 500cc (BOOK OF)
- MATCHLESS 1957-1966 SINGLES & TWINS (ALL) FACTORY WSM
- MONTESA 1962-1978 125cc to 360cc ALL MODELS WORKSHOP MANUAL
- NEW IMPERIAL ALL SV & OHV FROM 1935 ONWARDS (BOOK OF)
- NORTON 1932-1939 PREWAR MODELS (BOOK OF)
- NORTON 1938-1956 (BOOK OF)
- NORTON 1945-1963 MODELS 16H, Big4, ES2, 19 & 50 WSM'S & PARTS
- NORTON 1955-1963 MODELS 19, 50 & ES2 (BOOK OF)
- NORTON 1948-1970 DOMINATOR TWINS FACTORY WSM'S & PARTS
- NORTON 1955-1965 DOMINATOR TWINS (BOOK OF)
- NORTON 1960-1970 TWIN CYLINDER FACTORY WORKSHOP MANUAL
- NORTON 1970-1975 COMMANDO 850 & 750cc FACTORY WSM
- NORTON 1975-1978 MK 3 COMMANDO 850 cc FACTORY WSM
- PANTHER 1932-1958 LIGHTWEIGHT MODELS 250 & 350cc (BOOK OF)
- PANTHER 1938-1966 HEAVYWEIGHT MODELS 600 & 650cc (BOOK OF)
- PENTON-KTM-SACHS 1968-1975 100cc & 125cc WORKSHOP MANUAL
- PENTON-KTM 1972-1975 175cc, 250cc & 400cc WSM & PARTS MANUALS
- RALEIGH MOTORCYCLES 1919-1933 (BOOK OF)
- ROYAL ENFIELD 1934-1946 SINGLES & V TWINS (BOOK OF)
- ROYAL ENFIELD 1937-1953 SINGLES & V TWINS (BOOK OF)
- ROYAL ENFIELD 1946-1962 SINGLES (BOOK OF)
- ROYAL ENFIELD 1948-1962 350cc & 500cc PRE-UNIT BULLET WSM
- ROYAL ENFIELD 1948-1963 500cc TWINS FACTORY WORKSHOP MANUAL
- ROYAL ENFIELD 1952-1963 700cc TWINS FACTORY WORKSHOP MANUAL
- ROYAL ENFIELD 1956-1966 250cc CRUSADER & 350cc NEW BULLET WSM
- ROYAL ENFIELD 1958-1963 250cc & 350cc SINGLES (SECOND BOOK OF)
- ROYAL ENFIELD 1962-1970 INTERCEPTOR WSM'S & PARTS (Compilation)
- RUDGE 1933-1939 (BOOK OF)
- SACHS 1968-1975 100cc & 125cc ENGINES WSM & M/CYCLE PARTS LIST
- SUNBEAM 1928-1939 (BOOK OF)
- SUNBEAM 1946-1957 S7 & S8 (BOOK OF)
- SUZUKI 50cc & 80cc UP TO 1966 (BOOK OF)
- SUZUKI T10 1963-1967 FACTORY WORKSHOP MANUAL
- SUZUKI T20 & T200 1965-1969 FACTORY WORKSHOP MANUAL
- SUZUKI TWINS 1962 ONWARDS 125-500cc WORKSHOP MANUAL
- TRIUMPH 1935-1949 SINGLES & TWINS (BOOK OF)
- TRIUMPH 1937-1961 SINGLES SV & OHV 250cc-600cc + TERRIER & CUB
- TRIUMPH 1945-1955 PRE-UNIT 350cc, 500cc & 650cc TWINS WSM No.11
- TRIUMPH 1945-1959 TWINS (BOOK OF)
- TRIUMPH 1956-1969 TWINS (BOOK OF)
- TRIUMPH 1956-1962 PRE-UNIT 500cc & 650cc TWINS WSM No.17
- TRIUMPH 1957-1963 UNIT CONSTRUCTION 350-500cc WSM No.4
- TRIUMPH 1963-1974 UNIT CONSTRUCTION 350-500cc FACTORY WSM
- TRIUMPH 1963-1970 UNIT CONSTRUCTION 650cc FACTORY WSM
- TRIUMPH 1968-1974 TRIDENT T150 & T150V FACTORY WSM
- TRIUMPH 1971-1973 650cc OIL-IN-FRAME FACTORY WSM
- TRIUMPH 1973-1978 750cc BONNEVILLE & TIGER FACTORY WSM
- TRIUMPH 1979-1983 750cc T140, TR7 & TR65 FACTORY WSM
- VELOCETTE 1925-1970 ALL SINGLES & TWINS (BOOK OF)
- VELOCETTE 1933-1952 MOV-MAC-MSS RIGID FRAME FACTORY WSM
- VELOCETTE 1953-1960 MAC SPRING FRAME WSM & ILL PARTS LIST
- VELOCETTE 1954-1971 MSS-VENOM-THRUXTON-VIPER FACTORY WSM
- VILLIERS ENGINE UP TO 1959 INC. 3 WHEELERS (BOOK OF)
- VILLIERS ENGINE UP TO 1969 (BOOK OF)
- VINCENT 1935-1955 (WORKSHOP MANUAL)
- YAMAHA 1961-1967 YA5 & YA6 (WORKSHOP MANUAL & ILL PARTS LIST)
- YAMAHA 1968-1971 DT1 & MX SERIES Inc. GYT WORKSHOP MANUAL
- YAMAHA 1971-1972 JT1& JT2 (WORKSHOP MANUAL & ILL PARTS LIST)

VELOCEPRESS MANUALS – SCOOTERS BY MAKE

- BSA SUNBEAM SCOOTER WORKSHOP MANUAL 1959-1965
- BSA SUNBEAM SCOOTER 1959-1965 (BOOK OF)
- LAMBRETTA 1947-1957 ALL 125 & 150cc MODELS (BOOK OF)
- LAMBRETTA 1957-1970 LI & TV MODELS (SECOND BOOK OF)
- NSU PRIMA 1956-1964 ALL MODELS (BOOK OF)
- TRIUMPH TIGRESS SCOOTER WORKSHOP MANUAL 1959-1965
- TRIUMPH TIGRESS SCOOTER (BOOK OF)
- VESPA 1951-1961 (BOOK OF)
- VESPA 1955-1963 125 & 150cc & GS MODELS (SECOND BOOK OF)
- VESPA 1955-1968 GS & SS (BOOK OF)
- VESPA 1963-1972 90, 125 & 150cc (THIRD BOOK OF)

VELOCEPRESS MANUALS – MOPEDS & MOTORIZED BICYCLES

- CYCLEMOTOR (BOOK OF)
- NSU QUICKLY 1953-1963 ALL MODELS (BOOK OF)
- PUCH MAXI N & S MAINTENANCE & REPAIR (3 MANUAL COMPILATION)
- RALEIGH MOPEDS 1960-1969 (BOOK OF)

VELOCEPRESS MANUALS - THREE WHEELER'S

- BOND MINICAR THREE WHEELER 1948-1967 (BOOK OF)
- BMW ISETTA FACTORY WORKSHOP MANUAL
- BSA THREE WHEELER (BOOK OF)
- RELIANT REGAL THREE WHEELER 1952-1973 (BOOK OF)
- VINTAGE MORGAN THREE WHEELER (BOOK OF)

VELOCEPRESS TECHNICAL BOOKS – MOTORCYCLE

- 1930'S BRITISH MOTORCYCLE CARBS & ELEC COMPONENTS (BOOK OF)
- 1930'S BRITISH MOTORCYCLE ENGINES (OVERHAUL & MAINTENANCE)
- 1930'S BRITISH MOTORCYCLE GEARBOXES & CLUTCHES (BOOK OF)
- CATALOG OF BRITISH MOTORCYCLES (1951 MODELS)
- LUCAS ELECTRONICS BRITISH M/CYCLES REPAIR & PARTS (1950-1977)
- MOTORCYCLE ENGINEERING (P.E. Irving)
- MOTORCYCLE ROAD TESTS 1949-1953 (Motor Cycle Magazine UK)
- SPEED AND HOW TO OBTAIN IT (Motor Cycle Magazine UK)
- TUNING FOR SPEED (P.E. Irving)
- WIPAC (COMBO) MANUAL NUMBER 3 + M/CYCLE & SCOOTER MANUAL

www.VelocePress.com

VELOCEPRESS MANUALS – AUTOMOBILE BY MAKE

ALFA ROMEO GIULIA WORKSHOP MANUAL 1300 TO 2000cc 1962-1975
ALFA ROMEO GIULIA TECH MANUAL CARBURETED CARS FROM 1962
ALFA ROMEO GIULIA TECH MANUAL FUEL INJECTED CARS FROM 1969
ALFA ROMEO GIULIETTA & GIULIA 750 & 101 SERIES 1955-1965 WSM
AUSTIN-HEALEY SPRITE & MG MIDGET WORKSHOP MANUAL 1958-1971
BMW 600 LIMOUSINE FACTORY WORKSHOP MANUAL
BMW 600 LIMOUSINE OWNERS HAND BOOK & SERVICE MANUAL
BMW 2000 & 2002 1966-1976 WORKSHOP MANUAL
BMW 2500, 2800, 3.0 & BARVARIA WORKSHOP MANUAL
CORVAIR 1960-1969 WORKSHOP MANUAL
CORVETTE V8 1955-1962 WORKSHOP MANUAL
FERRARI HANDBOOK ROAD & RACE CARS (SERVICE/SPECS) 1948-1958
FERRARI 250GT SERVICE & MAINTENANCE by JIM RIFF 1956-1965
FERRARI 250GT & 250GTE FACTORY PARTS AND REPAIR MANUALS
FIAT 500 FACTORY WORKSHOP MANUAL 1957-1973
FIAT 600, 600D & MULTIPLA FACTORY WORKSHOP MANUAL 1955-1969
FORD MUSTANG 1965-1973 TRANSMISSION WORKSHOP MANUAL
JAGUAR E-TYPE 3.8 & 4.2 SERIES 1 & 2 WORKSHOP MANUAL
JAGUAR MK 7, 8, 9 & XK120, 140, 150 WORKSHOP MANUAL 1948-1961
MERCEDES-BENZ 230 SERIES 1963-1968
MERCEDES-BENZ 280 SERIES 1968-1972
METROPOLITAN FACTORY WORKSHOP MANUAL
MGA & MGB OWNERS HANDBOOK & WORKSHOP MANUAL
MG MIDGET TC, TD, TF & TF1500 WORKSHOP MANUAL
PORSCHE 356 1948-1965 WORKSHOP MANUAL
PORSCHE 911 2.0, 2.2, 2.4 LITRE 1964-1973 WORKSHOP MANUAL
PORSCHE 911 2.7, 3.0, 3.2 LITRE 1973-1989 WORKSHOP MANUAL
PORSCHE 912 WORKSHOP MANUAL
PORSCHE 914/4 & 914/6 1.7, 1.8, 2.0 LITRE 1970-1976 WSM
TRIUMPH TR2, TR3, TR4 1953-1965 WORKSHOP MANUAL
VOLKSWAGEN TRANSPORTER, TRUCKS & WAGONS 1950-1979 WSM
VOLVO 1944-1968 ALL MODELS WORKSHOP MANUAL

VELOCEPRESS TECHNICAL BOOKS - AUTOMOBILE

HOW TO BUILD A FIBERGLASS CAR
HOW TO BUILD A RACING CAR
HOW TO RESTORE THE MODEL 'A' FORD
MASERATI OWNER'S HANDBOOK
PERFORMANCE TUNING THE SUNBEAM TIGER
SOUPING THE VOLKSWAGEN
SOLEX CARBURETORS (EMPHASIS ON UK & EU AUTOMOBILES)
SU CARBURETORS (EMPHASIS ON UK AUTOMOBILES)
WEBER CARBURETORS (EMPHASIS ON ALFA & FIAT)

VELOCEPRESS BOOKS & GUIDES - AUTOMOBILE

COMPLETE CATALOG OF JAPANESE MOTOR VEHICLES
FERRARI 308 SERIES BUYER'S AND OWNER'S GUIDE
FERRARI BROCHURES AND SALES LITERATURE 1968-1989
FERRARI SERIAL NUMBERS PART I - ODD NUMBERS TO 21399
FERRARI SERIAL NUMBERS PART II - EVEN NUMBERS TO 1050
HENRY'S FABULOUS MODEL "A" FORD
MASERATI BROCHURES AND SALES LITERATURE

VELOCEPRESS BOOKS – AUTO RACING

BOOK OF THE 1950 CARRERA PANAMERICANA - MEXICAN ROAD RACE
DIALED IN - THE JAN OPPERMAN STORY
VEDA ORR'S NEW REVISED HOT ROD PICTORIAL
LIFE OF TED HORN – AMERICAN RACING CHAMPION

www.VelocePress.com